CONTEXTUALIZING SECTARIANISM IN THE MIDDLE EAST AND SOUTH ASIA

States across the Muslim world are faced with challenges associated with a perpetual cycle of conflict and violence organized along sectarian lines. To understand modern-day sectarianism, it is essential to move beyond explanations that focus predominantly on ancient Sunni-Shia animosities or a singular lens. It is important to engage in interdisciplinary and multidirectional examinations to better understand how sectarianism is strategically utilized by political entrepreneurs. Moreover, while religious identities and how individuals define themselves and their communities are important, it is also integral to analyze how identity has been utilized in historical and contemporary political contexts on state and non-state levels.

This volume seeks to fill gaps in understanding the complexities associated with sectarianism through a transnational interdisciplinary analytical framework to enhance understanding of the socio-political, religio-political, cultural, and security landscapes of the Middle East and South Asia. It also challenges narratives regarding sectarian divisions between Sunnis and Shias and deconstructs popular misconceptions about sectarianism, its spatial and temporal impact, as well as its influence on identities, conflict, and competition. The volume will be of interest to scholars and researchers of the Middle East and South Asia, and those interested in history, politics, international relations, international security, religion, and sociology.

Satgin Hamrah is a PhD Candidate in History at Tufts University, where she focuses on the Middle East, South Asia, the Iran-Iraq War, sectarianism, and Islamism, as well as state and non-state conflict and violence. She also focuses on the intersection of identity, memory, trauma and politics on local and transnational levels within the framework of her research interests. Hamrah has a Master of Arts degree in International Relations from Boston University, where her thesis focused on offensive strategies to protect critical infrastructure against terrorism. Hamrah also has a Master of Public Administration degree from the University of Southern California, with a focus on international development and state formation of post-Soviet states in the Caspian region during the 1990s with a focus on Azerbaijan. Hamrah was a Doctoral Fellow at The Fares Center for Eastern Mediterranean Studies at the Fletcher School of Law & Diplomacy at Tufts University between September 2016 and October 2018.

CONTEXTUALIZING SECTARIANISM IN THE MIDDLE EAST AND SOUTH ASIA

Identity, Competition, and Conflict

Edited by Satgin Hamrah

Designed Cover image: Getty Images

First published 2023
by Routledge
4 Park Square, Milton Park, Abingdon, Oxon OX14 4RN

and by Routledge
605 Third Avenue, New York, NY 10158

Routledge is an imprint of the Taylor & Francis Group, an informa business

© 2023 selection and editorial matter, Satgin Hamrah; individual chapters, the contributors

The right of Satgin Hamrah to be identified as the author of the editorial material, and of the authors for their individual chapters, has been asserted in accordance with sections 77 and 78 of the Copyright, Designs and Patents Act 1988.

All rights reserved. No part of this book may be reprinted or reproduced or utilised in any form or by any electronic, mechanical, or other means, now known or hereafter invented, including photocopying and recording, or in any information storage or retrieval system, without permission in writing from the publishers.

Trademark notice: Product or corporate names may be trademarks or registered trademarks, and are used only for identification and explanation without intent to infringe.

British Library Cataloguing-in-Publication Data
A catalogue record for this book is available from the British Library

Library of Congress Cataloging-in-Publication Data
A catalog record has been requested for this book

ISBN: 978-1-032-34627-4 (hbk)
ISBN: 978-1-032-35953-3 (pbk)
ISBN: 978-1-003-32951-0 (ebk)

DOI: 10.4324/9781003329510

Typeset in Bembo
by Taylor & Francis Books

CONTENTS

List of contributors   vii
Acknowledgements   xi

   Introduction: Untangling the Complexities of Sectarianism and
   Moving Beyond Misconceptions   1
   Satgin Hamrah

1 Unravelling Sectarianism in South Asia   8
   Ayesha Jalal

2 The Ahmadiyya Muslim Community's Identity as the "True
   Islam" through its Exclusion   20
   Misbah Hyder

3 Understanding the Long-term Impact of Mobilizing Militant
   Islamists in the Soviet-Afghan War: Strategies of the United
   States, Saudi Arabia, and Iran   38
   Satgin Hamrah

4 Advice Columnists in Egypt: Envisioning the Good Life in an
   Era of Extremism   52
   Andrea B. Rugh

5 Sectarianism's Ambiguity: Lebanon as a Case Study, 1843–1958   64
   Brittney Giardina

6 Falling Together: Identity and the Military in Fragmented Societies 77
Dylan Maguire

7 Accidentally Accelerating Sectarianism: Elections and the U.S. Role in the Iraqi Civil War 101
Frank Sobchak

8 Contextualization of Sectarian Conflict and Violence in Iraq: The Intersection of Identity, Power, and Conflict 117
Satgin Hamrah

9 Sectarianism and Counterterrorism: Explaining the "Silent Space" between Policy and Practice 135
Heidi E. Lane

10 Old Stately Friends, New Sectarian Foes: The Modern Saudi-Iranian Roots in Shia-Sunni Sectarianism 153
Pouya Alimagham

Conclusion: The Contextualization of Sectarianism: The Role of Identity, Money, and Competition 168
Ibrahim Warde

Index *173*

CONTRIBUTORS

Ayesha Jalal is the Mary Richardson Professor of History at Tufts University. After majoring in history and political science at Wellesley College, she obtained her doctorate in history from the University of Cambridge. Jalal has been Fellow of Trinity College, Cambridge (1980–1984); Leverhulme Fellow at the Centre of South Asian Studies, Cambridge (1984–1987); Fellow of the Woodrow Wilson Center for International Scholars in Washington, D.C. (1985–1986); and a Academy Scholar at the Harvard Academy for International and Area Studies (1988–1990). From 1998–2003 she was a MacArthur Fellow. Her publications include "The Sole Spokesman: Jinnah, the Muslim League and the Demand for Pakistan" (Cambridge: Cambridge University Press, 1994); "The State of Martial Rule: the Origins of Pakistan's Political Economy of Defence" (Lahore: Sang-e-Meel Publications, 1999); and "Democracy and Authoritarianism in South Asia: a Comparative and Historical Perspective" (Cambridge: Cambridge University Press, 1995). Jalal has co-authored "Modern South Asia: History, Culture and Political Economy" with Sugata Bose (3rd ed, London: Routledge, 2011). Her study of Muslim identity in the subcontinent is entitled "Self and Sovereignty: The Muslim Individual and the Community of Islam in South Asia since c.1850" (London: Routledge, 2000). Her most recent book is "Partisans of Allah: Jihad in South Asia" (Cambridge, Massachusetts: Harvard University Press, 2008).

Ibrahim Warde is an Adjunct Professor of International Business at the Fletcher School of Law and Diplomacy at Tufts University. He is a Carnegie scholar working on informal and underground finance in the Islamic world. His books include *The Price of Fear: The Truth Behind the Financial War on Terror* (London: I.B. Tauris, 2007), which has been translated into French, Italian, Japanese, and Czech, and was selected by Foreign Affairs as one of the best books of the year about economic, social, and environmental issues, and *Islamic Finance in the Global Economy*, now in its second edition (Edinburgh: Edinburgh University Press, 2010). He has previously taught at the University of California, Berkeley, at MIT's Sloan School of Management, and at other universities in the United States and abroad. He is also a writer for Le Monde Diplomatique and a consultant. He holds a B.A. from Université Saint Joseph in Beirut, Lebanon, an MBA from France's Ecole des Hautes Etudes Commerciales, and an M.A. and a Ph.D. in Political Science from the University of California, Berkeley.

Heidi Lane is Professor of Strategy and Policy and Director of the Greater Middle East Research Study Group at the U.S. Naval War College. She specializes in Comparative Politics and International Relations of the Middle East with a focus on security sector development, ethnic and religious nationalism, and rule of law in transitioning societies. Her co-edited book *Building Rule of Law in the Arab World and Beyond* (Boulder, CO: Lynne Rienner Publishers, 2015) was published in 2016. She is currently completing research on a book manuscript about counter-terrorism and state liberalization in the Middle East. Dr. Lane has served as a Visiting Research Affiliate with the Truman Institute for the Advancement of Peace at the Hebrew University of Jerusalem, a U.S. Fulbright scholar in Syria, and as a research fellow with the International Security Program at the Belfer Center for Science and International Affairs at Harvard University. She is currently a Senior Associate at the Center for Irregular Warfare and Armed Groups (CIWAG) at the Naval War College. She holds an M.A and Ph.D. in Islamic Studies from the Center for Near Eastern Studies, University of California, Los Angeles, and a B.A. from the University of Chicago and is trained in Arabic, Hebrew, and Persian and is proficient in German.

Col. Frank Sobchak, is an Adjunct Professor at the Joint Special Operations University and has taught at the U.S. Military Academy at West Point, Tufts University, The Fletcher School of Law and Diplomacy, and The Massachusetts Institute of Technology. He holds a B.S. in Military History from West Point and an M.A. in Arab Studies from Georgetown University and a PhD in International Relations from the Fletcher School of Law and Diplomacy at Tufts University. During his 26-year career in the U.S. Army, he served in various Special Forces assignments including leading teams and companies in 5th Special Forces Group in peace and in war and representing U.S. Special Operations Command as a congressional liaison.

Andrea Rugh has been a technical advisor for USAID development projects in the Middle East, South Asia, and Africa. She was a Research Associate at the Harvard Institute of International Development from 1987 to 1994 and worked for Save the Children and UNICEF in Pakistan and Afghanistan from 1998 to 2002. Over a period of 40 years residence and work in the Middle East, she has written on local culture and society. Her books include *Family in Contemporary Egypt*

(Syracuse, N.Y: Syracuse University Press, 1984), *Reveal and Conceal: Dress in Egypt* (Syracuse, N.Y.: Syracuse University Press, 1986), *Within the Circle: Parents and Children in an Arab Village* (New York: Columbia University Press, 1997), and two translated books: *Daughter of Damascus* (Siham Tergeman, Austin: University of Texas Press, 1994, trans. Andrea Rugh), *Folktales of Syria* (Samir Tahhan, Austin: University of Texas, 2004, trans. and introduction Andrea Rugh). Her latest books are *The Political Culture of Leadership in the United Arab Emirates* (New York: Palgrave Macmillan, 2007), *Simple Gestures: A Cultural Journey Into the Middle East* (Washington, D.C: Potomac Books, 2009), *International Development in Practice: Education Assistance in Egypt, Pakistan, and Afghanistan* (New York: Palgrave Macmillan, 2012) and *Christians in Egypt: Strategies and Survival* (New York: Palgrave Macmillan US, 2015).

Pouya Alimagham is a historian of the modern Middle East and a Lecturer at the Massachusetts Institute of Technology. He specializes on Iran, Iraq, and the Levant, focusing on such themes as revolutionary and guerrilla movements, imperialism, representation and Orientalism, political Islam and post-Islamism and the intersections therein. His dissertation titled "Contesting the Iranian Revolution: The Green Uprising," was the 2016 winner of the Association for Iranian Studies Mehrdad Mashayekhi Dissertation Award, which is presented biannually (Cambridge: Cambridge University Press, 2020). His other articles and book chapters (some in progress) cover the Arab Spring, Iranian protest music, women in Middle East revolution, sectarianism and the psycho-history of post-9/11 discourse.

Dylan Maguire is an analyst at the United States Department of Defense. Prior to joining the Department of Defense, he was the 2020–2021 Office of the Security of Defense Minerva Research Peace and Security Fellow. Maguire holds a PhD from the Department of Political Science at Northeastern University. His dissertation examined transnational political-military partnerships between militias and states and focused on the Lebanese and Syrian civil wars. He is now working on a book project that explores the roles of intelligence and ideology in militia decision-making.

Brittney Giardina is a recent graduate of Loyola University in New Orleans where she earned a degree in History and minors in Middle Eastern Peace Studies and Studio Art. Her historical interests include the politicization of religion and representations of religiosity in art. Her research interests include examining issues pertaining to sectarianism in Lebanon, as well as examining the dynamics of ethno-religious identity, tension and conflict in the Middle East and North Africa.

Misbah Hyder is a Ph.D. Candidate in Political Science, specializing in International Relations and Global Studies, at the University of California, Irvine. She studies how persecuted religious minorities respond to their marginalization from state and religious institutions through their religious practice. Her dissertation, "The Pen is Mightier than the Sword: How the Ahmadiyya Muslim Community Enacts Peacebuilding," focuses on how the global engagement of a marginalized Muslim minority necessitates a re-evaluation of theories on agency for religious actors.

ACKNOWLEDGEMENTS

This book is a product of collective efforts of the faculty and staff at Tufts University. I would like to thank the Fares Center for Eastern Mediterranean Studies at the Fletcher School of Law and Diplomacy at Tufts University, the Department of History at Tufts University, The Center for South Asian and Indian Ocean Studies at Tufts University, The International Security Studies Program at the Fletcher School of Law and Diplomacy at Tufts University, and the Center for Strategic Studies at the Fletcher School of Law and Diplomacy at Tufts University for their generous support of the 2018 conference on sectarianism, "Explaining Sectarianism: Community, Competition and Conflict," at the Fletcher School of Law and Diplomacy at Tufts University, which this edited volume is based on. I am also deeply indebted to Dr. Ayesha Jalal, Dr. James Rice, and Dr. Ibrahim Warde for their invaluable support and sage advice for both the conference and this book. I am also especially grateful for Annette Lazzara, Lori Piracini, Christopher Doyle, and Phoebe Sargeant.

I am enormously grateful to the contributors of this volume for their invaluable intellectual contributions and their patience over the long haul of the editorial process. I am deeply honored and thrilled to have worked with them on this project. Finally, I would also like to thank my husband and daughter for their unwavering patience and support as this book came to fruition.

INTRODUCTION

Untangling the Complexities of Sectarianism and Moving Beyond Misconceptions

Satgin Hamrah

Political Islam cuts across geographic boundaries, transcending national borders and political ideologies giving rise to growing Islamic activism and its instrumentalization within security, political, and cultural landscapes. It has also served as a catalyst for the surge in sectarianism since the 1980s with highly consequential results coinciding with the political change process that the Greater Middle East and South Asia have been experiencing since the late 1970s. Given the highly nuanced nature of sectarianism and its role in influencing tension, conflict, and violence in the wider region, the focus on sectarianism is a key framework by which most of the conflicts and violence in the Greater Middle East and South Asia are analyzed. Much of this stems from its strategic utilization by state and non-state political entrepreneurs for the advancement of their interests. It is often a key tool in conflicts between Sunnis and Shias in the wider region and can exist on both intrastate and interstate levels with each influencing the other. Moreover, the process by which political entrepreneurs strategically utilize sectarianism includes the decontextualization and deconstruction of a community or identity of any given size, and the construction of an imagined identity and an imagined community (Anderson 1991) along in-group/out-group paradigms.

To understand this phenomenon and its short-term and long-term impact, it is important to contextualize it within the framework of the country or region being examined, as well as the specific covert and overt factors that contributed to its rise. However, prior to the contextualization of this phenomenon it is highly beneficial to understand the theoretical prisms that are used to examine sectarianism. Moreover, this includes unpacking the theories by which it is framed, it is useful to ask how sectarianism should generally be identified. Sect is understood as a socio-religious grouping (Berger 1984: 367–385). By extension sectarianism occurs when members of a different denomination within the same faith experience prejudice, hatred, and/or discrimination based on being from a different sect. This religious or sect-based affiliation often exists as a differentiated relationship to power and may have socio-political and/or security-based consequences.

Sect-based religious identification and sectarianism have been recognized as having a so-called double function in terms of legitimation of power and privilege, as well as in protest and opposition. The utilization of religious or sect-based identity for the former has been evident throughout the greater Middle East and South Asia on state and non-state levels, including by Saddam Hussein who framed Iraq's nationalism within a Sunni context, Ayatollah Khomeini's framing his right to rule Iran within a Shia context, and General Zia-ul-Haq's use of his particular brand of Sunni Islam to add credibility and legitimacy to his rule in Pakistan. Non-state actors also use religious identification and sectarianism to enhance their credibility, legitimacy, position, and power. For example, within the context of Iraq, examples include Al-Qaeda in Iraq (AQI), the Islamic State of Iraq and the Levant (ISIL), and the Popular Mobilization Forces, among others. In terms of the use of religious sect to frame opposition, Ali Shariati comes to mind. He framed his opposition to Mohammad Reza Shah, the Pahlavi Dynasty, and U.S. influence in Iran within a Shia framework. Another prime example is Muhammad Iqbal, a South Asian Muslim writer and politician who framed his opposition to British colonial rule of India also within an Islamic framework. These categories illustrate that politics is often infused with religious symbols and rhetoric. Additionally, within the context of sect-based identity, focus is often placed on symbols, stories and history, among other factors, that fit within a specific framework that is deemed strategically beneficial to political entrepreneurs. Furthermore, in times of popular struggle, as well as with non-state actors in conflict zones, such as those in Iraq since 2003, religious or sect-based identity is often used as a resource to legitimize violent tactics. Therefore, the utilization of religion and religious identity is not based on spiritual ideology or the essence of religion. Rather, it is based on strategic planning, interests, and the goals of political entrepreneurs.

The ramifications associated with the instrumentalization of religious identity are highly nuanced, impactful, and overall detrimental to society on micro and macro levels. Before analyzing the causes and consequences of sectarianism, a brief theoretical framework of three schools of thought will be explained to better conceptualize this phenomenon. Establishing a theoretical framework by which to examine the strategic utilization of identity, particularly sect-based identity, by political entrepreneurs facilitates a blueprint by which to deconstruct covert and overt complexities associated with sectarianism and its ramifications. This is beneficial based on the need to examine sect-based strategies on both state and non-state levels through different frameworks and contexts to better ascertain and untangle relevant patterns and nuances regardless of geographic or temporal frameworks of analysis. This alongside a multi-directional and multi-dimensional interdisciplinary analytical framework helps bridge existing gaps in understanding how religious identity has been strategically utilized, as well as its associated ramifications on state and non-state levels.

The three primary schools of thought are primordialism, instrumentalism, and constructivism. According to Hashemi and Postel, it is important to understand these schools of thought to better explain and understand the rise of Islamic sectarianism, and the mobilization of sect-based groups, as well as the process of othering and subsequent conflict (Hashemi & Postel 2017: 1–13). Primordialism is the theory that identity is fixed, and individuals have one main ethnic identity which is neither malleable nor subject to change. More specifically, primordialism is arguably based on a shared sense of group identity and is deeply imbedded in human psychology, as well as in social relations. According to Smith, identity, particularly ethnic identity is based on a set of intangible elements rooted in biology, history and tradition that bind or connect an individual to a larger collectivity (Smith 1998). By extension, Stack argues that ethnic mobilization is often tied to emotional and often irrational notions of group solidarity and support (Stack 1986). Geertz furthers this argument by stating that primordial attachments are a given in social existence, overpowering in the context of ethnicity and religion (Geertz 1963) and by extension posits that these characteristics contribute to its rigidity and the non-malleable nature of identity.

According to Valbjorn, primordialists are highly influential. However, their view on ethnicity and identity are deeply flawed (Valbjorn 2020: 91–107) as people are less driven by religion or some ancient past than by issues of economics and politics (Matthiesen 2013). This is further reflected by the fact that both in historical and present day contexts, it is possible to identify countless examples of inter-sectarian cooperation and intra-sectarian divisions (Colgan 2015). Additionally, according to Hashemi and Postel, primordialists do not adequately address the link between identity and conflict and how identity is manipulated in such contexts and its impact (Hashemi & Postel 2017: 1–13). This is particularly problematic as there are countless examples including in Afghanistan, Pakistan, Yemen, Lebanon, and Iraq in which religious identity has been and continues to be manipulated and strategically utilized by political entrepreneurs who seek to advance their interests.

Instrumentalism on the other hand suggests that identity is malleable and can be manipulated by emphasizing in-group similarities and out-group differences. This theoretical framework posits that identity can also be utilized to invoke fear for strategic purposes by political entrepreneurs. This includes fear of assimilation, domination, or annihilation, which by extension can stimulate identity mobilization (Lake & Rothchild 1998b; Brass 1979: 35–77). Hashemi argues that for instrumentalists, identity mobilization, including mobilization based on ethnicity is a byproduct of political projects of political entrepreneurs who utilize identity to advance their political and economic interests. As such, in the context of conflict and violence, instrumentalism allows cross-comparisons between societies with similar social cleavages (Hashemi 2016: 65–76), on local, state or transnational levels. Moreover, Valbjorn argues that those who instrumentalize identity do not take identities and ideational factors seriously as these are reduced to some kind of surface phenomena under which the real drivers are present (Valbjorn 2020: 91–107). For example, in the modern context of Sunni-Shia sectarian conflict and violence the emphasis on differences in sects by political entrepreneurs is not based on ideological incompatibility, it is ideological constructs of identity that are manipulated and utilized for strategic purposes (Lynch 2013).

The third theoretical concept for the examination of sectarianism is constructivism. This concept adopts the middle ground between primordialism and instrumentalism (Hashemi & Postel 2017: 1–13). It borrows from Benedict Anderson (1991) by arguing that ethnicity is not fixed, but rather a political construct based on a dense web of social relationships (Young 1993). Valbjorn argues that for constructivists collective identities are imagined communities and as such are socially constructed (Valbjorn 2020: 91–107). This is conducive to the argument that people have multiple identities, including those that conflict with each other. The importance of each layer of identity varies in importance based on temporal and spatial circumstances (Valbjorn 2020: 91–107). Moreover, constructivism avoids essentializing sect affiliation and allows for human agency within the social context of group affiliation. Gaiser further argues that sect-based identity is only part of multiple intersecting identifications of a group or individual (Gaiser 2017). On one hand, constructivism recognizes the importance of seemingly rigid features of ethnic and religious identity. On the other hand, similar to instrumentalists, constructivists believe that political entrepreneurs manipulate identity, which often plays a critical role in the mobilization process of groups. However, they disagree with the extent to which identities can be manipulated (Hashemi 2016: 65–76) as they believe that conflict flows from "pathological social systems" and "political opportunity structures" that facilitate conflict and the manipulation of social cleavages (Lake & Rothchild 1998a).

Another important component in analyzing the complexities associated with sectarianism is examining the way issues pertaining to identity, including sectarianism, are framed and by extension analyzed, which assists one in understanding how information and knowledge have been constructed, assembled, and presented. According to Hashemi and Postel it is also beneficial to take into consideration the functional similarities between ethnic and religious mobilization as ethnicity and religion are often intertwined, overlap, and reinforce each other (Hashemi & Postel 2017: 1–13). An interesting example is how sectarianism is frequently framed as one between Persian Shia and Arab Sunnis, which lends credence to the salience of the literature on nationalism and ethnic politics in assessing religious sectarianism in Muslim societies today (Hashemi & Postel 2017: 1–13). A timely example of this intersection is Iraq during the Iran-Iraq War and after the 2003 invasion.

Sectarianism is on the rise across the Muslim world. Borders and boundaries have come under pressure, resulting in escalating tension, conflict, violence, and terrorism, as well as mass displacement and migration. States across the Muslim world – Yemen, Pakistan, Iraq, Afghanistan, Syria, Lebanon, among others – have faced challenges associated with a perpetual cycle of competition, conflict, and violence organized along sectarian lines. What is truly fueling its rise? Is it politics, faith, or competition? In this context a misconception has emerged in the literature about the nature of the relationship between politics and Islam. Conflict and violence within a Sunni-Shia context or the use of Islamic-based rhetoric is not necessarily related to or stem from a specific feature of Islam itself or the diverse cultures and people that identity with the faith. Rather, such rhetoric, conflict, and violence are based on the exploitation of religion for power, legitimacy, contestations, mobilization, and outbidding processes (Khatib 2015: 341–361) on state and non-state levels. To understand modern-day sectarianism, it is essential to move beyond explanations that focus predominantly on ancient Sunni-Shia animosities[1] and engage in multi-disciplinary and multi-directional examinations of this phenomenon that is shaping the political and security environments of the Islamic world on state and non-state levels.

While religious identities and how individuals define themselves and their communities are important, it is integral to understand how this identity has been utilized in historical and contemporary political contexts. It is also essential to understand how the role of sectarianism in modern conflicts on state and non-state levels has evolved and continues to evolve. As such, to enhance comprehensive understanding regarding the modern context of the surge of sectarianism and sectarian conflict in the Muslim world, it is important to critically examine the key individuals and major events that propelled this phenomenon forward and their transnational connectivity. It is also vital to examine the nuances that continue to influence changing political environments on national and regional levels, as well as transnational sect-based spaces and sectarian undercurrents. Whether in Lebanon, Pakistan, Iraq, Yemen, or elsewhere, sectarian identity in the modern context has served as a pretext to inflict injury and death upon countless individuals who have been "othered" for strategic purposes. Therefore, to understand modern-day sectarianism, it is essential to challenge many previously utilized conceptual frameworks by which it has been examined. As noted earlier, this includes moving beyond explanations that focus predominantly on ancient Sunni-Shia animosities or narrow examinations of sectarianism within broader political, security and religio-cultural contexts. According to Nasr, while history and theory may have established the identities of the different sects and rival groups "…the actual bones of contention are far less likely to be religious ideas than matters of concrete power and wealth…" (Nasr 2006).

By examining diverse themes, including the political economy of sectarianism, counterterrorism, issues pertaining to identity, Islamism, and the intersection of politics, identity, and sectarianism, this book seeks to challenge popular narratives that use sectarian divisions between Sunnis and Shias as an all-encompassing explanation for conflicts across the Muslim world. Through an interdisciplinary transnational approach the authors of this volume seek to deconstruct popular misconceptions regarding the complexities associated with sectarianism and its impact. The methodologies that are being utilized include historical analysis, securitization theory, case studies, as well as ethnographic and grounded theory approaches. The methodologies that are being employed, coupled with the diverse backgrounds of the book's authors, provides diverse perspectives and ideas that are highly valuable in examining this complex and nuanced phenomenon. This innovative way of examining sectarianism seeks to build upon and fill gaps in existing scholarship as the socio-political, geopolitical, and security landscapes of the greater Middle East and South Asia are notoriously complex and have been, and continue to be, influenced by a shifting mixture of domestic and international dynamics that affect the region on local and transnational levels.

Note

1 Sunni-Shia sectarian conflict is not rooted in ancient hatred nor is it based on primordial roots of shared identities with their specific sect fighting the perceived other. Rather, this new version of sectarianism across the region emerges predominantly from the recent political history of the Middle East.

Bibliography

Anderson, Benedict. *Imagined Communities: Reflections on the Origins and Spread of Nationalism*. New York: Verso, 1991.
Berger, Peter L. "The Sociological Study of Sectarianism." *Social Research* 15, no. 1/2, (Spring/Summer 1984): 367–385.
Brass, Paul R. "Elite Groups, Symbol Manipulation and Ethnic Identity Among the Muslims of South Asia," in *Political Identity in South Asia*, edited by David Taylor and Malcolm Yapp. London: Curzon Press, 1979, 35–77.
Colgan, Jeff. "How Sectarian Shapes Yemens War." *The Washington Post*, April 13, 2015.
Falk, R. "Religion and Politics: Verging on the PostModern." *Alternatives* 13, no. 3 (1988): 379–394.
Gaiser, Adam. "A Narrative Identity Approach to Islamic Sectarianism," in *Sectarianization: Mapping the new politics of the Middle East*, edited by N. A. Hashemi & D. Postel. London: Hurst Publishers, 2017.
Geertz, C. "The Integrative Revolution: Primordial Sentiments and Civil Politics in the New States, " in *Old Societies and New States: The Quest for Modernity in Asia and Africa*, edited by C. Geertz. London: Free Press, 1963.
Hashemi, Nader and Danny Postel. "Sectarianization: Mapping the New Politics of the Middle East." *The Review of Faith & International Affairs* 15, no. 3 (2017): 1–13.
Hashemi, Nader. "Toward the Political Theory of Sectarianism in the Middle East: The Salience of Authoritarianism over Theology." *Journal of Islamic and Muslim Studies* 1, no. 1 (2016): 65–76.
Khatib, Hakin. "Political Instrumentalization of Islam in a Violent State Crisis: The Case of Syria." *Journal of Applied Security Research* 10, no. 3, (July 2015): 341–361.
Lake, David and Donald Rothchild, eds., *The International Spread of Ethnic Conflict: Fear, Diffusion and Escalation*. Princeton: Princeton University Press, 1998a.
Lake, David and Donald Rothchild. "Spreading Fear: The Genesis of Transnational Ethnic Conflict," in *International Spread of Ethnic Conflict: Fear, Diffusion and Escalation*, edited by David Lake and Donald Rothchild. Princeton: Princeton University Press, 1998b.
Lynch, Marc M. "The Entrepreneurs of Cynical Sectarianism: Why the Middle East's Identity Conflict Go Way Beyond the Sunni-Shia Divide." *Foreign Policy*, November 13, 2013.
Matthiesen, Toby. *Sectarian Gulf: Bahrain, Saudi Arabia, and the Arab Spring that wasn't*. Stanford: Stanford University Press, 2013.
Nasr, Vali. *The Shia Revival: How Conflicts Within Islam Will Shape the Future*. New York: W. W. Norton & Company, 2006.
Smith, Anthony D. *Nationalism and Modernism: A Critical Survey of Recent Theories of Nations and Nationalism*. New York: Routledge, 1998.
Stack, John F.Jr. ed. *The Primordial Challenge: Ethnicity in the Contemporary World*. New York: Greenwood Press, 1986.

Valbjorn, Morten. "Beyond the beyond(s): On the (many) Third Way(s) Beyond Primordialism and Instrumentalism in the Study of Sectarianism." *Nations and Nationalism* 26, no. 1 (January 2020): 91–107.

Young, Crawford, ed. *The Rising Tide of Cultural Pluralism: The Nation-State at Bay?* Madison: University of Wisconsin Press, 1993.

1
UNRAVELLING SECTARIANISM IN SOUTH ASIA

Ayesha Jalal

Introduction

What exactly is "sectarianism"? Human beings have always been subject to processes of inclusion and exclusion throughout human history. Is "sectarianism" merely an analytical device for shifting social and political formations or an actual depiction of the historical dynamics that result in people excluding and hating "others," both internal and external. Perspective matters as does context and the interpretative approach. Take the famous hadith attributed to a Prophetic saying that there would be 73 sects after him and only one of these would go to paradise. The desire of Muslim sects to be the 73rd sect has historically fueled sectarian competition, heightening social conflict and the propensity for violence against those deemed to have gone beyond the pale. This bigoted impulse is reversed in another interpretation of the hadith cited by the 10th-century geographer Muqaddasi, according to which only one of the 73 sects would go to hell. The 12th-century theologian Al-Ghazali read this as "all are in heaven except the *zindiqs* (heretics)" (Mottahedeh 2006). While the stated number of sects is figurative rather than literal, there is little doubt about the religious pluralism implicit in this interpretation of the hadith, overturning the exclusionary thrust of the first one and allowing for more accommodative attitudes towards rival sects. Such an interpretation fully accords with the Quran where diversity of religious belief is described as divinely ordained.

How then has sectarianism come to be seen as the source of modern conflicts? We live in an age where wars between nation-states pose less of a threat than spiraling conflicts between state and non-state actors, some of whom harbor hopes of not only wresting state power but also gaining global domination. Seemingly inspired by engrained sectarian animosities, these conflicts have been threatening the fragile social orders and state structures of South and West Asia alike. While the factors driving the rise of sectarianism in the two regions are informed by

DOI: 10.4324/9781003329510-2

distinctive historical processes, aspects of the phenomenon have been conducive to comparative analysis attracting a vast and varied body of work of scholarly merit. Despite differences in points of emphasis, most of the scholarship on the subject defines sectarianism as a construction that entails exclusion if not outright bigotry and fanaticism, whether of the religious or sectarian varieties.

Sectarianism's negative connotations are a result of its departure from the dominant religious and political perspectives in any given context. This is exemplified today by the legal idioms of modern nation-states, which claim uniformity of purpose in contrast to sectarian divisiveness even while promoting discord along lines of community for political advantage. Historically, sects have rarely had the opportunity to define themselves as such and are given a separate designation to denigrate them for their aberrant, if not heretical, tendencies that break with the dominant ones. Longitudinal histories of sectarianism in different parts of the world attentive to local and regional dynamics are critically important at a time when sectarianism is coming to be invoked as a universal and universalizing category, one that can be sanguinely invoked to explain varied and complex political dynamics.

Insofar as Muslims are an interpretative community, the ideal of consensus and reality of contention are intrinsic to the practice of Islam (Ahmad 2017). Deployed loosely to describe religiously motivated disputes, sectarianism as a blanket category flattens out the complex and uneven story of fluctuating political fortunes, reflecting the perpetual see-sawing between Muslim unanimity and discord. Sectarian divisions among Muslims on closer analysis tend to be more personalized than a product of interpretative differences on specific religious issues. Shia-Sunni differences are a case in point. Far from being intrinsic to Muslim religiosity, whatever its conception and performance, Shia-Sunni conflicts have historically been political in nature. In more recent times Muslim sectarianism, and not just the Shia-Sunni divide, has been utilized to promote the imperious logic of state power in unstable post-colonial regions, leading to the misconception that sectarian fissures among Muslims are somehow religiously ordained. Competition between the two sects for political supremacy historically has never foreclosed the possibility of alliances of convenience or the forging of a broader unity, however fleeting in duration.

Using sectarianism to describe internal differences among Muslims as inherently religious ignores the often more important aspect of state formation, the challenges of consolidation and sustainability, and the international, regional, and domestic linkages informing that process. Deeming religion and state to be inexorably linked in Islam, orientalist scholarship has placed far too much weight on the writings of Muslim theologians and Muslim jurists. Alternative insights are conveniently occluded by the self-confident premises of categories like sectarianism, doing damage both to the subject and its history. The uncorroborated conflation of religion and sect in contexts where there is a distinction between faith and affinity to a community has done much to confuse matters. This lack of clarity invariably strengthens the moral superiority of the modern nation-state's normative homogenizing ideals against negatively portrayed religious sects, obfuscating the state's role in undermining its self-adopted idioms in political practice.

The contributions to this volume offer a wide range of insights into the local and regional characteristics of the global phenomena called "sectarianism." Despite differences in emphasis, they all bring out some of the key practical difficulties in viewing political conflicts in West Asia and also South Asia through the conceptual prism of "sectarianism". Historically grounded and analytically critical approaches help expose the conceptual limitations of "sectarianism" as a universal explanatory framework to explain politics and faith in Muslim countries. This in turn can go some way towards correcting the common misconception that places like West Asia and South Asia with their ancient tribal and sectarian affiliations are "exceptions" that can never be at peace other than under the jackboot of authoritarianism. While it is true to say that "sects", or groups of people who define themselves by constructing mental and physical boundaries with others have always existed, it is a historically moot question whether "sectarianism" is a product of "ancient hatreds" as some illustrious public figures are known to periodically pronounce. The modern antecedents of "sectarianism", a particular way of perceiving, creating, classifying, and controlling difference are traceable to the emergence of the modern nation state in the age of Western imperialism during the nineteenth and early twentieth centuries. This belies the stamp of historic antiquity often given to sectarian conflicts like Shia-Sunni contentions in the contemporary world.

Putting Sectarianism in its Place

There is ample evidence to reject the notion that sectarian differences between Shias and Sunnis have always and everywhere prevented social interaction and political alliances among Muslims. Based on his study of early sources, the renowned Indian Muslim scholar, Shibli Nomani, found that sectarian discord was present in the initial years of Islam and Muslims routinely referred to their opponents as infidel or heretic. However, personal animosities were not a barrier to the faithful negotiating their differences and making common cause since sectarian disputes were factional and not religious in nature. A tradition related to the Prophet of Islam recounted by a Shia, a Mutazilite or rationalist, an innovator or someone considered to be irreligious, was deemed to be reliable by Sunni collectors of hadith so long as the transmitter had a reputation for truthfulness. The differentiation between religious beliefs and honesty in hadith collection extended to the educational curriculum where it was common to teach the religious works of other sects along with explanatory notes of dissent. Religious differences were no barrier to the acquisition of rational and literary knowledge. Al-Farabi and Ibn Sina, considered to be beyond the pale, were a regular part of the school curriculum. Despite facing opposition, the Ahl-e-Sunnat wa Jamaat considered it legitimate to say prayers behind someone belonging to an opposing sect (Nomani 1930). The history of Islam in the Indian subcontinent has been informed by the dialectic of difference and accommodation among Muslim sects quite as much as between the faithful and non-Muslims. While politically motivated conflicts did lead to Shias and Sunnis as well as different Sunni sects coming to blows, especially after the weakening of central state authority in the late Mughal period, it was only with the end of Muslim sovereignty and the establishment of British colonial rule that sectarianism in India assumed some of its contemporary characteristics. The proclamation of religious freedom and neutrality by the British was not new to the subcontinent. The Mughal emperor Akbar's policy of "sul-e-kul," peace for all, extended respect and protection to the inhabitants of the empire regardless of caste or creed. What made the British different, as Shibli astutely observed, was a calculated policy of religious indifference, allowing the colonial rulers maximum leeway for intervention if and when necessary while projecting a semblance of religious neutrality. For instance, the state was neutral on issues concerning mosque and church but not when it came to razing a mosque to clear space for a road or build a military cantonment. It was the intrusive nature of the colonial state's secularity in matters to do with religion, not its retreat from the domain of religion, that stoked the fires of sectarianism. With the rulers declaring neutrality, if not indifference, Muslim sects responded to the absence of religious authority by creating their own places of worship and seeking adjudication of their disputes in colonial courts.

It is impossible to do complete justice to the complex underpinnings of sectarian contention among Muslims in India in a short chapter. But it is still worth outlining the key differences between the Mughal and the British periods. Unlike the Mughals who were keenly interested in religion, the British maintained a façade of religious neutrality, which as Shibli noted was effectively calculated indifference towards religion and never meant non-intervention. The Mughal ruler's religious inclinations were all important and, recognizing their subordination to temporal authority, the ulema generally did not seek to organize movements of religious reform or pose as social reformers. However, they contributed to Islamic knowledge and discourse, using new methodologies to interpret hadith, Quranic interpretations, and works on jurisprudence. With the loss of Muslim sovereignty, the British policy of religious freedom and neutrality created the illusion of opportunity for the more ambitious among the ulema. With the glistening prize of religious authority lifting the darkness in their hearts and minds, the internal power struggles among the ulema intensified.

Significantly, the quality of scholarship produced by Muslim ulema in the period of colonial rule was in inverse proportion to the ferocity of attacks on rival sects. Differences of interpretation on relatively minor matters like the correct way of standing to perform the ritual prayer, for example, provided impetus for opposition and outright conflict. Personality cults proliferated around these differences, verbal as well as performative, giving impetus to the establishment of new sects, each with its own notion of being Muslim. Sober minded Muslims considered sectarian disputes to be over matters that are secondary to the religious tenets of Islam on which, ironically, there has always been general agreement. Internal jostling among Indian Muslim maulvis for religious authority and control over urban spaces fueled a pamphlet warfare and an ensuing battle of fatwas which, together with the colonial courts, and the colonial state's bureaucratic manipulations of its decennial census-based assumptions, reconfigured the meaning of religion in India.

Muslims wary of sectarian divisions rarely escaped the fire and fury propelling the political ambitions of those aspiring to become the preeminent Islamic religious authority in British India. The ulema's hopes of exercising religious authority over Indian Muslims were misplaced as a cursory glance at history demonstrates the impossibility of exercising religious authority over Muslims without political sovereignty. The great Muslim reformer Saiyid Ahmad Khan, who won the respect and trust of the British through his diligent administrative service and loyalty, was well aware of the rift between political and religious power in the aftermath of 1857. Despite his access to the highest echelons of the colonial state, he became one of the main targets of the ulema's rage when he poached on their jealously guarded domain by venturing to interpret the teachings of Islam in light of the new education. A battery of fatwas was issued against him not only in India but also in Mecca and Medina, calling for his excommunication and even death for his perceived transgressions of Islamic principles. Contemporary sources reveal the ease with which signed fatwas – non-binding legal opinions – could be procured in India as well as the Holy cities of Mecca and Medina. The only difference was the language of the fatwas: Hindi-Urdu in India and Arabic in the Hejaz. Those giving the fatwas belonged to different sectarian affiliations. When not enticed by money to give made-to-order fatwas, they wrote treatises condemning rivals depending on which way the winds of political fate were blowing.

A zero-sum game for the participants, the contradictory fatwas advertised Muslim sectarian differences over and above the unities of a common faith, negating the already limited advantages of their status as a religious minority. Saiyid Ahmad Khan and his wide circle of associates in the Aligarh movement tried emphasizing Muslim unities over Muslim divisions in their writings and public speeches. Much like the role of social media in our own times, the relative ease of airing religious opinions through an expanding press and publications market intensified the sectarian divide, turning minor differences of opinion into major conflicts that required recourse to colonial courts. Since the British were less interested in curbing sectarian and communitarian hatreds than in censoring anti-imperialist points of view, the tussle within the Muslim community heightened internal tensions, making a travesty of the colonially guaranteed principle of religious freedom and neutrality.

The renowned Urdu novelist Deputy Nazir Ahmad, an ardent supporter of Saiyid Ahmad Khan despite differences with his interpretation of religion, was irked by the rifts among his co-religionists. His novel *Ruya-i-Sadiqa (True Dreams)* published in 1892 is a blunt expose of Muslim sectarianism. In choosing fiction over an ethical tract, he clearly was aiming for a broader audience even though the book, which is really a compendium of his religious point of view, was not a commercial success like his other novels. In Nazir Ahmad's opinion, Shia-Sunni differences had nothing whatsoever to do with religion. A misogynist religion in the eyes of the world, Islam's main sectarian division is remarkably on account of two women – Fatima, the Prophet's daughter; and Ayesha, the Prophet's favorite wife and daughter of his close friend Abu Bakar, who became the first caliph despite Ali's claim. With this personalized insight, Nazir Ahmad dismisses the religious basis of the Shia-Sunni conflict in its entirety. The tragedy of Karbala, which had nothing to do with religion, was a blot on the history of Islam. Sunnis erred in denying that Fatima and Ali, and their son Hussain and his family, were treated in the most appalling and inhumane manner (Ahmad 2014).

According to Nazir Ahmad, a deep reverence for the Prophet's immediate family lies at the heart of the Shia dispute with Sunnis. Shias revere the Prophet's extended family for their presumed inheritance of divine majesty. The Sunnis are divided into a multitude of sects, Ahl-Hadith, Wahabi, Barelvi, Muqallid – those following the authority of a religious school or an imam – and Ghair Muqallid who only follow the Quran and the hadith. But despite these divisions, Sunni sects are in accord with the Shias when it comes to the Prophet, whom they wrongly entangle with God and the minutia of religion and the world. Some Muslim sects sanctified the Prophet in a manner reserved exclusively for God. Despite clear and repeated warnings against making the same mistake as the Jews and the Christians, who had distorted the messages of their prophets, later Muslims started venerating the Prophet as much as, and at times more than, God. The Prophet had left categorical instructions to his followers not to turn his grave into a mosque. He could not have imagined that Muslims would not just worship at his grave but turn the graves of other saints into mosques. This is shirk, associationism, and a cardinal error that undermines Quranic teachings on the unity of creation. By ignoring the Prophet's teachings and equating him with God, Muslims are not just violating the principle of tawhid, the bedrock of Islam, but wrongly pitting religion against the world and ensuring constant friction between the two.

Nazir Ahmad deftly charts the interplay between the colonial policy of neutrality towards religion and the rising crescendo of Muslim sectarian disputations. Muslims are shown as exercising the right to religious freedom conferred on them by the British claim of neutrality by calling co-religionists infidels and apostates. These took the form of public disputations, or *munazaras*, essays in newspaper and journals, and pamphlets. Even casual utterances on religious issues inflamed tempers and could land colonial subjects in financially and emotionally draining lawsuits in colonial courts. In a marvelous kaleidoscope of Muslim life in Delhi following the 1857 rebellion, Nazir Ahmad captures the fatuity of sectarian divisions. The medley of idle, good for nothing mischief makers, whom he holds responsible for creating unnecessary divisions among believers included someone who proposed splitting the city's mosques between those who followed a school (*mazhab*) of Muslim thought and those that did not, and issuing tickets at the entrance to check the entry of strangers. Another troublemaker believes Muslims belonging to a school of religious thought cannot perform prayers behind an independent minded *imam* as their prayers will become invalid. There is a chauvinist who had sent his wife to her maternal home only because they participated in the city's inter-religious festival of flower growers. Then there is a sermon giver who stands at the entrance of the Fatehpuri mosque, supposedly to counter Christian priests, but tells Muslims coming for sunset prayers that listening to him takes precedence over prayer. A self-styled religious warrior, who lives outside the city, says his morning and sunset prayers at a mosque in a Hindu neighborhood, deeming this to be equivalent to a jihad. A lawyer who has dedicated his life to fighting court cases whenever he hears of a religious dispute, regardless of their merit, is among this company of horrors. So is an agitator bent upon destroying any Hindu temple that does not have a mosque in its vicinity and, finally a crusader who hates *necharis*, but lacking the intellect to take them on himself collects all the negative criticisms against them that he can find in newspapers and other publications.

Flouting the dictum of live and let live, this picture of the Muslim penchant for futile disputes in pursuit of worldly matters might be a novelist's entertaining depiction of the underpinnings of sectarian divisions in colonial India's capital city. But its finer insights can help in navigating the infinitely more complex landscape of sectarian enmities formed by the coming together of individual warriors of the faith with those wielding state power in the newly independent states of formally British India.

Sectarianism in Post-Colonial South Asia

The irony of the British policy of religious freedom leading to an intensification of sectarian rivalries among Indian Muslims serves as a warning against considering these fissures to be inherent in the teachings of Islam. A broader and more extensive reading of South Asian sources reveals that "sectarianism," as in West Asia, is a product of a particular way of seeing and being that has less to do with clashing conceptions of religion than with belonging to a particular community as in the Pakistani case of the heterodox Ahmadi sect. Posing as the 73rd sect, they offended the sentiments of non-Ahmadi Muslims with their proselytization and exclusionary group practices. Despite efforts by a loose coalition of right-wing parties, posing as guardians of Islam, both before and immediately after the creation of Pakistan, Ahmadis continued to be considered equal citizens and were entitled to the same legal protections as the others.

It was only in the dramatically changed context of post-1971 when Pakistan lost its eastern wing with the breakaway of Bangladesh that the so-called religious lobby secured the assistance of their patrons in Saudi Arabia to force Zulfikar Ali Bhutto's elected government to declare Ahmadis non-Muslims. The quadrupling of oil prices following the Arab-Israeli war of 1973 gave the oil rich Arab states unprecedented political muscle internationally, which they deployed to promote their preferred versions of Islam globally. Pakistan was one of the earliest to fall into line (Jalal 2011). Not only were Ahmadis ostracized from the Muslim community in 1974, they were subsequently also legally banned from using Islamic terminology and practicing Islamic rituals on the grounds that Muslims have a patent on them akin to Coca-Cola as a brand name. In its four against one ruling in *Zaheeruddun vs.the State* in 1993 the Supreme Court of Pakistan redefined the very meaning of religious freedom by accepting the proposition that Muslims have exclusive proprietary rights over Islam (Siddiq 1995). Reduced to the unenviable status of second-class citizens, and their lives, property, and places of worship under threat from self-styled Islamic vigilantes, Ahmadis face criminal charges just for giving the Muslim call to prayer or referring to their own call to prayer as an *azan*.

The denial of elementary citizenship rights to Ahmadis required overturning decades of social, political, and legal resistance to demands to banish the community from the fold of Islam. This was made possible by skirting around civil law and making it criminal for an Ahmadi to claim to be a Muslim or behave like one. In a frenzied judgment the learned justices of the supreme court made a complete mockery of the law with a ruling deriving its rationale from religious sentiment. On the grounds that Ahmadis offended Muslim religious sensibilities, Section 298 (C) of the Pakistan Penal Code destroyed the very basis of religious freedom. Ahmadis are barred from posing as Muslims, propagating their faith, or referring to it as Islam. Speaking, writing, or making visual representations offensive to Muslim religious feelings can result in up to three years in prison and a fine. The weaponization of Islam as a proprietary brand name like Coke and Pepsi may well be one of the judicial master strokes of the independent Muslim state of Pakistan that has had expected as well as unintended consequences.

Ahmadis are not the only targets in the sham of religious freedom existing in post-colonial Pakistan. The blasphemy law has been deployed as a favored weapon by the religious right. Together with the urge to grab expensive urban land, the blasphemy law has been used by self-interested individuals looking to enhance their power and pelf. The state's strategic interests have melded with the interests of these self-seekers in consequential ways. The Iranian revolution and Ayatollah Khomeini's fiery rhetoric vowing to export radical Shia thinking to the rest of the Muslim world alarmed the military caretakers of predominantly Sunni Pakistan, especially after Shias laid siege on the federal capital in July 1980 to protest General Zia-ul-Haq's military government's enforcement of Islamic taxes under the Zakat and Ushr ordinance. The government's retraction of its decision, exempting Shias from paying the additional taxes, inflamed vocal sections of the Sunni majority community. This was the shot from the starter's pistol that set two communities, joined in faith and cultural traditions, against each other. While Sunni-Shia tensions had the most immediate impact on domestic politics, Pakistan's strategic concerns vis-à-vis the new clerical regime in Iran was a primary driving factor.

The Soviet invasion of Afghanistan in December 1979 further altered the political matrix of military dominated Pakistan. A mainly Barelvi Muslim country, the Pakistani state's patronage of Deobandis, who were in the ascendance in the North West Frontier Province (renamed Khyber Pakhtunkhwa in 2010) where recruits for the "jihad" against the Soviets were being procured, reconfigured the playing field. With their deep roots in Pakistani society, Barelvis assisted by lucrative transnational links hotly contested the sudden rise of the Deobandis, heightening conflict between the two groups. The outbreak of the Iraq-Iran war in September 1980 added another layer of complexity to the sectarian scene. On the backfoot after its concession to the Shia community, Zia-ul-Haq's military regime allowed hidebound Sunni groups to flex their muscle unhindered. Jhang district in Pakistan's largest and most powerful province of Punjab where elite Shia families enjoyed considerable political clout on account of their dual role as landlords and hereditary leaders of shrines, became the new epicenter of sectarian tensions that were directly linked to the Iran-Iraq war. In 1984 an organization called the Anjuman-i-Sipah-i-Sahaba, literally the army of the Prophet's companions, who drew support from less privileged and marginalized social groups, emerged in Jhang with the explicit purpose of spreading hatred against Shias.

Guided by its strategic calculations in the aftermath of the Iranian revolution and the Soviet invasion of Afghanistan, the Zia regime looked the other way as the Anjuman-i-Sipah-Sahaba persisted with its highly inflammatory anti-Shia discourse. By 1986 the Sipah-i-Sahaba had embarked upon a campaign of the targeted killing of Shias. In December 1990 it went so far as to engineer the assassination of the Iranian Consul General in Lahore with dire consequences for Pakistan's relations with Iran. But with the Sipah-i-Sahaba's spread of madrasas in Punjab serving as recruiting grounds for a state-supported "jihad" in Afghanistan, nothing was done to curb its noxious narratives and violent activities. The sectarian outfit forged an alliance with the Deobandis to become an even more potent force in Pakistan's politics. Shias for their part forged their own militant outfits to stave off their Sunni counterparts. While militant groups of Sunnis and Shias vied with one other in the urban jungles of Pakistan, the state recruited and trained would-be jihadis to fight the ungodly occupiers of Muslim Afghanistan and by the early 1990s also in Indian held Kashmir. Becoming a frontline state in the war against the Soviets in Afghanistan and then fighting a proxy war in Kashmir helped Zia-ul-Haq to become the longest surviving military ruler in Pakistan's history. The feat was achieved at great cost – ripping apart the social matrix of Pakistan, leaving indelible mental and emotional scars that are making it increasingly difficult for the country to achieve a modicum of political stability and economic prosperity.

There was a time when neighboring India flaunted its "secular" claims and democratic credentials with much fanfare. Today it is succumbing to a dangerous blend of nationalist bigotry and authoritarianism. Backed by the big bags of Indian business, the Hindutva brigades are fomenting their version of "sectarian" conflicts with Muslims and Christians as targets. If lynching Muslims to death for the mere suspicion of eating beef or passing legislation prohibiting conversions on suspicion of these being part of a so-called "love jihad" by Muslim men against Hindu women can be considered a measure of religious sentiment, India's civil society is giving its counterparts in Sunni orthodox Pakistan tough competition. There has been a disturbing rise in anti-Muslim feelings in India, all of them deliberately orchestrated to offer maximum mileage to Hindutva protagonists. The trend has grown by leaps and bounds since the rise of Narendra Modi at the helm of the ruling Bharatiya Janata Party (BJP) in 2014. Whatever the evidence of soft Hindutva in the early decade when India was seemingly wedded to the ideals of secularism, democracy and religious freedom, there can be no denying the qualitative changes that are underway to chip away at the fundamental rights of those outside the fold of Hinduism.

New Delhi's shocking disregard of constitutional norms in its unilateral abrogation of Article 370 in August 2019 did not fail to raise concerns internationally. But it is the inhuman treatment of Kashmiri Muslims – stripped of their citizenship rights, kept under a lockdown, and denied Internet access and thrown into jail without due process – that has brought India's secular-democratic façade crashing down. Matters do not stop in Kashmir, a long-standing dispute between India and Pakistan. The BJP's implementation of the National Register of Citizens in Assam has led to the exclusion of two million people. Among those facing statelessness, a high proportion are women. Shedding all pretense at secularism, the Modi government enacted the highly divisive Citizenship Amendment Act (CAA), giving Hindus, Jains, Buddhists, Sikhs, and Christians escaping persecution from India's neighboring countries citizenship in India. The deliberate exclusion of Muslim makes for a particularly insidious kind of state sectarianism whose main premise is that India belongs to the Hindus. The Supreme Court's ruling on the Ayodhya dispute greatly strengthened this narrative. Favoring Hindu nationalist religious sentiments, the court's decision on the contentious Ayodhya issue is strikingly similar in its reasoning to the 1993 Coca Cola judgment in Pakistan. It remains to be seen whether the effects will be the same as Ahmadis are miniscule in comparison to Indian Muslims.

Bangladesh, where secularism is enshrined in the constitution, is also showing growing signs of sectarian differences. Once again, the primary reason is political rather than religious. The global assertion of Islam has impacted Bangladesh's political landscape far more than is often acknowledged (Riaz 2008a, 2008b). In recent years the secular ideology of the country has come under growing pressure after targeted attacks on Shia Muslims, Ahmadis, and Christians by right wing groups. Even Sri Lanka, which perceives itself as a secular country and was witnessing relative calm after a three-decade-long civil war, has been rocked by sectarian violence directed at the island's religious minorities, especially Muslims and Christians. While the spike in sectarian violence in each of Britain's former colonies is informed by new political impulses, they also carry the weight of a colonial past that saw a privileging of religious categories for census and bureaucratic purposes that have yet to be decolonized and replaced by narratives of equal rights of citizenship. If Pakistan is sitting on a powder keg of pent-up sectarian feelings, "secular" India is sinking under the weight of a state promoted religious bigotry, Bangladesh has been witnessing attacks linked to the Islamic State on atheist bloggers, and Sri Lanka is being slowly transformed into a hub of sectarianism by extremist Buddhist propagandists. With democracy facing unprecedented challenges, South Asia's sectarian landscape looks anything but hopeful.

Should sectarianism in its pejorative connotation then be construed as a necessary condition of contemporary life in South and West Asia? There is no doubt that division and divisiveness have been in the political ascendance even as globalization binds us into interconnectivities of which we may or may not be conscious. It would be interesting to consider how sectarianism has fared in Arab nation-states wedded to the principle of secularism. Defining who can and cannot be a Muslim and then laying down an elaborate infrastructure of discrimination for all those who failed to meet the legally laid down criteria, the military dominated Pakistani state has fueled a conflict between the Sunni majority and other sects that is not about religious doctrine but is inherently political in nature. Much the same can be said of India, Bangladesh, and Sri Lanka, and also West Asia. Official state secularism did not end sectarian politics in many formerly colonized countries in South and West Asia, not because of religion but because of secular state policies using colonial schemes of classifying and controlling social groups with confessional beliefs that are at variance with the political purposes of the dominant narrative.

"Sectarianism" then is less a manifestation of religious differences and more the result of a concerted politics of exclusion and discrimination amid heightened competition. It is imperative to approach issues of religious pluralism and diversity in the contemporary world without essentializing religiously defined cultural differences and turning sectarianism into a self-fulfilling prophecy. There is great elasticity in sectarian relations in everyday social and political practice that anyone who has visited these countries would know. Discursive claims of difference can be sustained in carefully crafted narratives of "sectarianism" but cannot wholly undermine the infinitely more flexible everyday interactions between those who happen to be Sunni, Shia, Copt, Druze, or Ahmadi. We can either take the self-definitions of these groups at face-value or, going beyond the stifling constraints of identity politics, decide to view them as an expression of a God-given human diversity, one worthy of respect and understanding, not exclusion and elimination based on sect or religion. One can take an expansive and broad-minded approach and celebrate diversity or a narrow minded and bigoted one by rejecting difference as intolerable.

The choice is there for us to make. We need to choose judiciously, keeping in mind the ties that bind and remain open to understanding and those that divide. Disagreement does not have to entail opposition, far less rejection and execration. In conclusion, the uplifting poetry of the master sage Jalaluddin Rumi is the perfect overture to the spirit of Islam on human diversity. Together with a historically nuanced view of sects, his grand vision provides a corrective to state supported modernist attempts at creating, classifying, and controlling differences and imbuing them with eternal essences.

Bibliography

Ahmad, Nazir. "Ruya-i-Sadiqa", in *Majmua Deputy Nazir Ahmad*. Lahore: Sang-e-Meel, 2014.
Ahmad, Shahab. *What is Islam: The Importance of Being Islamic*. Princeton: Princeton University Press, 2017.
Jalal, Ayesha. "An Uncertain Trajectory: Islam's Contemporary Globalization, 1971–1979", in *The Shock of the Global: The 1970s in Perspective*, edited by Nial Ferguson, Charles S. Maier et al. Cambridge: Harvard University Press, 2011.
Mottahedeh, Roy P. "Pluralism and Islamic Traditions of Religious Divisions." *Svensk. Teologisk Kvartalskrift*. År g. 82, 2006.
Nomani, Shibli. *Maqalat*, vol.1. Azamgarh: Darul Musannefin, 1930.

Riaz, Ali. *Faithful Education: Madrassahs in South Asia*. New Brunswick: Rutgers University Press, 2008a.
Riaz, Ali. *Islamist Militancy in Bangladesh: A Complex Web*. USA and Canada: Routledge, 2008b.
Rumi, Jalaluddin. "Only Breath." Translated by Coleman Barks, in *The Essential Rumi*. San Francisco: Harper Collins, 2004.
Siddiq, N. Nadeem Ahmad. "Enforced Apostasy: Zaheeruddin V. State and the Official Persecution of the Ahmadiyya Community in Pakistan." *Law & Inequality* 14, no. 1 (1995): 275–.

2

THE AHMADIYYA MUSLIM COMMUNITY'S IDENTITY AS THE "TRUE ISLAM" THROUGH ITS EXCLUSION

Misbah Hyder

> Since its emergence, Jama'at-i Ahmadiyya has reinvigorated the debate on Islamic orthodoxy among the Muslim mainstream.
>
> *(Khan 2015: 2)*

> In a certain sense, [Ahmadis] occupy a liminal space between the internal other and the external other, as a minority that does not agree with that characterization and that hence constantly threatens the stability of the boundaries separating self and other.
>
> *(Tareen 2017: 137)*

Introduction

In response to the increasing sectarian disputes among Muslims worldwide, and the September 11, 2001 attack on the World Trade Center, over 200 members of the world's leading Islamic scholars from 50 countries gathered in Jordan to discuss and sign a "Universal Islamic Consensus" that "amounts to a historical, universal and unanimous religious and political consensus (*ijma'*) of the Community (umma) of Islam in our day, and a consolidation of traditional, orthodox Islam" for the "first time in over a thousand years" (Ghazi 2007). In this message, released in 2004 by King Abdullah II of Jordan, global Islamic scholars agreed on the "Three Points of the Amman Message": (1) recognized the validity of eight *Mathhabs* (legal schools) of *Sunni*, *Shia*, and *Ibadhi* Islam; of traditional Islamic Theology *(Ash'arism)*; of Islamic Mysticism (*Sufism*), and of true *Salafi* thought, with a "precise definition of who is a Muslim;" (2) forbade *takfir* (declarations of apostasy) between Muslims, based on the definition; (3) provided guidelines for issuing *fatwas* (Islamic religious declarations). Summing up points one and two, the Amman Message declares:

DOI: 10.4324/9781003329510-3

it is neither possible nor permissible to declare as apostates any group of Muslims who believes in God, Glorified and Exalted be He, and His Messenger (may peace and blessings be upon him) and the pillars of faith, and acknowledges the five pillars of Islam, and does not deny any necessarily self-evident tenet of religion.

("The Ammam Message" 2009)

This message was designed to speak to both Muslim and non-Muslim audiences about how the global Muslim *ummah* is "formally and specifically coming to such a pluralistic mutual inter-recognition" (Ghazi 2007).

One group excluded from the religious leaders consulted on the Amman Message was the Ahmadiyya Muslim Community – an allegedly apostate community that has been excluded from conceptualizations of Islamic "orthodoxy" among many global Muslim leaders since the community's founding. This was exacerbated after the Pakistani state's legal designation of the Ahmadiyya as a non-Muslim minority (Iqtidar 2012; Khan 2015; Qasmi 2015; Saeed 2017, 2007). Despite this exclusion, the Ahmadiyya identify not only as a community of Muslims, but Muslims that practice "True Islam" and therefore actively participate in debates defining "real" Islam. As such, the Ahmadiyya plays an important role in debates defining "an Islamic orthodoxy."[1] The community claims inclusion within the Muslim *ummah* despite the community's exclusion from a constructed, monolithic "Islamic orthodoxy" by many global Muslim leaders, especially those from South Asia. As such, Adil Hussain Khan asserts that this "illustrate[s] how the Ahmadi controversy has helped shape the discourse of orthodoxy in contemporary Islam more broadly" (Khan 2015). In this chapter, I analyze how the Ahmadiyya Muslim Community has participated in debates on defining the "real" Islam since its founding during the late nineteenth century under British colonial rule of the Indian subcontinent and how this continues today in the context of global persecution.

The Ahmadiyya community claims that it adheres to the core tenets of Islam with its five pillars, as outlined in the Amman Message, and does not dispute the sanctity and finality of the Prophet Muhammad. However, the latter in particular is challenged by many non-Ahmadi Muslims based on the Ahmadiyya belief in its founder, Mirza Ghulam Ahmad, as the "Promised Messiah."[2] According to the Second Amendment of the Pakistani Constitution, the Ahmadiyya rejects *khatam-i-nabuwwat* (the finality of Prophet Muhammad) and believes in a "false prophet." This legally designates Ahmadis as a non-Muslim minority. The accusation that the Ahmadiyya does not believe in *khatam-i-nabuwwat* has spread across the global Muslim *ummah,* leading to anti-Ahmadi violence and persecution across Muslim-majority contexts, including in Bangladesh, Indonesia, Saudi Arabia, Malaysia and in Muslim-majority areas of the UK (Acquah 2011; London Mosque warned 2019; Burhani 2014; Haron 2018; Irawan 2017; Samwini 2006; Soedirgo 2018). However, Ahmadis reject the accusation that their belief in the Ahmadiyya's founder as the Promised Messiah delegitimizes the Ahmadiyya concurrent belief in the Prophet Muhammad's finality.

Constructing the boundaries of a "real" Islam was at stake in debates about *jihad* and the sanctity of the Prophet among the Muslim *ulema* (religious scholars) during British colonial rule of the Indian subcontinent. Indian Muslim scholars were leaning on centuries-old debates about the proper interpretations and uses of *jihad*, as well as the role of the Prophet Muhammad within Islamic practice.[3] While this chapter does not seek to discuss the broader discourses on Islamic orthodoxy, it attempts to trace *how* some of these central debates seeking to draw the contours of what is the "True Islam" have impacted the Ahmadiyya Muslim identity today.

First, I will describe some of the ways the Ahmadiyya Muslim Community responds to its contested Muslim identity. After outlining how the community faces exclusion today, from state and religious institutions, I will present how the Ahmadiyya defines who is a "true" Muslim. The second and third sections will outline two central debates among Indian Muslims during the late nineteenth century, particularly given the rise of British colonial power on the subcontinent, and how both debates corresponded to two controversial Ahmadiyya beliefs: the absolute rejection of violent *jihad* and Ghulam Ahmad's messianic and prophetic status. The debates among Indian Muslims about the appropriate use and interpretation of *jihad,* as well as the sanctity of the Prophet Muhammad, were particularly controversial in the late nineteenth century, after the 1857 Rebellion and the increasing threat of Christian missionary activity. This context was the backdrop for Mirza Ghulam Ahmad's initial writings and the reason for founding of the Ahmadiyya Muslim Community in the 1880s. Both controversial beliefs addressed in this chapter have defined how the Ahmadiyya positions itself within the global Muslim *ulema* as the "True Islam" since its founding. In the fourth section, I briefly delineate how both beliefs continue to shape the Ahmadiyya's own Islamic identity today by taking a closer look at a recent speech given by an Ahmadi leader in 2019. The Ahmadiyya interpretation of *jihad* and Ghulam Ahmad's prophetic status continue to illustrate Ahmadis' Muslim identity.

More broadly, this chapter highlights how the Ahmadiyya is often ignored in discussions of sectarianism within South Asian Islam,[4] despite participating in core Islamic debates while facing persecution from Muslims globally. Most of the literature on the Ahmadiyya focuses on the marginalization and violence that Ahmadis face due to sectarian claims of heresy.[5] While this continues to be important research, current discussions on sectarianism in South Asia miss how Ahmadis enter core Islamic debates on the sanctity of Prophet Muhammad and the appropriate interpretations and uses of *jihad* to make their case as the "True Islam" through their ongoing global persecution.

The Ahmadiyya's Contested Muslim Identity

Despite being characterized as a heterodox community, even by scholars who are not denouncing the faith,[6] the Ahmadiyya actively participates in debates about defining an Islamic "orthodoxy," delineating who is a "real Muslim," and centers itself as the "True Islam." While I do not dive into the theorization of the term "orthodoxy" in this chapter, I seek to frame this discussion as such because this term continues to hold a great deal of power, as it is deployed to exclude the Ahmadiyya community from the limits of Islam, and this power has life and death consequences for adherents. As such, I find anthropologist Talal Asad's treatment of the term useful, as "not a mere body of opinion but a distinctive relationship – a relationship of power to truth. Wherever Muslims have the power to regulate, uphold, require, or adjust *correct* practices, and to condemn, exclude, undermine, or replace *incorrect* ones, there is the domain of orthodoxy" (Asad 2009). The key here is the *power* in what is regarded as orthodox and heterodox, and how the ubiquitous understanding of the Ahmadiyya as outside of Islamic orthodoxy puts the community outside the limits of the "real" Islam. This claim, however, is deeply contested by Ahmadis who, in fact, see themselves as the "True Islam," and therefore at the center of an Islamic "orthodoxy." Before diving into the historical debates that animated the origins of the Ahmadiyya, in this section, I will first outline some ways that the Ahmadiyya face exclusion from conceptualizations of Islamic "orthodoxy" by the Muslim mainstream today. Second, I will present how the Ahmadiyya Muslim Community (as the representative global institution) envisions Islam more broadly and its own position within the Muslim *ummah* through the Community's flagship "True Islam" public relations campaign.

The Exclusion of the Ahmadiyya

The most notable form of persecution faced by Ahmadis is perpetrated by the Pakistani state, as the community's exclusion is institutionalized within the Pakistani Constitution, voting and citizenship rights, and blasphemy laws (Khan 2003, 2015; Iqtidar 2012; Qasmi 2015; Saeed 2007, 2017). According to the Second Amendment of the Pakistani Constitution, Ahmadi adherents are legally designated as non-Muslim based on *khatam-i-nabuwwat*,[7] which also means that Ahmadis are prohibited from running for office under Islamic political parties and voting or receiving citizenship as Muslims in Pakistan.[8] When voting or applying for a Pakistani passport, citizens are asked to indicate their religious affiliation, and if one puts down "Islam," they must sign a declaration that reads,

"...I hereby solemnly declare that:

1. I am Muslim and believe in the absolute and unqualified finality of the prophethood of Muhammad (peace be upon him) the last of the prophets.
2. I do not recognize any person who claims to be a prophet in any sense of the word or of any description whatsoever after Muhammad (peace be upon him) or recognize such a claimant as prophet or a religious reformer as a Muslim.
3. I consider Mirza Ghulam Ahmad Qadiani to be an imposter nabi and also consider his followers whether belonging to the Lahori or Qadiani group to be non-Muslim."[9]

This, in effect, disenfranchises Ahmadi voters and citizens who must choose between identifying as non-Muslim or denouncing their founder.[10] Ahmadis also face vandalism of their mosques in Pakistan, burning down of Ahmadi-run businesses, and exclusion from the educational system ("Beleaguered Community" 2020).

In addition to exclusion and persecution from state institutions and societal violence, Muslim religious leaders have issued declarations, or *fatwas,* that disclaim the Ahmadiyya as Muslim. Such *fatwas* have been issued since Ghulam Ahmad's time, including from his teachers and classmates (Khan 2015). One example of a more contemporary anti-Ahmadi *fatwa* is from the Muslim World League, a non-profit Muslim organization based in Mecca, Saudi Arabia, which cites "nefarious methods" used by Ahmadis:

1. Construction of mosques with the assistance of the anti-Islamic forces wherein the misleading Qadiani thoughts are imparted to the people.
2. Opening of school institutions and orphanages wherein the people are taught and trained as to how they can be more anti-Islamic in their activities. They also published the corrupted versions of the Holy Quran in different local and international languages (Dawat-o-Irshad 2020).

This *fatwa* outlines the activities by Ahmadis that are seen by the Muslim World League as threatening and blasphemous: their acts of teaching and spreading their interpretations of Islam through social welfare institutions and translations of the Quran (and other publications). The *fatwa* highlights the community's missionary work (*tabligh,* or outreach) and the use of *jihad* through the written word (or, as Ahmadis call it, "*jihad* by the pen") as not only important features of the Ahmadiyya practice of Islam, but also urges Muslims to view Ahmadi religious practices as suspicious. Furthermore, a term used in the *fatwa,* "Qadiani," is an epithet also used by the anti-Ahmadiyya Pakistani movements to refer to Ahmadis, particularly within the context of the passing of the Pakistani 1984 Ordinance XX blasphemy law.[11]

The Ahmadiyya's Self-Identity as the "True Islam"

While the message that the Ahmadiyya Muslim Community embodies the "True Islam" is global, the "True Islam" public relations campaign, is primarily based in the United States (though it is also used by the community in the United Kingdom ("Introducing Ahmadiyyat" 2022), and is part of the Ahmadiyya's "Nationwide campaign to educate Americans on Islam's true teachings" ("The Revival" 2020). This campaign was launched in 2015, originally titled "True Islam and the Extremists" and its aim is to "correct some of the most common misconceptions about the religion and educate Muslims, non-Muslims and Americans of other faiths about the correct meaning of Islam" (Westcott 2015). The "True Islam" campaign has also stated that it "actively counters the menace of extremism that has resulted from inconsistent Muslim leadership" ("The Revival" 2020). The reference to the "menace of extremism" because of "inconsistent Muslim leadership" displays how the Ahmadiyya community distances itself from "Other Muslims," their "inconsistent leadership," and terrorist extremism that has been largely associated with Islam after 9/11. Through this distancing, the Ahmadiyya community clarifies eleven misconceptions held about Islam by non-Muslims, but through the perspective of "True Islam."

One of the misconceptions Ahmadis claim that non-Muslims might hold about Islam is regarding *jihad*. The "True Islam" campaign states that "True Islam believes in non-violent *jihad* of the self and of the pen… [and] rejects violent *jihad*" ("The Revival" 2020). The use of the terms "*jihad* by the sword" or "violent *jihad*" serves to reinforce the trope that there are "Bad Muslims"[12] who interpret *jihad* through violent means, and that the Ahmadiyya Muslim Community does not. While they do reference verses of the Qur'an to cite how Islam teaches *jihad*, the framing continues to be through a rejection of "Other Muslims." Here we see a deliberate choice to not only distance itself from "Other Muslims," but to also display that "the menace of extremism" today is because of their "inconsistent leadership." This messaging associates some blame of contemporary religious fundamentalism to Muslim leadership.

While the Ahmadiyya Muslim Community will characterize itself as the "True Islam," and work to distance itself from "Other Muslims," the Ahmadiyya also make it very clear that they are not the *only* Muslims. This is often framed through the accusations they face as being a non-Muslim minority: "[w]ith many Muslim scholars declaring other Muslims as non-Muslims in this day and age, it can be difficult to ascertain as to who is a true Muslim" (Noman 2020). In this piece titled "Definition of a True Muslim" in the Ahmadiyya-run periodical *Review of Religions,* the author cites several verses of the Qur'an and Hadith that indicate "anyone who believes in Islam, is entitled to call themselves Muslim" (Noman 2020). The threat of persecution for "false" Muslims was a theme throughout this piece, especially when the author cited some *hadith* in which the Prophet Muhammad: "…has given a warning to the Muslims." He knew that in the future some extremist Muslims would persecute other Muslims over their differences. He warned such extremists that by persecuting such innocent Muslims, they would be betraying Allah. The definitions given today by some Muslims are completely opposite to the words of the Prophet Muhammad. Ahmadi Muslims believe all who recite the *kalima* [declaration of faith] to be Muslims. Anything else spread in the media is either out of context or propaganda (Noman 2020).

This declaration of how the Ahmadiyya define a "true" Muslim, including anyone who recites the *kalima* – the proclamation of faith in one God and that Muhammad is his Prophet – seeks to provide the baseline understanding of Islam, within which the Ahmadiyya has included itself. In this chapter, the term Ahmadiyya is very explicitly referring to the community's own experiences of exclusion and persecution today by other Muslims, especially with the definitions provided today by some Muslims, which are the complete opposite to the words of the Prophet.

In the subsequent analysis, I focus on how the Ahmadiyya has participated in debates about defining Islam, and in particular the "true" Islam, since its origins in the late nineteenth century under British colonial rule on the Indian subcontinent.

As the community developed, especially in its controversy, its positions within debates on the appropriate use of *jihad* and the sanctity of the Prophet Muhammad became more explicit in reference to the Ahmadiyya's exclusion from conceptualizations of a "true" Islam.

The Case for "Jihad by the Pen"

In this section, I demonstrate how Ghulam Ahmad, with the Ahmadiyya community more broadly, placed himself in vitriolic debates on *jihad* during the British colonial period in India. Scholars have noted that it was not just his stance against enacting violence in the name of *jihad* that made the Ahmadiyya stance on the issue controversial (Jalal 2008; Khan 2015) – the community also aligned itself with the British when the colonial government conflicted with segments of the Indian Muslim population. I will first provide context about Indian Muslim stances on *jihad*, especially considering British colonial rule, through the 1857 Rebellion and highly contested debates between Indian Muslims in its aftermath. Then, I will briefly outline some ways that Ghulam Ahmad engaged in these debates in the late nineteenth century and how the community continued to engage in discourses on *jihad* after his death. Finally, I will connect this historical context to how the Ahmadiyya discusses *jihad* today, especially in light of a post-9/11 Islamophobic global political era.

"Jihad" under British Colonial Rule

The advent of British colonial rule marked a shift within debates on *jihad* among Indian Muslim scholars, especially when Indian Muslims, largely, mobilized to resist British rule in the 1850s. Religious Studies scholar Ilyse Morgenstein Fuerst contend[s] that "the 1857 Rebellion marks a dramatic and palpable moment in which *jihad* comes to signify Muslims broadly and definitionally as religious actors and as (potential) subjects of empire" (Morgenstein Fuerst 2017). British understandings of Islam often conflated rebellion and *jihad* (Morgenstein Fuerst Fuerst 2017), especially in the direct aftermath of the 1857 Rebellion, and has only expanded to a global scale today.

The meaning and power of *jihad* – a term that literally translates to "striving" – became intertwined with violence, especially in the eyes of the British. Violent *jihad*, in particular, was externally viewed as a core component to Islamic identities and practices. This context created the conditions for heated debates among Muslims about the meaning of *jihad* within an "authentic" Islam and how a Muslim ought to relate to political governing authorities. During the 1857 Rebellion, the Muslim *ulema* could not agree on whether to declare *jihad* against British rule, and so political engagement as *jihad* took on a different meaning under British colonial rule. To quote Morgenstein Fuerst again, "the nineteenth century [began] the discourse about jihad as a concern of empire and as a fixation of British rule in South Asia" (Morgenstein Fuerst 2017). In her rich account of the polemics about *jihad* among the Muslim ulema in pre-, during- and post-colonial South Asia, Historian Ayesha Jalal notes that:

Fatwas were often obtained by force, forged, or attributed to people without their knowledge, thereby provoking opposition from Sunni and Shia ulema, who issued rulings of their own. The contradictory fatwas on jihad illustrate how religiously informed cultural identities were articulated in the early struggles against colonialism. Recourse to jihad invariably established the outer limits of Muslim identity.

(Jalal 2008)

The discourse about *jihad* among the Muslim *ulema* was complicated by how religious rulings (*fatwas*) were issued – especially on whether India under British rule was considered *dar-ul-harb* (land of war) or *dar-ul-islam* (land of peace) (Morgenstein Fuerst 2017) – and the imminent threat of the rise of British rule in South Asia, which deeply affected the ways that a coherent Indian Muslim identity was constructed. Defining the nature of an Islamic "orthodoxy" was at stake here.

Mirza Ghulam Ahmad's Stance on Jihad

In her discussion of Ghulam Ahmad's writings on *jihad,* Jalal notes that: "Although violating the rights of God is the worst possible form of crime, Ghulam Ahmad was more concerned about the violation of human rights by Muslims" (Jalal 2008). In particular, Ghulam Ahmad was concerned about the use of violence in the name of *jihad* during this time in Indian history, which was contentious, but not so much that it warranted the use of violence. In his writings on *The British Government and Jihad*, Ghulam Ahmad clearly states his absolute rejection of violent forms of *jihad* and makes the case that, because he, as the Promised Messiah, is now here, there is surely no reason for the use of violence. He says:

> If you still do not abstain from such blood-thirsty deeds and hold your tongues from such preachings, you shall be deemed to have turned your backs upon Islam... Had I not come, the error would, to some extent, have been pardonable. But now that I have come... those who take up the sword under the pretense of the support of religion... shall be called to account before their Lord... for their false hankering after Paradise.[13]

Ghulam Ahmad's writings against the use of violence for the sake of *jihad* was not just a moral plea for Muslims to reassess their interpretations of *jihad*. It became a way to carve out who had the authority to call themselves Muslims. According to Ahmadis, he has the authority to make such claims as the proclaimed Promised Messiah. This debate, for Ghulam Ahmad and Ahmadis after him, was no longer just between learned scholars of Islam. Instead, it was between scholars who may have been experts in Islam arguing against a divinely appointed authority. This type of power warranted the right for Ghulam Ahmad to make pronouncements of who was and was not considered to be within the fold of Islam.

The Ahmadi understanding of Ghulam Ahmad's divine authority continues to be highly significant in understanding the Ahmadiyya Islamic identity, because of how both Ahmadi and non-Ahmadi Muslims have participated in debates on where this community falls within the normative boundaries of Islam. Ahmadis calling themselves the "True Islam" was not a reaction to being called non-Muslims by the Pakistani government. It was a stance that defined the origins of the community itself. Ghulam Ahmad was actively responding to vitriolic debates among Indian Muslim scholars during the British colonial period, before and during his formation of an Ahmadiyya sect. His participation in debates about how to understand and practice *jihad,* among others,[14] has shaped the conceptualization of an Ahmadi vision of Islam – one that is still practiced today.

According to the Ahmadiyya, *jihad* must be enacted based on the circumstances of the time and the necessity of violence that existed during the time of the Prophet, which no longer exists today.[15] This can be seen, for example, in a 2013 press conference in which the current *Khalifah* (global religious leader) of the Ahmadiyya is describing the Ahmadiyya practice of *"jihad* by the pen":

> Today religious wars are not being waged against Islam. Rather, Islam is being attacked in the media and in print. Thus, the *Jihad* of today is to publish literature and books in favor of true and peaceful Islam. That is what the Ahmadiyya Muslim Jamaat is doing – we are publishing literature in various languages explaining the true teachings of Islam.
>
> *("True Khilafat" 2013)*

This stated approach to *jihad* stemmed from the origins of the community, given Mirza Ghulam Ahmad's prolific writings. Mirza Ghulam Ahmad penned over 80 books, ranging from defenses of Islam through Quranic verses and Hadith to the relationship between Islam and democracy. In addition to his books, Ghulam Ahmad submitted several articles and notes to the editors in a variety of Indian newspapers – which is a practice that continues across the global Ahmadiyya community today, with national campaigns to submit "letters to the editor."

In this section, I have demonstrated that how this community engages in debates on *jihad* today is based on the historical moment of its origins, namely sectarian conflict within Islam emerging at the start of British colonial rule. Mirza Ghulam Ahmad took controversial stances on the absolute rejection of non-violent *jihad,* as well as how Muslims ought to respect and obey British governance of the subcontinent. While this, in and of itself, did not directly lead to the persecution that Ahmadis would face not soon after, it did set the stage for polemical exchanges between Mirza Ghulam Ahmad and his Muslim counterparts.

Prophet Muhammad's Buruz: Ahmadiyya Piety through Persecution

What might be considered the most universal of Islamic beliefs across global sects is known as the *shahadah* or *kalima* – Islamic profession of faith – which usually is translated as: "I bear witness that there is no God but Allah, and Muhammad is the Messenger of Allah."[16] The belief in the Prophet Muhammad as Allah's final messenger, or *khatam-i-nabuwwat*, is drawn from this proclamation of faith. Since the formation of the Ahmadiyya sect, and especially after the Ahmadiyya's persecution in Pakistan, this issue of whether Ahmadis believe in *khatam-i-nabuwwat* is the most prominent fault line between the Ahmadiyya and mainstream approaches to Islam. Declarations that claim Ahmadis are not Muslims, including the Second Amendment of the Pakistani Constitution, will cite the Ahmadiyya belief in Ghulam Ahmad's prophetic status as the reason for Ahmadiyya exclusion from Islam. According to Ahmadis, the accusations about their lack of belief in the finality of Prophet Muhammad based on mainstream Muslims' misunderstandings of Ahmadiyya interpretations of prophethood.[17] Additionally, for the Ahmadis, their persecution affirms that they represent the "True Islam" and the accusation of heresy itself continues to be their measure of piety. In this section, I discuss how the Ahmadiyya portrays the status of Ghulam Ahmad against the backdrop of highly contentious debates about the significance of the Prophet Muhammad during the advent of British colonial rule in India. Just as the debates about how to appropriately engage in *jihad* during the late nineteenth century shaped Ahmadi beliefs about "*jihad* by the pen" today, the Barelvi-Deobandi debates about the sanctity of the Prophet shaped how Ghulam Ahmad positioned himself as an imitation (*buruz*) of Prophet Muhammad.

Debates about the "Normative Muhammad" in Colonial India

The debate about the significance of Prophet Muhammad within Islam has defined the nature of Islamic orthodoxy, especially in contemporary South Asia (Khan 2015; Tareen 2017). According to Religious Studies scholar SherAli Tareen, "in the context of Islam in colonial India, the normative model of the Prophet emerged as a synecdoche representing the entirety of law, *sharia*. The locus of normativity was now firmly established in the figure of the Prophet" (Tareen 2017). Discourses on orthodoxy and heresy were based on whether it was appropriate for Muslims to celebrate *mawlid* (celebration of the Prophet's birthday), for example, as a means to debate the type of divine power that the Prophet held. While such debates had a history that goes further back than the late nineteenth century, the Barelvi-Deobandi polemical encounter in the advent of British colonial rule in India marked a turning point for Islamic discourses on the subcontinent.

Named after their places of origin, the Deobandi and Barelvi Sunni schools of thought have engaged in vitriol within India for centuries. The debates between these Sunni sects were particularly heightened in the late nineteenth century, during the advent of British colonial rule. Within this context, Tareen asks: "What image of the Prophet should anchor a Muslim's normative orientation and everyday life?" (Tareen 2017). This question animated "the logics, archives, and terrain of the controversy [that has] indelibly informed the critical question of what counts as Islam and what counts as a normative Muslim identity in the modern world, in South Asia, and indeed globally" (Tareen 2017). There was a sense of urgency within the debate about the normative power of the Prophet Muhammad due to the onset of British colonial rule in India, in which "the condition of being colonized generated tremendous anxiety as well as anticipation about the aspiration of constructing an ideal Muslim subject and public" (Tareen 2017). While the anxiety of British rule more obviously led to debates on the meaning and use of *jihad* – specifically whether to fight for the reestablishment of Muslim rule in India (Jalal 2008; Morgenstein Fuerst 2017) – the debates on the sanctity of the Prophet and the normative role that He plays within Islam led to "terms and stakes [that] pervade the everyday performance of Islam and shadow conversations ranging from defining blasphemy to organizing the choreography of a community's moral and devotional life" (Tareen 2017). The Barelvi-Deobandi debates fueled vitriol that eventually led to the exclusion of the Ahmadiyya from the orthodoxy of a South Asian Islam and later persecution of the community, such as through Pakistan's blasphemy laws. These debates about the "normative Muhammad" continue to hold very real and severe stakes within South Asian and global Islam today.

Ghulam Ahmad's Claim as a Buruz

In the heat of the late nineteenth century Barelvi-Deobandi debates that "animated opposing imaginaries of prophetic authority in South Asian Islam" (Tareen 2017). Mirza Ghulam Ahmad was beginning to write *Barahin-e-Ahmadiyya*, a five-part volume that "used logical arguments…in support of the Holy Qur'an & the Prophethood of the Holy Prophet Muhammad" (Ahmad 1880). In the fifth volume, published in 1905, Ghulam Ahmad crystallized his position as the "Promised Messiah" of Islam. Thereafter, he continued to write about his divinely appointed position, especially in relation to the Prophet Muhammad. While his claims were inconsistent, the overall takeaway was that he likened himself to be an imitation or *buruz* of the Prophet. This continues to hold great symbolic value for the Ahmadiyya Muslim Community today, especially in how it led to the division between Lahori and Qadiani Ahmadis.[18]

For his prophetic claims, Mirza Ghulam Ahmad relied on the distinction between legislative prophets (*anbiya tashri*) and non-legislative prophets (*anbiya la tashri'a lahum*) from Ibn al-'Arabi, a highly influential Sufi Islamic thinker (Friedman 1989). Prophet Muhammad, who brought a new scripture and code of law to humanity through the Quran, was the last of the legislative prophets. However, Mirza Ghulam Ahmad regarded himself as inferior to Prophet Muhammad, as he was ordained with the task of reinforcing the Qur'an as the final scripture and not bringing a new code of law. Put another way, Ayesha Jalal notes that Ghulam Ahmad gave a "modernist twist to the Quranic *surah* telling Muslims that God had sent *nabis* (literally prophets) throughout the ages, [and] argued that while Muhammad was the seal of the prophets, his task had to be continued by others" (Jalal 2002). According to Ghulam Ahmad, *khatam-i-nabuuwat* remains intact, because of the distinction between law-bearing and non-law-bearing prophets. Ghulam Ahmad claimed to be sent by

God to rectify the ways that the Quran has been misconstrued and misinterpreted within the modern age. More specifically, he was allegedly sent to correct how Muslims were interpreting the Quran and practicing Islam during British colonial rule of India, and conceded that he did not have the same canonical powers as Prophet Muhammad.[19] However, according to Muslim discourses that address the Ahmadiyya belief in Ghulam Ahmad's messianic character and, even if inferior, prophetic status as the crux for why adherents of this faith are not able to identify as Muslims.

The similarities and differences between the sanctity of the Prophet Muhammad and Mirza Ghulam Ahmad is critical to understand Ahmadiyya Islamic theology, as well as the sectarian divides between Ahmadis and "other Muslims." How Ahmadis revere the Prophet Muhammad is one way that they illustrate their interpretation of Islamic orthodoxy – especially when Ahmadis see themselves as the "True Islam," because Mirza Ghulam Ahmad was the *buruz*, or manifested spiritual imitation, of Prophet Muhammad. With this unique spiritual standing, "Ghulam Ahmad imitat[ed] the Prophet Muhammad so closely [that he] identified with Muhammad's very being and thereby acquired his own prophetic status through the Prophet Muhammad…[he] was only ascribed the prophethood through his pure and perfect spiritual imitation (*buruz*) of Muhammad" (Khan 2015). This claim that Ghulam Ahmad was the spiritual imitation of the Prophet Muhammad meant to communicate Ahmad's pious, but inferior, status. Ghulam Ahmad as Prophet Muhammad's *buruz* also allowed him and his followers to draw parallels between these two pious figures.

Symbolism of Prophet Muhammad's Persecution

In observing the contentious religious landscape of the British colonial period, Ghulam Ahmad's first writings in the five-volume *Barahin-e-Ahmadiyya* speaks to Muslims and non-Muslims within Punjab on how the Qur'an is the only pure source of religious teachings. He offers his audience a reward for refuting his "logical arguments" that defend the Qur'an and the Prophet Muhammad. By the end of the fourth volume, Ghulam Ahmad crystallizes his own spiritual status as the "Promised Messiah." While the excerpt below is prior to his claim as the "Promised Messiah," the narrative about Prophet Muhammad's persecution and his patience in continuing to preach Islam became a cornerstone narrative for the Ahmadiyya religious ethic:

> Just think how, to his last breath, the Holy Prophet steadfastly and unwaveringly held on to his claim of Prophethood in the face of countless perils and so many enemies, detractors and threateners. The persecution and hardship he endured for years seemed to preclude all possibility of success and were increasing day by day. His patient response to them clearly rules out any plans for material gain. On the contrary, the very moment he made his claim to Prophethood, he lost even the little support he already had. With a single

announcement, he made innumerable enemies and brought upon himself countless tribulations…The severe hardship he endured for so long and with such fortitude could not have been tolerated by a deceiving imposter…His own kith and kin were the first to oppose him when he forbade them from worshipping idols.

(Ahmad 1880)

This narrative centers the trials faced by the Prophet Muhammad, based on his claim of Prophethood. Ghulam Ahmad notes that those who opposed the Prophet the most were his own followers and those to whom he was closest. Moreover, despite facing bitter persecution, Prophet Muhammad remained steadfast in the mission to spread Islam globally. Ghulam Ahmad stresses that this is the model from which Ahmadis ought to pursue *tabligh*, the propagation of the faith, which includes their missionary and humanitarian work. Rather than discouraging their practice, the opposition from non-Ahmadi Muslims serves as an *affirmation* that Ahmadiyya Islam is the "True Islam."

"Promised Messiah" as the Fulfillment of Prophecies

Much of the Ahmadiyya theology draws on the importance of prophecies. For example, the central justification for Ghulam Ahmad's claim as the "Promised Messiah" rested in a Quranic prophecy that claimed the coming of a future leader that would steer mankind back toward the right path after the death of Prophet Muhammad. In a speech given at the 2019 West Coast *Jalsa Salana* (annual gathering) in California (Husain 2019), Sohail Husain, a leader in California's Ahmadiyya community discussed prophecies as "early detection warnings," such as those for natural disasters and presented three examples to his audience: a prophecy that occurred before Prophet Muhammad's time, one that was fulfilled during His time, and one that was destined to be fulfilled after His time. I will focus on the latter two.

For the second prophecy, the Prophet had a vision that he and his followers were circling the Kaaba in Mecca. This is while he was living in Medina, taking refuge after being persecuted by the Meccan tribe Quraysh, in particular. After this vision, the Prophet began his travels to Mecca and was stopped before getting there by Meccans who prohibited Him from entering the city. To resolve the dispute, rather than engaging in violence, the Prophet agreed to the Treaty of Hudaybiyyah, a landmark treaty in the early days of Islam, and agreed to perform pilgrimage to Kaaba the following year. After two years of peace between the Muslims and the Meccans, the tribe Quraysh broke the treaty and necessitated the Prophet and his followers to march back into Mecca. Again, instead of engaging in violent warfare, the Prophet chose to forgive the Meccans for over two decades of oppression and gave amnesty to all Meccans. This was the Prophecy fulfilled – the Prophet entered Mecca, performed pilgrimage, and the tides were turned with Muslims gaining victory over Mecca through strategies of peace. This prophecy demonstrated how Prophet Muhammad responded to oppression and persecution, and how the wait for the fulfillment of prophecies is key to long term success and piety.

Similar lessons have been communicated to Ahmadis when discussing their persecution in Pakistan and other Muslim-majority societies today. The first response, if possible, is to emigrate and seek refuge elsewhere – as the community's leadership did in 1984 when fleeing from Pakistan to the United Kingdom. The second response is to engage in efforts of reconciliation through peaceful means, rather than through violence. Often, this story of the Prophet Muhammad's response to persecution by the Meccans and His efforts to reconcile are used to justify the Ahmadiyya's absolute rejection of violent *jihad* today, in the pursuit of peaceful forms of *jihad*. The third prophecy that Husain described in his speech was on the victory of Islam in the latter days through a deputy of Prophet Muhammad. He outlined various verses in the Quran that predicted the dominance of Islam globally through the guidance of a Promised Messiah of the latter days. This would be a "subordinate reflection" of the Prophet, that would "mirror the light of the Prophet as though he returned in the latter age." It was the task of a divine leader to spread Islam globally, not through warfare, but instead by "reestablishing the relationship between Man and God." To further demonstrate this point, Husain quotes Mirza Ghulam Ahmad: "the work for which Allah has appointed me, my function as the Promised Messiah is that I should remove the estrangement that has taken place between God and Man and reestablish Man's connection of purity and love with his Creator" (Husain 2019). The claim that Mirza Ghulam Ahmad is the Prophet's "subordinate reflection" is central to Ahmadiyya theological claims as the "True Islam," especially because of the analogies made between the Prophet's own persecution from Mecca and Ahmadiyya persecution globally today. Moreover, the prophecies outlined in this speech by an Ahmadi adherent encapsulates the importance of the debates on *jihad* and on the significance of the Prophet Muhammad for Ahmadis globally. The political and religious contexts of the late nineteenth century British rule of India deeply shapes the Ahmadiyya's identity as the "True Islam" today as the community continues to respond to varying forms of state- and societal-based persecution. In particular, Ahmadis are still largely considered to be non-Muslims based on *khatam-i-nabuwwat,* and face global exclusion within Islam and violence from Muslims based on this accusation; while simultaneously, Ahmadis actively engage in intra-Muslim discourses on how one ought to approach *jihad*.

Conclusion

Mirza Ghulam Ahmad found the late nineteenth century's bitter sectarian divides during the British colonial rule of India to be a fruitful time for Muslims to re-establish the connection with God. During this time, he found that Muslims were too caught up in vitriolic debates with each other about defining the boundaries of Islam through the status of Prophet Muhammad and whether Muslims should enact violent *jihad* against the British. Ghulam Ahmad began his response to interreligious and Muslim sectarian violence and debates with a defense of the Qur'an and Prophet Muhammad – getting back to the basics of Islam – before establishing his own status as the "Promised Messiah" divinely appointed to resolve these conflicts. In other words, the

Ahmadiyya Muslim Community was founded during the late nineteenth century on the Indian subcontinent, given the advent of British colonial rule, in response to interreligious conflict and sectarian divides among Muslims.

As Adil Hussain Khan has stated, "Since its emergence, Jama'at-i Ahmadiyya has reinvigorated the debate on Islamic orthodoxy among the Muslim mainstream" (Khan 2015). Contours of South Asian Islamic orthodoxy are often drawn through the exclusion of the Ahmadiyya. What does it mean for one to be a "true" Muslim? Questions about the sanctity of Prophet Muhammad, in particular, continue to thrive in light of the Pakistani state's active refusal to incorporate Ahmadis into the country's Muslim majority. However, this community also continues to be important in sectarian debates today because it continues to claim itself as the "True Islam" through its strong institutional support and a global reach. Despite being excluded from the folds of Islam internally, this chapter outlines how the Ahmadiyya started carving spaces for themselves amid bitter sectarian divides among Muslims that continues to see them as heterodox and how the community continues to shape contemporary discourses on Islam globally.

Notes

1 Tareen tackles his issues with the term "orthodoxy" in his recent book *Defending Muhammad in Modernity* when discussing the deployment of the term *bid'a* (innovation/invention) by the Muslim *ulema* (scholars) when debating the celebration of Prophet Muhammad's *mawlid* (birthday). He instead "prefers the category of normativity over orthodoxy because it affords greater fluidity and ambiguity in the location of religious authority among a set of competing claimants…The binary construct of orthodoxy/heterodoxy is quite unhelpful in capturing the range of contesting opinions on the borders separating the normative from the heretical" (Tareen 2017, 137–141). On a personal level, I am completely on board with Tareen's conceptualization. Doing away with notions of "orthodoxy" can only benefit how scholars of Islam study the diverse and vast corpus of, often conflicting, discourses among and about Muslims. For the purposes of my analysis of the Ahmadiyya's participation in these debates, the term "orthodoxy" holds a great deal of power in the exclusion and persecution of this community, so I am using it here for those purposes.

2 In this chapter, I focus on the theological significance of Mirza Ghulam Ahmad for the "Qadiani" branch of the Ahmadiyya, represented by Jama'at-i-Ahmadiyya, or the Ahmadiyya Muslim Community. (The use of the term "Qadiani" here is not through the derogatory connotation; this is just to distinguish them from the "Lahori" branch.)

The other branch, known as the "Lahoris" split from the "Qadiani" branch in 1910 based on disputes about the future leadership of Ahmadis after the death of the second *khalifah* and about the "correct interpretation of Ghulam Ahmad's mission and claim." According to Adil Hussain Khan, the "Lahoris had adopted a softer position [on the prophetic status of Mirza Ghulam Ahmad], which was more consistent with Sunni orthodoxy. The Qadianis continued to emphasize controversial aspects of Ghulam Ahmad's prophethood, which fundamentally enabled his inner religious experiences to serve as the basis of newly formed doctrine" (Ahmad 2015: 70). In sum, I will be engaging with the interpretation of Ghulam Ahmad's prophethood according to the Qadiani branch of the Ahmadiyya.

3 For more in-depth analyses of debates about *jihad* in South Asia, see: Jalal (2008). And for more in-depth analyses of debates about the sanctity of Prophet Muhammad, and the Barevli-Deobandi polemic in particular, see: Tareen (2017).

4 Apart from Ayesha Jalal's *Partisans of Allah* and *Self and Sovereignty* (Jalal 2002, 2008) other scholarship about the debates among Muslim scholars during the British colonial period mention Ghulam Ahmad or Ahmadis in passing, such as Tareen's *Defending Muhammad in Modernity* (2017) and Ilyse Morgenstein Fuerst's *Indian Muslim Minorities and the 1857 Rebellion* (2017).
5 For some examples of research about Ahmadi exclusion in Pakistan, see: Khan (2003); Iqtidar (2012); Qasmi (2015); Rahman (2014: 408–422); Saeed (2007, 2017). Notable exceptions to this are: Khan (2015) and Friedmann (1989).
6 For example, when reviewing Adil Hussain Khan's take on the development of the Ahmadiyya, Tareen takes issue with Khan's passive regard of Ahmadis as outside of "Islamic orthodoxy" without theorizing the term itself. Tareen asks: "if Ahmadis don't consider themselves non-orthodox or heterodox, why should a scholar of their tradition judge them to be so? Moreover, what exactly is orthodox Islam?" (2017, 140).
7 The text of this amendment is as follows: "A person who does not believe in the absolute and unqualified finality of The Prophethood of Muhammad (Peace be upon him), the last of the Prophets or claims to be a Prophet, in any sense of the word or of any description whatsoever, after Muhammad (Peace be upon him), or recognizes such a claimant as a Prophet or religious reformer, is not a Muslim for the purposes of the Constitution or law."
8 For example: "Beleaguered Community" 2020; Gottshalk 2018; Imam 2016; Sayeed 2018.
9 A photo of the declaration can be seen in Imam 2016.
10 For example: Gottshalk 2018; Sayeed 2018.
11 The literal translation of "Qadiani" is "someone from Qadian," referring to the birthplace of the Ahmadiyya's founder. This term is now associated with the anti-Ahmadi movements in Pakistan; the Jama'at disavows this term and considers it derogatory.
12 I am using this term based on Mahmood Mamdani's noteworthy analysis of the "Good" and "Bad" Muslim tropes within the Global War on Terror. See: Mamdani (2005).
13 Cited in Jalal (2008: 164); originally Ahmad (1880: 4–5).
14 While in this chapter I only talk about how Mirza Ghulam Ahmad engaged in debates about *jihad* and the sanctity of Prophet Muhammad, he also confronted Christian missionaries and Hindu revivalists – debates with the missionaries shaped Ahmadi practices of *tabligh* [preaching] that continue to thrive today. For more detail on Ghulam Ahmad's polemics, see: Khan (2015) and Jalal (2008).
15 In the debates about whether British colonial rule was classified as a land of war (*dar-ul-harb*) or land of peace (*dar-ul-islam*), Mirza Ghulam Ahmad stood firmly that the British deserved loyalty from Indian Muslims. For more detail on Ghulam Ahmad's stance on loyalty to the British, see: Khan (2015) and Jalal (2008).
16 Some of the Shia community will add "and Ali is his protector" to the *shahadah*.
17 In an April 2022 interview conducted with the author, an Ahmadi stated that the difference in how Ahmadis and other Muslims interpret "*khatam-i-nabuwwat*" rests in how the word "*khatam*" is translated between Urdu and Arabic. He claimed that in Urdu, the word "*khatam*" is translated as "finish," or "final," while in Arabic it is translated as "sealed." As such, he claimed that the term "*khatam-i-nabuwwat*" does not mean imply that Prophet Muhammad is the final prophet, and instead means that there is a seal on the laws bestowed by the prophets. Given his status at a *buruz*, Ghulam Ahmad is not offering any new laws, which sustains Prophet Muhammad's status as "*khatam-i-nabuwwat*." For a general explanation, see: Al-Islam.org (2020).
18 See a brief explanation of this split in fn. 2. For further explanation, see: Khan (2015).
19 Admittedly, this account of Mirza Ghulam Ahmad's prophetic claims make them sound much more consistent and straightforward than they truly were. Adil Hussain Khan provides an authoritative account of how the Ahmadiyya grew in prominence and controversy, under British colonial rule through the formation of Pakistan, and has done an excellent job in tracking the inconsistencies within his claims of prophethood.

Bibliography

Acquah, Francis. "The Impact of African Traditional Religious Beliefs and Cultural Values on Christian-Muslim Relations in Ghana from the 1920 to the Present: A Case Study of the Nkusukum-Ekumfi-Enyan Traditional Area of the Central Region." PhD Diss, University of Exeter, 2011.

Ahmad, Mirza Ghulam. *Barahin-e-Ahmadiyya, Parts I and* II. London: Islam International Publications Ltd., 1880.

Al-Islam.org, "What Is the Difference between Ahmadi Muslims and Other Muslims? | Islam Ahmadiyya," accessed October 2, 2020, https://www.alislam.org/question/difference-between-ahmadi-muslims-others/.

Asad, Talal. "The Idea of an Anthropology of Islam." *Qui Parle* 17, no. 2 (Spring/Summer 2009): 1–30.

"Beleaguered Community: Jamaat-i-Ahmadiyya to Stay Away from Forthcoming Polls." *The Express Tribune*, accessed October 2, 2020, https://tribune.com.pk/story/980272/beleaguered-community-jamaat-i-ahmadiyya-to-stay-away-from-forthcoming-polls.

Burhani, Ahmad Najib. "Treating Minorities with Fatwas: A Study of the Ahmadiyya Community in Indonesia." *Contemporary Islam* 8, no. 3 (2014): 285–301.

Friedmann, Yohanan. *Prophecy Continuous: Aspects of Ahmadi Religious Thought and Its Medieval Background*. Oxford: Oxford University Press, 1989.

Ghazi, H.R.H. Prince. "On the Amman Message," The Official Website of the Amman Message. Last modified July 22, 2007. https://ammanmessage.com/on-the-amman-message/.

Gottshalk, Peter. "Why a Pakistani Community has Boycotted Elections for 30 Years." *Quartz India*, August 9, 2018.

Haron, Muhammed. "Africa's Muslim Authorities and Ahmadis: Curbed Freedoms, Circumvented Legalities." *The Review of Faith & International Affairs* 16, no. 4 (2018): 60–74.

Husain, Sohail. "The Holy Qur'an – Prophecies Fulfilled by Sohail Husain – Jalsa Salana West Coast USA." December 22, 2019, https://www.youtube.com/watch?v=oKeAjPhw_38.

Idara Dawat-o-Irshad. "The 1974 Declaration of Muslim World League (Rabita al-Alam al Islami)," accessed October 2, 2020, http://irshad.org/exposed/fatwas/rabita.php.

Imam, Zainab. "The Day I Declared My Best Friend Kafir Just So I Could Get a Passport." *Dawn*, June 1, 2016.

"Introducing Ahmadiyyat: The Renaissance of Islam." *True Islam*. Last modified April 22, 2022. https://trueislam.co.uk/.

Iqtidar, Humeira. "State Management of Religion in Pakistan and Dilemmas of Citizenship." *Citizenship Studies* 16, no. 8 (2012): 1013–1028.

Irawan, Andi Muhammad. "'They Are Not Muslims': A Critical Discourse Analysis of the Ahmadiyya Sect Issue in Indonesia." *Discourse & Society* 28, no. 2 (2017): 162–181.

Jalal, Ayesha. *Self and Sovereignty: Individual and Community in South Asian Islam since 1850*. London:Routledge, 2002.

Jalal, Ayesha. *Partisans of Allah: Jihad in South Asia*. Cambridge: Harvard University Press, 2008.

Khan, Adil Hussain. *From Sufism to Ahmadiyya: A Muslim Minority Movement in South Asia*. Indiana: Indiana University Press, 2015.

Khan, Amjad Mahmood. "Persecution of the Ahmadiyya Community in Pakistan: An Analysis Under International Law and International Relations." *Harvard Human Rights Journal* 16 (2003).

"London Mosque Warned over 'kill Ahmadis' Leaflets." BBC News. March 21, 2019.

Mamdani, Mahmood. *Good Muslim, Bad Muslim: America, The Cold War, and the Rootsof Terror*. London: Harmony/Rodale, 2005.

Morgenstein Fuerst, Ilyse. *Indian Muslim Minorities and the 1857 Rebellion: Religion, Rebels, and Jihad*. London: Bloomsbury, 2017.

Noman, Raziullah. "The Definition of a True Muslim." The Review of Religions. Last modified May 10, 2020. https://reviewofreligions.org/22137/the-definition-of-a-true-muslim/.

Qasmi, Ali Usman. *The Ahmadis and the Politics of Religious Exclusion in Pakistan*. London: Anthem Press, 2015.

Rahman, Fatima Zainab. "State Restrictions on the Ahmadiyya Sect in Indonesia and Pakistan: Islam or Political Survival?" *Australian Journal of Political Science* 49, no. 2 (2014): 408–422.

Saeed, Sadia. *Politics of Desecularization: Law and the Minority Question in Pakistan*. Cambridge: Cambridge University Press, 2017.

Saeed, Sadia. "Pakistani Nationalism and the State Marginalization of the Ahmadiyya Community in Pakistan." *Studies in Ethnicity and Nationalism* 7, no. 3 (2007): 132–152.

Samwini, Nathan. "The Muslim Resurgence in Ghana since 1950: Its Effects upon Muslims and Muslim-Christian Relations." PhD Diss., University of Birmingham, 2006.

Sayeed, Saad. "The Town that Doesn't Vote: Pakistan's Ahmadis Say Forced to Abstain." Reuters, July 20, 2018.

Soedirgo, Jessica. "Informal Networks and Religious Intolerance: How Clientelism Incentivizes the Discrimination of the Ahmadiyah in Indonesia." *Citizenship Studies* 22, no. 2 (2018): 191–207.

Tareen, SherAli. "Review of From Sufism to Ahmadiyya: A Muslim Minority Movement in South Asia, by Adil Hussain Khan," *Nova Religio: The Journal of Alternative and Emergent Religions* 21, no. 2 (November 2017): 137–141.

"The Amman Message," The Royal Aal Al-Bayt Institute for Islamic Thought. Last modified 2009. https://rissc.jo/wp-content/uploads/2018/12/Amman_Message-EN.pdf.

"The Revival of Islam." True Islam. Accessed October 2, 2020, https://trueislam.com/.

"True Khilafat Compatible with Democracy – Head of Ahmadiyya Muslim Jamaat," Ahmadiyya Muslim Community: Press & Media Office, September 30, 2013, https://www.pressahmadiyya.com/press-releases/2013/09/true-khilafat-compatible-democracy-head-ahmadiyya-muslim-jamaat/.

Wescott, Lucy. "U.S. Muslim Group Launches Campaign to Reclaim the Meaning of 'True Islam' From Extremists." Newsweek, December 30, 2015.

3

UNDERSTANDING THE LONG-TERM IMPACT OF MOBILIZING MILITANT ISLAMISTS IN THE SOVIET-AFGHAN WAR

Strategies of the United States, Saudi Arabia, and Iran

Satgin Hamrah

Introduction

In the 1970s there was a significant shift towards political Islam, throughout all levels of society on local, national, and regional levels. A facet of this region wide shift was an increase in the instrumentalization of sect-based identity for strategic purposes by state and non-state political entrepreneurs from North Africa to Afghanistan. Thus, giving rise to the direct and indirect use of Islam for strategic purposes, including the utilization of sect-based identity. The variation depended on the framework or purposes Islam was being used for. The broad shift and the highly sectarian focused landscape that emerged were connected with the larger economic, security, and political challenges that the wider region experienced in the 1970s and into the 1980s. According to Nasr, such shifts generally stemmed from economic, political, and security challenges (Nasr 2006) rather than issues of ideological compatibility or ancient hatred. As such, the utilization of political Islam and sectarianism as tools for the advancement of interests is highly strategic in nature and immensely provocative, as it not only advances false narratives of "us versus them," but it also promotes conflict under the guise of religion during challenging periods, often with devastating consequences. Interestingly while before 1979 political Islam was increasingly being utilized by political entrepreneurs, neither political Islam nor sectarian conflict or violence were a common factor throughout the region (Warde 2016). However, in the 1980s the wider region experienced a major surge in the use of political Islam and by extension the strategic utilization of sectarianism by state and non-state political entrepreneurs resulting in a cascading effect with long-term negative ramifications. To have a thorough understanding of the modern historical context regarding the surge of political Islam, particularly sectarianism in the greater Middle East and

DOI: 10.4324/9781003329510-4

South Asia during the latter part of the 20th century and today, it is essential to critically assess key watershed events that influenced this phenomenon. There are numerous examples across the region from Afghanistan to North Africa in which political Islam and sectarianism were increasingly used as a vehicle of change during this period (Roy 2001) on top-down and bottom-up levels.

The socio-political and security landscapes of the greater Middle East and South Asia are complex and have been influenced by domestic and international dynamics that affect the region on local and transnational levels. This was evident in the 1980s as multiple conflicts converged in the wider region within the same period, including the Iran-Iraq War, the Cold War, and the Soviet-Afghan War. Each of these conflicts influenced the other and added a thread of complexity to a region already undergoing a highly nuanced change process, which was increasingly characterized by the more extreme elements of Islam. This was evident during this period as the wider region was increasingly characterized by the strategic use of sect-based identity by political entrepreneurs who instrumentalized identity to influence members of their specific sect and effectively "othered" those that did not share their sect-based identity. The focus of this chapter is to provide a brief examination of this phenomena within the context of the Soviet-Afghan War and its influence on the rise of political Islam, sectarianism, and by extension terrorism, which emerged in subsequent years. This relates to the fact that modern militant Islamism, as well as sectarian conflict and violence partly stem from the policies and practices that were utilized during the final years of Cold War by the United States, Saudi Arabia, and Iran within the context of the Soviet-Afghan War. For example, central to U.S. strategy in its fight against Soviet influence in Afghanistan was the strategic utilization of militant Islamists in its war against the Soviet Union. However, it is important to note that the United States was not alone in its instrumentalization of Islamists in this capacity.

Both Saudi Arabia and Iran were also key figures in couching their interests and strategies in religious terms and sect-based identity. This was evident as both countries used their specific sect to advance their interests and depth of power both at home and abroad. In terms of Afghanistan this existed within the framework of foreign support of Sunni and Shia mujahideen that poured into the country from throughout the Muslim world. In the short-term Sunni and Shia mujahideen were both fighting a jihad against Soviet "infidels." This not only gave domestic and foreign fighters a common cause, but also a type of crusade for which they were religiously inspired and willing to die for. Their fervor along with their training and resources ultimately led to a victory against the Soviets. In the short-term the ramifications associated with this victory were positive. However, in the long-term, complexities of this security landscape contributed to the rise of sectarian conflict and violence, as well as terrorism that has been plaguing the wider region for decades. Additionally, this landscape helped both Saudi Arabia and Iran enhance the strategic layers and transnational linkages needed to engage in their long-term competition for regional hegemony. Afghanistan was one of the first theaters in which the two countries instrumentalized their Islamic sect in competition with each other, while simultaneously pursuing their mutual goal of defeating the Soviets. As such, the changes that occurred during this period were profound and established deep roots of sectarian tension and conflict both related to the Soviet-Afghan War and other important events, including the Iran-Iraq War. When the Soviet Union pulled its last troops out of Afghanistan in 1989, ending many years of direct involvement and occupation (Taylor 2014) it left behind a cycle of tension, conflict, and violence that continues to not only plague Afghanistan and its people on socio-political and security levels, but also the wider region. To thoroughly understand the complexities of sectarianism and militant Islamism today, it is essential to examine factors that contributed to their rise and expansion. This chapter provides a brief analysis of the Soviet-Afghan War and the strategic use of militant Islamism within this context, as well as the utilization of this war as a pretext to enhance division within the Muslim world based on sect-based identities.

The Soviet Invasion

The Soviet-Afghan War was triggered by the Soviet invasion of Afghanistan. The Soviet Union had exerted its influence inside Afghanistan for decades prior to invading the country in 1979. In April 1978 Afghanistan's centrist government, headed by President Mohammad Daud Khan, was overthrown by left-wing military officers led by Nur Mohammad Taraki. Power was shared by two Marxist-Leninist political groups, the People's (Khalq) Party and the Banner (Parcham) Party. They had earlier emerged from a single organization, the People's Democratic Party of Afghanistan and reunited to form a coalition shortly prior to the coup. The new government had little popular support from the people of Afghanistan. To strengthen its position the nascent government forged close ties with the Soviet Union, launched ruthless purges of all domestic opposition, and began extensive land and social reforms that were immensely resented by the devoutly Muslim and largely anti-communist population. What ultimately resulted was a rise in insurgencies against the government among both tribal and urban groups.

Collectively members of the insurgencies were known as the mujahideen. The rise in insurgencies, along with fighting between the People's and Banner factions were among the motivating factors that prompted the Soviets to invade the country to secure its interests. On December 24, 1979, the Soviet Union invaded Afghanistan under the pretext of upholding the Soviet-Afghan Friendship Treaty of 1978 and supporting a pro-Soviet regime in Kabul. They sent in thousands of troops toppling the short-lived presidency of People's leader Hafizullah Amin ("Major News" 1980). However, according to archival records of a conversation between the Soviet Ambassador Puzanov and Amin on November 3, 1979, it is likely that the depth of Soviet dissatisfaction regarding Afghanistan's domestic policies and circumstances was unknown to him.[1] The Ambassador had informed Amin just a month before he was toppled that the Soviet leadership was satisfied with the measures undertaken by the Afghan leadership in the area of party and state building.[2]

Despite the Ambassador's statement of support for Hafizullah Amin's government in November, Amin was deposed on December 27, 1979, three days after the Soviet Union's airborne division had landed. He was subsequently executed (Middleton 1982).

The invasion also aimed to prop up and support Babrak Karmal, who had positive views of Soviet involvement in Afghanistan and was seemingly thankful for their substantial economic and political support. Moreover, he was also a proponent of integrating Soviet economic reforms into the Afghan economy.[3] However, Karmal was unable to attain significant popular support among the Afghan people. In regards to Soviet involvement in Afghanistan, the Soviets incorrectly assessed that the invasion would be a short and successful campaign and one that would easily allow them to not just solidify their power and influence in the country, but also to expand it (Matthews 2011). Consequently, the Soviets found themselves in a quagmire as they did not understand the complexity of the country and underestimated the opposition they would face. Consequently, within weeks of the invasion they found themselves engulfed in a rapidly escalating war characterized by Islamism, guerilla warfare, and highly effective asymmetric tactics (Matthews 2011).

The invasion was the first large-scale military operation by the Soviet military since 1945. Initially the Soviets sent in approximately 80,000 troops.[4] However, by mid-1986 this figure had increased to about 118,000 to 225,000 and an additional 20,000 to 40,000 military personnel were supporting the war in the Soviet Union. Incorrectly thinking the invasion and occupation would be relatively easy and fast, Moscow's basic goal was to ensure the continuation of a pro-Soviet Communist regime that it could easily control without a large Soviet military presence. In essence they wanted Afghanistan to be a satellite state under their control. This proved to be one of the most poorly judged foreign policy decisions in Soviet history (Brown 2013) as the mujahideen fought back effectively with the help of foreign support. Moreover, the invasion angered many people in Afghanistan, as well as members of the global Muslim community as evidenced by its condemnation by the Islamic Conference in early 1980 (Pentz 1988), the burning of Soviet flags in countries such as Iran, Turkey, Pakistan, and India and the converging of Sunni and Shia Islamists in Afghanistan to fight against the Soviets ("Major News" 1980).

What resulted was a coming together of Islamists from both inside Afghanistan and from other countries who converged into the country to fight the Soviets and prevent the spread of communism. They did so with the help of Muslim and non-Muslim states who entered the war for the advancement of their own interests. Consequently, the Soviet invasion of Afghanistan served as a catalyst for a brutal war and a theater for Cold War politics with long-term consequences that continue to shape the local, regional, and international arena today. This was related to the Afghan resistance that was rooted in approximately 36,000 villages and hamlets in about 29 provinces (Kamrany 1986). It was also deeply rooted in the strategic role that Islam, including sectarian identity played in the advancement of the resistance against the Soviets. As the mujahideen was fueled by religious fervor and its members were willing to die in their fight against the "infidel," they became an unpredictable force that countered the Soviets and ultimately defeated them through the utilization of asymmetric strategies and tactics. Who were the mujahideen? The majority component of the mujahideen were Sunni and backed predominantly by the United States and Saudi Arabia and supported by Pakistan. The second largest component of the mujahideen were Shia and supported by Iran. Based on the widescale and comprehensive support they received, they were able to effectively fight the Soviets. The Soviets were unable to emerge victorious as originally predicted. As such, by 1988 the Soviets were ready to pull out and stop the metaphoric bleeding that they were experiencing on military, economic and political levels.

Why Did the Soviets Eventually Pull Out of Afghanistan?

Despite the release of official announcements of victories over the mujahideen (Middleton 1982), the Soviets failed to achieve victory in the war and sought an exit. According to Roy, the withdrawal of the Soviets from Afghanistan (Tempest & Parks 1988) was not only a watershed event within the historical context of Afghanistan or the rise of transnational Islamist networks, but it also symbolized the end of confrontation between the United States and the Soviet Union (Roy 1991). The Soviet Union signed a set of accords with the United States, and its allies in April 1988 agreeing to the withdrawal of its troops which was completed by February 1989 (Ottaway 1988). The government in Kabul had been excluded from the meetings presumably due to the Soviet Union agreeing to the conditions set forth by the mujahideen, the United States, and its allies (Kamm 1988). While formal talks were primarily with the United States, Afghanistan, and Pakistan and they were the signatories of the accords, the Soviet Union also engaged in talks with other members of the Afghan opposition and their supporters. For example, on February 3, 1989, the Soviet Ambassador Vorontsov met with the Shia arm of the mujahideen, representatives of the alliance of Tehran Eight. According to the Ambassador "...the leading Iranian representatives took a pragmatic matter of fact approach in talks with him"[5] and the primary subject of the talks were about ceasing the war and creating a provisional government. According to this resource the Soviets believed it was important to create a "consultative council which would include representatives of the 'Seven' and the 'Eight'."[6] The fact that they met with the representatives of Tehran Eight, including its head Khalili, despite the fact that Iran would not be a signatory on the accords as it was increasingly internationally isolated, illustrates the rise of two distinct groups in the region – and the wider influence of external stakeholders in the Soviet-Afghan war. Iran's involvement regarding the Soviet Union's withdrawal and its direct and indirect influence on Afghanistan in the post-war landscape was wider in scope than meeting with the Soviet ambassador and what is often noted in existing scholarship on the subject. For example, as the final withdrawal date was approaching,

Khamene'i, Rafsanjani, and Mousavi made several attempts at negotiating with representatives of Pakistan- based Afghan parties to try to win them over to their point of view. At a January 1989 conference in Tehran, Khamene'i, Rafsanjani, and Mousavi secured commitments both from the loose alliance of Pakistani-backed mujahidin (the Peshawar Seven) and from their own alliance of Afghan groups (the "Tehran Eight") to declare the establishment of an Islamic Republic that would adhere to a foreign policy of "neither East nor West."

(Nunan 2022: 3)

Overall, it was arguably in the Soviet interest to end the war as they were increasingly bogged down in a guerilla war while the mujahideen they had installed as the government remained weak and ineffective (Directorate of Intelligence 1987). Since the invasion of Afghanistan in 1979, the war had become increasingly costly to the Soviet Union – politically, financially, and militarily. The Soviet leadership viewed it as death from a thousand cuts and according to General Secretary Gorbachev it was a "bleeding wound" (Directorate of Intelligence 1987). Politically it had cost the Soviets immensely. For example, according to an unclassified Intelligence Assessment from the Central Intelligence Agency dated 1987, the war had led to periodic censure within the United Nations, had become an obstacle to improving Sino-Soviet relations, and created challenges for Soviet policy towards nations in the non-aligned movement (Directorate of Intelligence 1987). Soviet involvement in Afghanistan proved to be politically disadvantageous for the Soviets domestically as well. For example the country began to experience "…pockets of social unrest related to Afghanistan, the diversion of energies from pressing economic problems, and dissatisfaction in the political hierarchy over the failures to end the war" (Directorate of Intelligence 1987). Additional negative political ramifications associated with the war included the reawakening of national-ethnic and Islamic identity in Central Asia based on their belief that the invasion was an immoral act committed by the Soviets (Brown 2013) against a Muslim nation. The impact of the political fallout had profound ramifications for the Soviet Union.

The Soviet-Afghan War also had a detrimental impact on the Soviet Union from a financial perspective. By 1985 costs associated with the war were up from $2 billion to $12 billion (Kamrany 1986). According to reports, much of the rising costs were associated with increases in their air operations and a significant number of aircraft losses (Directorate of Intelligence 1987). Overall the financial costs of the war steadily increased adding a further burden to an already difficult war for the Soviets. From a military standpoint, on one hand the army's credibility and morale had decreased, and on the other desertion rates had increased and some soldiers from Muslim Soviet Turkistan joined the Afghan resistance (Kamrany 1986). In terms of the human cost of the war, on the Soviet side approximately 15,000 had been killed, about 45,000 wounded and some 650,000 soldiers rotated in Afghanistan (Kamrany 1986). The numbers were much worse for the Afghan population. Over 1.3 million Afghans died, countless were injured, and over a third of the population became refugees due to the war. According to a study by the

National Institute of Health (NIH), the brutal military campaign resulted in one of the biggest humanitarian crises in modern history with over 5 million refugees fleeing to Pakistan and Iran and another 2 million displaced internally (Bhutta & Dewraj 2002).

Fierce Resistance Against the Soviets

Afghanistan's mujahideen were diverse. They consisted of Sunni and Shia fighters, each group being influenced and organized by different stakeholders. On one hand, Sunni fighters were primarily supported by the United States and Saudi Arabia and based in Pakistan. On the other hand, Shia fighters were sponsored by Iran, and based in Iran. Initially, the mujahideen arose out of local militias, led by regional warlords who independently took up arms across Afghanistan to fight the Soviet invasion. In addition to Afghan fighters, Muslims from other countries volunteered to join the mujahideen ranks, including fighters from Chechnya and Arab countries, among others. A majority of foreign fighters were from Arab countries, and they were called Afghan-Arabs, such as Osama bin-Laden. Thousands of Muslim recruits from across the Middle East and North Africa were encouraged by their governments, religious institutions, and Saudi recruitment campaigns to go to Afghanistan and fulfill what they came to see as a religious duty in the fight against the Soviet Union – the "infidels." Within this framework it is important to note the key role of transnational Islamic religious networks that were assembled around ulemas and institutions. According to Kepel, ulemas and institutions such as the Muslim World League and conservative Salafists, among others, had an important role in this regard in addition to key states. Nonetheless, after the invasion of Afghanistan, the United States, Saudi Arabia, and Pakistan created a highly effective coalition that is commonly referred to as the Washington-Riyadh-Islamabad triangle (Steinberg & Woermer 2013) in support of the Sunni arm of the mujahideen. Once in the mujahedeen training camps, the recruits became ideologically charged with the desire for holy war, became fixated on the return to the Golden Age of Islam, and were willing to die for their cause. According to Kepel, the mixing of Arabs with Afghans and other Muslims from every corner of the world meant that there was an exchange of ideas based on their different traditions (Kepel 2003). Consequently, in these gatherings of international militant Islamists a brotherhood emerged, and many unexpected ideological cross-fertilizations were facilitated leading to heightened levels of radicalization and the creation of transnational Islamist networks that transcended borders and boundaries and connected individuals based on their sect, and level of militancy. As the Soviet occupation dragged on, the Afghan resistance became increasingly united in its opposition of the Soviet Union. Meaning linguistic, ethnic, and cultural divisions were put aside for the time being to fight a common enemy. By 1985, the majority of the mujahideen were fighting as part of a broad alliance known as the Islamic Unity of Afghanistan Mujahideen under the banner of the Peshawar Seven. This was an alliance made up of fighters from the armies of seven major Sunni warlords. After the war ended, members of the mujahideen – those whose stayed in Afghanistan and others that returned home – were highly trained, battle hardy men, were proponents of Jihad as it was their mantra during the Soviet-Afghan War, had access to transnational extremist networks that were honed during the war, and sought to bring about a return to the Golden Age of Islam. This had and continues to have immense consequences across the wider region and in the global community.

Sunni Mujahideen

According to Kepel, the Afghan jihad as it was commonly known, was the central militant cause of the 1980s. For the United States, it meant that as part of a policy of containment of Soviet advancement it would provide massive aid and support to the mujahideen (Kepel 2003), which Ronald Reagan referred to as "freedom fighters in 1981" (Raines 1981). More specifically, when speaking about the mujahideen fighting in Afghanistan, he stated that, "those people are fighting for their own country and not wanting to become a satellite state of the Soviet Union, which came in and established a government of its choosing there…" (Raines 1981). This translated to a major international operation to arm the mujahideen with weapons, intelligence, and other things that they needed to drive the Soviets out of Afghanistan. The American operation to contain Soviet advancement in Afghanistan and arm the mujahideen was called "Operation Cyclone" (Williams 2008). According to an unclassified National Security Decision Directive on relations with the Soviet Union from 1983, the policy of the United States towards the U.S.S.R. consisted of three main elements: exerting external resistance to Soviet expansion, internal pressure within the country to weaken it domestically, and engaging in negotiations to eliminate disagreements.[7] U.S. support of the mujahideen in Afghanistan in essence engaged directly with two of these elements. It exerted external resistance to Soviet expansion, and it helped destabilize the country's domestic landscape based on its inability to emerge victorious in the war. Thus, U.S. policy and strategies in this context were able to effectively shape the Soviet Union's internal and external environment to one that was beneficial to U.S. interests and the destabilization of the U.S.S.R.

The United States supplied money, arms (Sciolinos 1989), and other resources to the mujahideen through intermediaries in Pakistan for the duration of the conflict. Pakistan's government distributed aid, funds and was a conduit for the rebels and controlled nearly all of the money and supplies sent from the United States to the mujahideen (Pentz 1988). The Zia regime was also involved in the active training of rebels in refugee camps located in Peshawar, Pakistan (Pentz 1988). Seemingly overnight, the invasion had made Pakistan of immense interest to the United States and it became a vital facet in the fighting against Soviet expansion into Afghanistan (Pentz 1988). More specifically, when the Soviets invaded Afghanistan, Pakistan suddenly became a "front-line" state (Pentz 1988) as it now shared a 13,000-mile border with Afghanistan and given the war this was now a Soviet border (Pentz 1988). Consequently, Pakistan emerged as a major player within the context of the Soviet-Afghan War and U.S. Cold War policies, particularly in the context of training and helping arm the majority of the militant Islamists that fought against the Soviets. It also served as a key entry point into Afghanistan during the war. This was evident in the experiences of Islamists in Peshawar, Pakistan where "Arabs mixed with Afghans and other Muslims from every corner of the world and exchanged ideas based on their different traditions" (Kepel 2003).

> For the international jihadists, the journey to Peshawar was above all an initiation. A socialization of the Islamist network; thereafter for some of them, it turned into a radicalization process, as they came into contact with militants who were much more extreme than their Saudi sponsors
>
> *(Kepel 2003)*

The Soviet invasion of Afghanistan in 1979 provided Saudi Arabia with a valuable opportunity to strengthen its relations with the United States, to enhance its Islamic legitimacy at home and abroad, to expand its sphere of influence, to increase the spread of the Wahhabi doctrine (which it was also doing in Pakistan during the same period), and to counter what it saw as the Shia threat from Iran. An interesting point from a religious angle – in January 1980 it was reported by the U.S. State Department that a Saudi ulama had issued a fatwa authorizing the payment to Afghan mujahideen fighters to engage in a jihad against the Soviets (*Aboul-Enein*, January 1, 2008). Moreover, the Saudi Grand Mufti, Bin Baz, endorsed Azzam's fatwa resulting in the creation of a collection of literature that made it religiously sanctioned to engage in jihad due to "…assaults on Muslim lands like Palestine and Afghanistan fard ayn,[8] meaning a compulsory duty incumbent upon all Muslims until these lands are liberated" (Aboul-Enein 2008). Thus, sanctioning militant and extremist interpretations of how to respond to global events and "challenges" (Aboul-Enein 2008). In terms of direct tangible support of the mujahideen, "until the mid-1980s, international Islamic solidarity was expressed largely in financial terms" (Kepel 2003) including by Saudi Arabia and others. Additionally, the Saudi government subsidized travel and training. In terms of funding the government of Saudi Arabia generally matched U.S. financial contributions, providing money in a joint fund with Washington. They paid the mujahideen in cash. In addition, several wealthy Saudi princes and other private citizens made contributions to the Mujahideen as well. "Besides the US, Saudi Arabia became the main financier of the mujahideen and from the mid-1980s built its own contacts and client networks among the Afghan opposition" (Steinberg & Woermer 2013).[9] It also actively engaged in the recruitment of jihadi fighters from around the world. This complimented U.S. support of the Afghan mujahideen.

Shia Mujahideen

The Sunni arm of the mujahideen comprised the biggest group fighting the Soviets. However, there was another coalition of Islamists that also fought the Soviets and was the second largest mujahideen force after the Peshavar Seven. They were smaller in scale and were restricted from fighting alongside the Peshawar Seven as there were clear sectarian based divisions between Sunni and Shia fighters. These were the Shia mujahideen who were supported by Iran – signifying one of the early theaters in which sectarianism was instrumentalized within a Shia framework after the fall of the Pahlavi Dynasty. While much is known about the Sunni arm of the mujahideen, less is known about its Shia arm, which comprised a political union called the Tehran Eight. This coalition was headquartered in Iran and supported by Iran. A Soviet dossier regarding the Tehran Eight documents the eight organizations that comprised this coalition. The organizations included the Organization of Fighters of Afghanistan for Islam, The Movement of the Islamic Revolution (DIR), The Council of Islamic Accord (SIS), The Islamic Movement of Afghanistan (IDA), The United Front of the Islamic Revolution (OFIR), The Corps of Guardians of the Islamic Jihad of Afghanistan (KSIRA), The Party of Victory ("Nasr"), and The Party of Allah ("Hezbe Allah") (Dossiers of Political Parties 1999). The core fighters of the Shia mujahideen were from the Fatemiyoun Brigade, which was founded in the early 1980s. The Fatemiyoun Brigade is an Iranian led Shia militia consisting of Afghan Shia's who were and still are predominantly Hazara. During this period, not only did they fight against the Soviets in Afghanistan, but they also fought on Iran's side (Heiat 2016) during the Iran-Iraq war (Hassan 2021).[10] This is highly significant as the Fatemiyoun Brigade continues to be utilized by the Iranian state to advance its strategic interests in the region and is an example of a long-term consequence regarding the use of political Islam in the context of fighting against the Soviets. While they continue to be an important element of Iran militarily, the Brigade has grown in size and importance to Iran since the 1980s with their current numbers believed to be between 40,000 and 60,000 fighters (Jamal 2019). Members of the Brigade are drawn from both Afghan Shia refugees, as well as members of the Hazara community in Afghanistan (Heiat 2016). With the rise of ISIL, Iran restructured the Fatemiyoun as a professionalized proxy force (Heiat 2016) and today this Brigade is a part of Iran's force in Syria.

Overall, Iran's support of the Shia arm of the mujahideen, was framed along the lines of Shia identity and similar to the Sunni arm of the resistance, it used an outbidding process to compete for support and influence within an Islamic framework. It also aimed to further embed itself within the transnational Shia community subsequently creating cohesive religio-political and security-based landscapes in Afghanistan and elsewhere. As such, on one hand the emergence of Iran during the 1980s as a Shia regional power seeking to project its influence through the strategic use of Shia identity across the wider region in competition with Saudi Arabia signified a major geopolitical fracture, as it severed the type of relationship that had existed between the two countries under the Nixon Doctrine until the success of the Iranian Revolution (Keynoush 2016). This was evident across the region, including within the larger context of the Soviet-Afghan War. On the other hand, with the ousting of the Pahlavi Dynasty in Iran and the shift in Iranian foreign policy, Saudi Arabia sought to establish a Sunni wall around Iran to contain its advancement on socio-political, religio-political, and security levels. The establishment of fissures between members of the mujahideen was arguably a facet of this overall strategy of both countries. This had widescale ramifications across the region, including in Afghanistan where members of the two sects did not generally fight alongside each other despite fighting the same enemy. However, there were exceptions. One of the exceptions to the divisions between Sunni and Shia mujahideen as they fought the Soviets occurred in April 1983, on the outskirts of Herat, near the Iranian border where they united to effectively fight the Soviets. According to the *New York Times*,

> There three rival Afghan rebel factions were said to have united for an ambush on April 1 of a large Soviet-Afghan military convoy. Many soldiers were reported killed and many others captured. The three rebel groups involved in what the diplomat said was a rare display of unity were identified as the Hezbe-i-Islami, The Jamat-i-Islami and the Harakat-i-Islami.
>
> *("Major Soviet-Led Drive" 1983)*

The coming together of Shia and Sunni mujahideen in this context further illustrates that the sectarian framework utilized among members of the mujahideen and their external supporters was simply based on strategic objectives rather than ideological incompatibility or ancient hatred. More specifically, it illustrates that Islam and sectarian identity were simply tools to avert Soviet advancement and communist ideology, while simultaneously advancing Shia and Sunni leaders in the Muslim world – Iran and Saudi Arabia.

Conclusion

The strategies utilized against the Soviet Union by the United States in its proxy war were successful in curtailing the spread of Soviet influence and power into Afghanistan. Indeed, this war not only prevented the spread of Soviet influence into Afghanistan, given the depth of loss that the Soviet Union sustained, it also arguably set in motion the eventual dismantling of the Soviet Union. For example, by 1986, for non-Russians the war became a unifying symbol of opposition to Soviet rule and demonstrated the overall vulnerability of its army, by extension influencing questions of legitimacy (Reuveny & Prakas 1999) and the ability of non-Russians to resist the status quo. However, it also resulted in the strengthening of transnational Islamist networks, the spread of Islamic revivalism and significantly deepened the rift between Shias and Sunnis (Roy 1991). The holy war waged by the mujahedeen against the "infidel" communists was successful and the long-term impact of the invasion and subsequent war was immense. Not only did it result in the Soviets leaving Afghanistan, but it also provided a fertile environment for the rise of militant Islamists throughout the world. It was one of the key watershed events in the 1980s that contributed to the surge of sectarianism that continues to exist across the Muslim world today with immense consequences. Moreover, the mujahideen's victory empowered Islamic extremists to believe that in essence the sky was the limit and with God on their side they could turn against the other enemy – the governments and societies in their home countries and later the West which they considered to be Jahiliyya.

The Soviet-Afghan War was also successful in bringing together extremely well trained, transnationally connected Islamic extremists, who continued their drive for jihad after the war ended. Moreover, since an empire was defeated, they felt empowered and kept pushing forward under the banner of jihad and extremism. But this time as noted earlier not to fight the Soviets, but rather to return to the glory days of the "Golden Age of Islam" in Afghanistan and the wider Muslim world. Given the long-term legacy of Islamic extremism and terrorism stemming from this war, as well as its cascading effect on the surge of sectarianism, it is important to contextualize the complexities associated with this war within a modern historical framework. Therefore, within this framework it is crucial to recognize that U.S. and Soviet intervention in Afghanistan and the subsequent proxy war has had and continues to have drastic long-term consequences. In addition to the countless lives lost and mass displacement during the Soviet-Afghan War, the conflict solidified the concept of global jihad and provided a platform for the emergence of a number of terrorist organizations, including the Taliban, GIA in Algeria, Al-Qaeda, and by extension the Islamic State of Iraq and the Levant (ISIL).

The Soviet-Afghan War was also significant from a sectarian perspective. The 1970s and 1980s were a period of Islamic revivalism and according to Roy, this contributed to the deepening the rift between Shias and Sunnis, including in Afghanistan. This was evident in the nature of Sunni and Shia mujahideen in fighting against the Soviets and in the socio-political and security landscapes of Afghanistan after the war (Roy 1991), as well as in the emergence of two distinct groups of mujahideen fighters that emerged – Sunni and Shia Islamists. While both groups fought against the Soviets, they generally did not fight alongside each other as they were divided along sectarian lines. This distinct division was solidified based on the competition that had emerged between Iran and Saudi Arabia after the fall of the Pahlavi Dynasty in Iran and the demise of the Twin Pillar policy. As such, both Saudi Arabia and Iran instrumentalized not only Islam for strategic purposes within the context of the Soviet-Afghan War, but each also strategically utilized their specific sect to advance their interests and level of influence among members of their respective Islamic sect within Afghanistan and elsewhere across the wider region.

Two levels of "us versus them" and in-group/out-group paradigms were used – one against the Soviets and the other against each other. Consequently, it can be argued that this arena also contributed to the fomentation of sectarianism for strategic non-ideological purposes between transnational Sunni and Shia communities as the nature of fighting was highly polarized and indicative of the existing hegemonic aspirations of the two major players in the Muslim world – Iran and Saudi Arabia. Therefore, Afghanistan became one of the first landscapes in which competition between Saudi Arabia and Iran was explicitly evident and consequently facilitated the strengthening of transnational sect-based networks. As such, political entrepreneurs successfully cultivated distinct sectarian identities and projected their influence through the utilization of their specific identity in Afghanistan and elsewhere during this period with long-term temporal and spatial consequences. This includes the emergence of distinct sect-based transnational Islamist networks that approximately 40 years later continue to have immense local, regional and global influence. As noted by Kepel, once the Islamists, "…were prepared to go beyond their local bases into the arena of international Islam; and as they did so, many unexpected ideology cross-fertilizations and grafts emerged" (Kepel 2003) ultimately contributing to the surge of militant Islamism, sectarian conflict and violence in the Muslim world.

Notes

1 "Record of Conversation Between Soviet Ambassador Puzanov and Amin," November 03, 1979, History and Public Policy Program Digital Archive, Notes by O.A. Westad at TsKhSD, f. 5, op. 76, d. 1045.
2 Ibid.
3 "Soviet briefing on the talks between Brezhnev and B. Karmal in Moscow," October 29, 1980, History and Public Policy Program Digital Archive, National Archives of Hungary (MOL), M-KS 288 f. 11/4391.o.e., Translated by Attila Kolontari and Zsofia Zelnik.
4 Directorate of Intelligence, "The Costs of Soviet Involvement in Afghanistan," February 1987.
5 "Report of the Soviet Ambassador Y. M. Vorontsov, concerning the current political situation inside Afghanistan and the possibilities of solving the Afghan question," February 03, 1989, History and Public Policy Program Digital Archive, State Central Archive Prague, File 02/1, CC CPCz Politburo 1980–1989, 103rd Meeting, 3 February 1989, in Czech. Translated by Todd Hammond and Derek Paton. Obtained by Oldrich Tuma. https://digitalarchive.wilsoncenter.org/document/113128.
6 Ibid.
7 Secret, The White House, "NSDD 75 on U.S. Relations with the USSR," January 17, 1983. Executive Registry 83–0331; A National Security Decision Directive on Relations with the USSR.
8 Fard al-ayn refers to legal obligations that must be performed by each individual Muslim, including prayer, charity, fasting and pilgrimage. Individual obligation is contrasted with fard al-kifayah (communal obligation).
9 The Saudi involvement did not end after the war ended. Rather it was slightly scaled down and followed a different agenda after the Soviet withdrawal in 1989.
10 During the Iran-Iraq War, these fighters were stationed in the mountainous areas of Loolan and Navcheh.

Bibliography

Aboul-Enein, Youssef. *The Late Sheikh Abudullah Azzam's Books: Radical Theories on Defending Muslim Land through Jihad.* West Point, NY: The Combating Terrorism Center, US Military Academy, 2008.
Bhutta, Zulfiqar Ahmed and Husein Lalji Dewraj. "Children of War: The Real Casualties of the Afghan Conflict," *British Medical Journal* 324, no. 7333 (February 9, 2002): 349–352.
Brown, James D. J. "Oil Fueled? The Soviet Invasion of Afghanistan," *Post-Soviet Affairs* 29, no. 1 (2013): 56–94.
Directorate of Intelligence. "The Costs of Soviet Involvement in Afghanistan," February 1987.
"Dossiers of Political Parties Intent on Exporting an Islamic Revolution." History and Public Policy Program Digital Archive, in A. A. Lyakhovskiy's *"Plamya Afgana"* ("Flame of the Afghanistan veteran")." Translated by Gary Goldberg. Moscow: Iskon, 1999.
Hassan, Lila. "What is the Fatemiyoun Brigade and Why Does It Make the Taliban Nervous?" *PBS: Frontline,* July20, 2021.

Heiat, Saumaun. "The Hazara community in Afghanistan is stuck in the middle between Iran and the Taliban." *Atlantic Council*, October 22, 2021.

Jamal, Ahmad Shuja. "The Fatemiyoun Army: Reintegration into Afghan Society." United States Institute of Peace, March 19, 2019.

Kamm, Henry. "Soviet-Afghan Rebel Talks Adjourned." *New York Times*, December 6, 1988.

Kamrany, Nake M. "The Continuing Soviet War in Afghanistan." *Current History* 85, No. 513 (October 1986): 333–336.

Kepel, Gilles. *Jihad: The Trail of Political Islam*. Cambridge: Belknap Press, 2003.

Keynoush, Banafsheh. *Saudi Arabia and Iran: Friends or Foes?* New York: Palgrave Macmillan, 2016.

"Major News: Soviet Invasion of Afghanistan Derails Detente Waldheim Mission Goes and Comes Flight to Gold, Destination Unsure," *New York Times*, January 6, 1980.

"Major Soviet-Led Drive is Reported in Afghan War." *New York Times*, April 21, 1983.

Matthews, Matt M. *"We Have Not Learned how to Wage War there": The Soviet Approach in Afghanistan, 1979–1989*. Fort Leavenworth, Kansas: United States Army Combined Arms Center Combat Studies, Institute Press, 2011.

Middleton, Drew. "Afghan War: Soviet Options After 3 Years: Afghan War: Soviet Options After 3 Years." *New York Times*, December 25, 1982.

Nasr, Vali. *The Shia Revival: How Conflicts Within Islam Will Shape the Future*. New York: W.W. Norton & Company, 2006.

Nunan, Timothy. "'Doomed to Good Relations:' The USSR, the Islamic Republic of Iran, and Anti-Imperialism in the 1980s."*Journal of Cold War Studies* 24, no. 1 (Winter 2022): 39–77.

Ottaway, David. "Agreement on Afghanistan Signed in Geneva," *The Washington Post*, April 15, 1988.

Pentz, Peter A. "The Mujahidin Middleman: Pakistan's Role in the Afghan Crisis and the International Rule of Non-Intervention." *Dickinson Journal of International Law* 6, no. 3 (1988): 377.

Raines, Howell. "Reagan Hinting at Arms for Afghan Rebels: Monroe Doctrine Invoked." *New York Times*, March 10, 1981.

Reuveny, Rafael and Aseem Prakash, "The Afghanistan War and the Breakdown of the Soviet Union." *Review of International Studies* 24 (1999): 693–708.

Roy, Olivier. "Introduction." *Adelphi papers* 31, no. 259 (1991): 3–5.

Roy, Oliver. *The Failure of Political Islam*. Cambridge: Harvard University Press, 2001.

Sciolinos, Elaine. "U.S. Divided on Soviet Afghan Stand: Some Hints of Doing without Najibullah are Read Two Ways." *New York Times*, December 16, 1989.

Steinberg, Guido and Nils Woermer. "Exploring Iran and Saudi Arabia's Interest in Afghanistan and Pakistan: Stakeholders or Spoilers – A Zero Sum Game?" Barcelona Centre for International Affairs, April, 2013.

Taylor, Alan. "The Soviet War in Afghanistan." *The Atlantic*, August 4, 2014.

Tempest, Rone and Michael Parks. "Soviets' Afghan Pullout Begins Armored Convoy Departing as Moscow Winds Down 8-Year War." *Los Angeles Times*, May 16, 1988.

Warde, Ibrahim. "Wagering on Sectarianism: The Political Economy of Extremism." *The Muslim World* 106, no. 1 (January 2016): 205–216.

Williams, Brian Glyn. "Talibanistan: History of a Transnational Terrorist Sanctuary." *Civil Wars* 10, no. 1 (2008): 40–59.

4
ADVICE COLUMNISTS IN EGYPT
Envisioning the Good Life in an Era of Extremism

Andrea B. Rugh

Introduction

Letters to advice columnists are a revealing way of penetrating people's thinking without violating their privacy. Historians and political scientists write about general trends but not much about the way these trends affect the personal lives of individuals. Letters to advice columnists show the personal pain these trends cause, and columnists' responses show culturally acceptable ways of mitigating their suffering. In short, the columns provide a window into a culture at a particular time and place. In the Egyptian context this has been highlighted by the intersection of advice columns and religious extremism, particularly in the 1980s as this was a period of Islamic revival. To examine the intersection of culture, religious extremism, and columns, data for this study has been derived from over 200 full and partial columns collected from Egyptian newspapers in the 1980s and early 1990s. Overall, there were two kinds of columnists: the self-described humanist, Abdul Wahab al-Muttawa, and religious commentators most of whom were scholars trained in religious interpretation. The questions of concern, beyond general insights into Egyptian culture, are how these columnists envisioned the *good life* and addressed the main issue of the day – extremism. This is an important point, as Egypt increasingly experienced acts of extremism in the 1980s, while many ordinary Egyptians were turning to religion to solve their problems. The increase in the level of religiosity has steadily increased since the 1980s. This has been evident by the steady rise in the number of mosques in the country. For example, there was one mosque for every 6,031 Egyptians in the 1980s and by the mid-2000s the number significantly increased to one for every 745 Egyptians (Osman 2010).

The decade of the 1980s saw the culmination of poorly conceived and implemented government policies after independence in 1952 (Richards 1991). The result was an intensification of trends building in Egyptian society since independence. Moreover, Nasser proposed reforms intended to uplift the poor

DOI: 10.4324/9781003329510-5

of Egypt – but land reforms, expansion of the urban industrial sector, and universal education with guaranteed government jobs for graduates had unintended ripple effects (Joya 2020). These initiatives were never fully funded or implemented, and as a result waves of rural Egyptians migrated to cities causing rapid urbanization and many went abroad in hopes of finding jobs, resulting in major social and economic dislocations. These dislocations and some of his other policies, including those aimed at suppressing Islamist politics and further empowering state security forces to limit assembly and speech, ultimately had immense socio-political ramifications.

After Nasser's death in 1970, Sadat took over, expelled the Soviets from the country, attempted to recreate the government, and was more open to Islamist groups than his predecessor (Sheehan 1972). To protect against Egyptian leftists, he encouraged the rise of the religious right[1] and opened the Egyptian economy to the West (Kepel & Rothschild 1985). In 1974 Sadat announced the country's open door policy and the freeing of Egypt's economy from previous restrictions and in 1975 he reopened the Suez Canal to international navigation (Baker 1981). Sadat had firmly moved Egypt into the Western sphere while simultaneously shifting Egypt's internal policies. Although opening the economy had some positive effects, the policy wreaked havoc on the poor and middle classes from inflation and the lure of consumer goods that most could not afford. These factors coupled with Sadat's immensely unpopular trip to Israel in search of peace, lay the groundwork for extremism increasing in Egypt in the 1980s.

The 1980s began with President Sadat's assassination by Muslim extremists, highlighting the change in the country's socio-political, cultural and religio-political landscapes. Consequently, when his vice-president, Hosni Mubarak came to power he modified Sadat's more unpopular economic policies, consolidated his control over the security services, clamped down on extremists (Marfleet 2013 and created space for more moderate Islamists. Ultimately, Mubarak reversed the latter as it became a space for Islamists who sought to delegitimize his regime and promote extremism (Al-Wadi 2005). The latter two prongs of his approach included the imprisonment of thousands of activists as well as targeting members of Islamist groups implicated in the assassination of President Sadat. In regards to the former, he gradually adopted measures proposed by the IMF subsequently resulting in more cuts and increased popular resistance (Al-Wadi 2005).

The Advice Columnists

A few months after Sadat's assassination, an advice column appeared in the quasi-government *Al-Ahram* newspaper. The columnist, Abdul Wahab al-Muttawa,[2] was born in 1940 in a small town about 40 miles east of Alexandria. He was one of the first waves of rural students to take advantage of Nasser's policy of universal education. In 1961, he graduated with a journalism degree from Cairo University and began working for *Al-Ahram* where he rose through the ranks, first as a sportswriter and ultimately becoming editor-in-chief. In the summer of 1977, the newspaper sent him for training to England. Al-Muttawa recalled[3] being extremely lonely there, especially on weekends when he spent hours reading the *Sunday Times*. He especially enjoyed the columns advising readers about their problems although not being from the same culture, he felt he did not always understand the advice that was given. He concluded that although circumstances may differ in everyone's life, people everywhere have the same fears and concerns including those related to death, disease, poverty, losing family, friends, and lovers (Rugh 2019).

During this period Abdul Wahab began to think about writing a column himself – one that would appeal to an Egyptian audience. He felt the answers in the British papers were too short to address the real suffering expressed by letter-writers. After a few lines, the British columnists would tell their readers to "seek a psychologist," advice he felt would not satisfy Egyptian audiences. Given his humanist approach Abdul Wahab's columns became enormously popular with Egyptians during the 1980s and until his retirement in the 1990s (Rugh 2019). He continued to write short stories and novels inspired by the problems sent in by his readers and hosted a TV show where people from all over the Middle East called in seeking his advice. He died in 2014 at the age of 64. Also appearing at the time were columns written by members of the religious establishment, usually sheikhs trained at and often still affiliated with Al-Azhar University, a main center of Sunni learning in the Muslim world. In contrast to Abdul Wahab who drew predominantly from his humanistic leanings, the sheikhs drew mainly from the writings of Islamic scholars and traditional sources and as such were anchored in religious sources. It is only possible to describe a small number of these many writers. Three in particular stand out because of their positions at Al-Azhar, while the fourth was a TV preacher. In the 1980s, Sheikh Gad al-Haq, was Grand Imam at Al-Azhar (1982–1996) while the second, Sheikh Muhammad Sayyid Tantawy was Grand Mufti (1986–1996). The third younger one, Sheikh Ahmed El-Tayeb, served as Grand Mufti (2002–2003), and then became Grand Imam (2010 onwards). The fourth sheikh, Muhammad al-Sharawy became the Arab World's most charismatic preacher of Islam during the 1970s, 1980s, and 1990s. Sheikh Sharawy was an immensely popular mainstream preacher, who had a major television presence in the Arab world (Alrawi 1994).

The early lives of these men were similar. They grew up in small rural villages or towns, where they studied at Al-Azhar primary and secondary schools and later attended and graduated from Al-Azhar University. Additionally, the first three rose through the ranks of Al-Azhar, while Sheikh Sharawy turned to preaching on TV (Alrawi 1994). As a result, Al-Azhar University is significant in this context as it had great influence on the advice given in the religious columns. Moreover, religious columnists presented themselves as models of conventional establishment Islam quoting from the Koran and the Prophet's examples, as well as citing scholars from early Sunni schools of jurisprudence. They mostly supported government policies, but not always, which raises an important question of this study. Why did they occasionally risk their safe government jobs to oppose government policies? Their waffling on these matters became most noticeable during the tenure of Sheikh Ahmed as Grand Imam in the 2000s.

The Columns

Abdul Wahab described his process for writing columns as choosing a problem that was familiar to Egyptians, then taking two or three letters on the topic and rewriting them into a single narrative. Often, he said, letter-writers were not able to write clearly or took lengthy detours away from the story line. He was aware they would naturally present their side of the story better than the other side. But felt he had to accept what they wrote, since he had not witnessed the events himself. If they were lying, they would not take his advice anyway. "One has to believe in people to help them," he said and added "readers expect answers to the facts given in the columns."[4] Abdul Wahab wrote about people's problems at several levels, the most basic being the airing of their complaints about government inefficiencies. As to their personal problems, the columns covered such topics as finding marriage partners, spousal and family relations, financial and employment concerns, reputation, and general values. Sometimes his columns appeared as full-length narratives containing multiple problems, while at other times, they were fragments consisting of a few sentences where his audience had to read between the lines to understand the problem. Occasionally he used a column to comment generally on the ills of the world.

On a practical level, at *Al-Ahram*, he organized "Red Agenda Nights" to connect benefactors with people needing help, including finding jobs and marriage partners, or needing charitable gifts, such as wheelchairs, leg braces, a desk for a student, or support for orphans. These nights indirectly challenged the government's inefficiency by showing that it did not take much effort to solve people's problems – just organization. The columns of the religious sheikhs were usually more narrowly focused. Most began with a question about how Islam viewed a particular behavior, followed by a sheikh commenting on Islamic doctrine and opining on the permissibility of a practice. Occasionally, the sheikhs commented on issues of concern to Islam generally or as they related to modern life.

Edited examples of these columns show the different approaches. In the first short fragment[5] below, Abdel Wahab uses sarcasm to show how he feels about the government. The column was called "Before we fall over from happiness." He wrote,

> These two months brought civilization to Manial District when the Municipality decided to pave some streets. We were going mad with joy and feeling grateful to officials until they began digging up the same streets to put in a cable for telephone service and left large holes to avoid having to repave them.

The second example[6] is typical of his longer narratives. A reader wrote to him stating:

I am writing for advice on a topic of concern to many wives and husbands. I have been married more than ten years after a long love story. We were able to marry because my father gave us from the little, he had, even though my husband's family was not able to help. We were proud of the fact that we made miracles happen without much help. Our happiness increased with the birth of our children. But soon my husband began complaining that my parents had not helped us enough and that they preferred my eldest sister, because they gave her more money at marriage. The reason was that my parents' circumstances were better at the time, so they gave her more. I was upset that he insulted my parents. At first, I remained silent but then started insulting his parents to restore my family's dignity. This bothered him so much that he beat me and our relationship worsened. He almost divorced me, but only renounced me once, so I knew he wanted to keep me. So, I stopped trying to humiliate him since it only made things worse. Our views continue to differ over this problem.

I hope you will tell me who is right. He says the husband-wife relationship is so deep they do not need to be respectful to one another. Couples should be natural, and since he likes insults, I should accept him without getting upset. I however feel daily life exposes couples to so many potentially divisive problems that respect is essential to lighten their differences. Without respect, life is a hell. How can he respect office colleagues and not respect those at home? Is it right that he should utter hateful words in front of our children who hold him up as a model?

"We see my mother regularly, and despite the fact that she comes from an old family, she treats him well. She made a mistake he will never forgive, which is that she refused him when he first asked to marry me. But since she was no longer rich, she had to accept his proposal. I persist in my belief about respect because I watched an old Arab film recently where a husband and wife respected one another even after he divorced her. The ex-wife respected him as father of her children and he her as mother of his children. He addressed her politely as *"Hanem"* (lady). "I have little experience of the world to know if I am right. I always ask his permission when I go out, thank him if he gives me something, and apologize if I do something wrong. Yet he continues his insults. How do I convince him that a good marriage needs more than love?"

Abdul Wahab answered:

I do not know if most husbands ignore respect in their marriages. I do know that the happiest marriages are those where spouses respect the personality and character of one another. I am not of your husband's opinion that marriage allows all barriers to drop. Yes, it is true the barriers of strangeness and shyness drop away, and a feeling of familiarity and trust develops from the understanding that disagreements will be forgiven. This is the respect I mean. It does not need expression – it should be internal and reflected upon. It is not loving to hurt a partner's feelings or use language that shatters a person. It is wrong if a person is respectful to others and hurts those closest to him. Some spouses have two personas – loving and respectful in their social life and rude and cursing in their private life. This is an odd contradiction.

I suggest you keep your opinion to yourself and behave respectfully toward your husband as the sacred bond of marriage demands, even if he does not respond as you would like. The person who treats others with respect, respects himself, and the one who mistreats others, does not, nor is he respected by them. To change the character of another person is difficult if not impossible. The way to convince them to change is to provide a good example. Maybe as time passes, he will learn from you that love is not all that is important in a relationship.

In another example (shortened),[7] Abdul Wahab uses a question to comment on an issue that interests him. The letter-writer is skilled in martial arts and complains about aggressiveness on Cairo streets. He dislikes defending himself or others and asks why people cannot be peaceful.

Abdul Wahad responded:

Your letter opens a wound in me related to people's suffering in society, and the aggressiveness that exists in many relationships today. I feel this comes from population explosion where the qualities of gentleness, care, and justice recede and are replaced with selfishness, individualism and enmity. If two people stand before a narrow door, one will politely ask the other to go through first. But if there are thousands, they push through the door. Cairo now is overcrowded just like all Egyptian cities and villages. We are imprisoned in the strip of land bordering the Nile. When population increases, values flee, and the law of the jungle prevails where only the fittest and strongest survive.

But the picture is not completely bleak. The ultimate solution is to expand into the mighty desert. Until that happens each of us must stick to our religious values in dealing with others. We must cultivate a spirit of justice, so we are not unjust nor willing to tolerate injustice. I am not talking about laws but about personal commitment in our hearts that does not need monitoring. God imposed the law on humans to love others as they would want to be loved themselves. People should not deprive others of their rights nor attack their dignity, and they should be free to go in public without hearing aggressive remarks. Concerning your question about goodness and weakness, it reminds me of an Indian story about a snake who no longer wants to hurt others. He goes to an Indian monk who tells him to go live in a remote area as repentance for his previous crimes. The snake does so but fails when boys come and throw stones at him. When he does not respond the boys throw more stones. So, he goes back to the monk and the monk says, "Hiss in the air once a week so the gang knows you can retaliate." The snake hisses and the boys leave him alone.

The circumstances of our lives are such that we need to separate strength from weakness and goodness. The writer, Naguib Mahfouz, says there are three kinds of people: the lion who never begins a quarrel but answers one, the wolf who begins and answers quarrels and the lamb who neither begins nor answers quarrels. The lamb is easily eaten. Life feels insecure now because wolf behavior is increasing. But where lion behavior exists, there is stability and life goes on. Goodness does not mean you should not respond to aggression–just do not use your strength in ways that have legreal consequences. Be like a lion—do not start fights but defend your rights. Go my friend! Know your goodness is not weakness. Hiss in the air to let others know you can defend yourself, as long as the hiss does no harm. Forgiveness is important above all.

In contrast, the tone and style of religious columns were different. Religious columns were of two kinds, those commenting on issues of general concern to Islam, and those describing Islam's views regarding the permissibility of behaviors. The general columns report on such issues as trying to convince prison youth to return to mainstream Islam or discussing the glories of Islamic civilization and decrying the current decline of Islamic values. The remedy, claims one writer, is education programs that give youth a correct understanding of Islam. Also in this category are columns declaring the Koran better than science at knowing the age of the cosmos or predicting the start of the calendar year. Another admonishes those who look at earlier traditions (perhaps extremists) to choose carefully between what is good and evil.

The largest share of the religious columns were devoted to describing Islam's view of practices concerned with personal relationships, gender issues, family obligations, financial concerns, and relations between Muslims and Westerners or with "People of the Book," (Christians and Jews). They define the seven deadly sins,[8] describe how to gently discipline children, and say the danger in music is its incitement of immoral behavior. They claim people in all sects of Islam can be good Muslims. One column approves photos if they do not incite sexuality or veneration. Another forbids smoking because it is addictive and rejects drugs and alcohol because they might cloud the mind during prayer. Whether killing is allowed is the subject of several columns. One says retaliating for murder is good if it prevents further murders, but a person who kills a believer will go to hell. Another column encourages people to kill those who abandon Islam and says adulterers should be stoned to death if married and lashed if single.[9] Several columns describe what is required for ablutions before prayer, including the parts of the body to wash, and whether a man needs to wash again if he accidently touches a woman.

Many columns address gender and family relations. They stress the importance of marriage, discuss the permissibility of certain kinds of marriages, state that a woman should not be married without her permission, and explain situations when a divorcee or widow can legitimately remarry. Several columns discuss the conditions for divorce. A number describe when a husband can lawfully exert authority over his wife. He should not for example make decisions about her finances. Other sheikhs say she may disobey him – if what the husband asks is contrary to what God wants. Several columns note that she has the right to work, but her salary should not be used for household expenses. Two columns stress good relations with parents. The gender columns describe the Prophet's behavior towards women and say that males and females enjoy equal status in the Koran after allowing for their different biological natures. Several condemn violations of women: physically, through slander or by looking at them with evil intent. Other columns discuss women's impurities related to prayer or handling the Koran. Two deal with female circumcision, saying it is not required but one saying it dignifies women.[10]

About Jews and Christians, one sheikh says if they pay taxes, follow Islamic rules, and do not disparage Islam they should be protected. God gives people the ability to choose their religion but if they are defiant, they will suffer on Judgement Day. People who live where Islam is unknown are not infidels and children of nonbelievers will be saved. One says not to imitate Westerners unless the practice is useful like wearing a hat. Another says to take what is good from Westerners since Islam calls for seeking knowledge wherever that may lead. These examples show the range of topics and kinds of detail that appear in the columns. They are rich in cultural detail which of course is the main reason for studying them. To note a persistent refrain: Abdul Wahab and the sheikhs both promote strong family ties, even when restoring them may be uncomfortable. American advice columnists by contrast focus on letter-writers' comfort, and often suggest abandoning stressful relationships even if they are family members.

The Good Life

At first glance the columnists seem to present two very different visions of the requirements for the good life. Abdul Wahab says people should adhere to a framework of social traditions and the sheikhs to a framework of correct religious practices. Both reach into widely accepted repositories of values that if followed would presumably lead to the good life. And in them the columnists find enough ambiguity to fit almost any situation or question asked. Abdul Wahab supports his advice with references to religious and philosophical luminaries all the way back to Confucius and St. Francis, as well as many others. The religious scholars stress that their learning makes them uniquely capable of interpreting Islamic sources[11] and they utilize a significant amount of column space describing the sources they use to support their judgements. An example is the sheikh who responds to a question about whether a man should marry a woman who cannot bear children. The sheikh responds that the Prophet answered the same question by saying it was better to marry a woman who could have children to increase the number of believers. But the sheikh notes that since the Prophet himself had wives who were barren, he could not be opposed to marrying such women. He says that the Prophet in this case probably intuited that the man wanted children and gave him an answer based on his desires. From this he concludes that the Prophet's advice was not always meant to be applied universally, but sometimes it was meant to address a specific case.

A closer look at the columns shows that both forms of advice have some similarities. Both couch the details in terms of obligations, the sheikhs as religious duties and Abdul Wahab as traditional obligations owed people in certain relationships such as kin, colleagues, or strangers. When Abdul Wahab sees violations – such as a mother who abandons a child to remarry, or a son who rejects his parents' advice about marriage – he says their mistakes are a result of flouting time-tested obligations. He however understands the complexity of modern life, and often offers alternatives if the preferred options do not work. The choice is up to the individual. In certain ways, the sheikhs' descriptions of Islamic duties overlap with Abdul Wahab's social obligations especially where family roles and cohesiveness are concerned. But extenuating circumstances mean little to the sheikhs. Once the morally correct behavior is determined they feel people must comply. One can imagine that this is not always possible in the real world. What we see here are two types of columnists recommending moral frameworks that, because they already are widely approved, make any advice derived from them feel right to readers.

Conclusion: The Columnists' Approaches to Extremism

Finally, there is the question of extremism. Did the columnists address this issue and if so, how? What shaped or constrained their approaches? Abdul Wahab started his column shortly after Sadat's assassination by Islamists, so he was acutely aware of the problem. He was also intensely concerned, unlike the sheikhs, with the root causes of social turmoil such as people's frustrations over government policies and the difficulties of daily living (Rugh 2019). In an interview in 1989, Abdul Wahab claimed that he was not against the growing religiosity, which he believed made young people seek their happiness in family life and not immoral activities outside marriage. At the same time, he deplored those who got carried away with unrealistic dreams. In one column[12] he tells the story of a dreaded monster that threatens a village, and no one can vanquish it. Hercules goes to his father Zeus and asks for advice on how to destroy the monster. Zeus says the secret of the monster's strength is that he is a son of the earth. As long as his feet touch the ground no one can hurt him. So, Hercules goes out and with one arm lifts the monster from the earth and with the other slays him. The moral of this story, according to Abdul Wahab is that successful people are down-to-earth and do not stray from reality. People, he says, lose faith in people with too much imagination. His readers see this as a veiled message to Islamists who want to return to a life at the time of the Prophet – a totally unrealistic dream as far as Abdul Wahab is concerned.

Why did Abdul Wahab not directly challenge Islamists? The obvious reason was that, as Sadat's assassination demonstrated, it was extremely dangerous to anger extremists. But there were other reasons as well. Egyptian press rules prohibited insulting the Egyptian president, his policies, or blaming bureaucrats for failing in their duties. He was able to maneuver around these prohibitions by publishing complaints without inserting himself or assigning blame. More to the point, President Mubarak's anti-terrorism laws let the government restrict publication of any content that "disrupted social peace" – meaning content offending "public decency" or criticizing Islam. The category was so vague that reporters knew to stay away from such topics – especially after even the mention of re-examining meanings in the Koran led to accusations of apostasy against public figures.[13]

By refraining from religious judgements, Abdul Wahab tried to avoid antagonizing either Al-Azhar or those in his audience who sympathized with extremists. To be on the safe side he often ended his columns with conventional religious phrases such as "God is the ultimate judge" or "God is compassionate and looks favorably on sincere repentance." There was little doubt that Abdul Wahab was devout or that his advice appealed to Egyptians looking for less extreme but obviously moral ways of solving their problems. By offering them these peaceful alternatives he may well have prevented some from turning to extremist approaches. The more complicated question is why the sheikhs did not openly challenge extremists. They were in direct competition for the hearts and minds of Egyptians. Moreover, what they wrote often contradicted extremist views without doing so in an explicit manner. As government-salaried employees, they were pressured to promote moderate versions of Islam. Yet looking like lackeys of the government was also not in their interest. The reasons for their reluctance to challenge extremists became clearer in the decades that followed the 1980s, as violence increased in Egypt (Kepel & Rothschild 1983; Kepel 2003). By the time of the al-Sisi presidency, Grand Imam Ahmed al-Tayeb was being publicly rebuked for not more aggressively challenging extremist views or, for example, not declaring ISIS members heretics, as President al-Sisi asked. Sheikh Ahmed explained that if ISIS members had made the declaration of faith –the *shahada* – they were Muslims by definition and it was up to God to decide whether they were good or bad ones, not him.

Why would Sheikh Ahmed support extremists like this? Again, the answer seems to be fear. His reasoning was undoubtedly affected by events like the near assassination in August 2016 of Ali Gomaa (Amr 2016), an ex-Grand Mufti of Al-Azhar. In trying to curry favor with the government where he was up for renewal, Sheikh Ali had released two controversial fatwas: one that declared it was a Muslim's obligation to be loyal to President al-Sisi and another declaring all members of the Muslim Brotherhood apostates. In his desperation to please both sides he released two additional fatwas, this time supporting extremist positions: one calling on Muslims to support Jihad for religion's sake and the other declaring all Christians infidels (Osman 2014). President Sadat's assassination in 1981 turned out to be the first in a series of events that showed officials the dangers of challenging extremists, or even of siding too much with government positions. In 1992, for example, some Al-Azhar sheikhs tried to appease the government[14] by accusing a human rights activist, Farag Foda, of blasphemy, and shortly thereafter extremists assassinated him.

The Al-Azhar sheikhs, including many who wrote advice columns, were already in the 1980s hedging their bets – by supporting government policies sufficiently to maintain their official relationships[15] and salaries and Islamists enough to appease them and show their independence from the government. All three of the establishment clerics I described earlier, waffled on such issues as correct banking procedure, usury, female circumcision, divorce requirements, abortion, the uses of violence, how to define a Muslim, and how to treat Christians, depending on who they wanted to please at the moment.

In summary the advice columns of the volatile 1980s not only provide insights into personal and cultural details of Egypt at the time, but also show how the columnists approached the sensitive issue of extremism. Their covert approach was consistent with the veiled ways Egyptians smooth communication and keep out of trouble. They also show how advice columnists modelled moderation and some of the influences that motivated them. What strikes the reader is that all those involved – both letter-writers and columnists alike – were looking for moral solutions to their problems. They were not just looking to make themselves comfortable but wanted to live lives that were morally correct by recognized religious or social standards.

Notes

1. Egyptians embraced religious conservatism at higher levels in the 1960s. The numbers increased significantly in the 1970s under President Sadat.
2. Technically his name should be spelled Abd Al-Wahab in translation but I have simplified it to Abdul Wahab.
3. In an interview with Abdul Wahab in 1989.
4. In an interview with Abdul Wahab in 1989.
5. *Al-Ahram*, December 9, 1982.
6. *Al-Ahram*, January 16, 1987.
7. *Al-Ahram*, May 1, 1990.
8. Denying the oneness of God, black magic, murder, usury, taking an orphan's money, neglecting jihad, and falsely accusing women of adultery.
9. The Egyptian government does not enforce these punishments.
10. Female circumcision is banned in Egypt but currently UNDP estimates roughly 72% or more of women are circumcised in Egypt.
11. The sources being mainly the Koran, the example of the Prophet, and early scholars' interpretations of these.
12. *Al-Ahram*, January 9, 1987.
13. Among the cases was that of Professor Nasr Abu Zayd at Cairo University in the early 1990s where comments he made in class led to him being tried and convicted of apostasy. More recently in 2015 a popular TV host, Islam al-Beheiry, was labelled an apostate by Al-Azhar for suggesting the Koran be re-examined for its correct meanings. His program was cancelled, and he was sentenced to a year's imprisonment for "contempt of religion." President al-Sisi eventually pardoned him.
14. Among other accusations Foda was charged with advocating the separation of religion and state, and the use of a state legal system rather than Sharia law. An Al-Azhar sheikh, Muhammad al-Ghazali said it was not wrong to kill an apostate and, as a result, 8 of the 13 accused of his murder were acquitted.
15. In the 1980s Al-Azhar officials were still being appointed by the head of state.

Bibliography

Amr, Dina. "3 Suspects arrested for assassination attempt of Ali Gomaa." *Daily News Egypt*, August 10, 2016.

Alrawi, Karim. "Goodbye to the Enlightenment." *Index on Censorship* 23, no. 1–2 (1994): 112–116.

Al-Wadi, Hesham. "Mubarak and the Islamists Why Did the Honeymoon End?" *Middle East Journal* 59, no. 1 (Winter 2005): 62–80.

Baker, Raymond William. "Sadat's Open Door: Opposition from Within. Social Problems," *Development Process & Problems* 28, no. 4 (April 1981): 378–384.

Joya, Angela. *The Roots of Revolt: A Political Economy of Egypt from Nasser to Mubarak*. Cambridge: Cambridge University Press, 2020.

Kepel, Gilles., and Jon Rothschild. *Muslim Extremism in Egypt: The Prophet and Pharaoh*. Berkeley: University of California Press, 1985.

Marfleet, Philip. "Mubarak's Egypt – Nexus of Criminality." *State Crime* 2, no. 2 (2013): 112–134.

Osman, Amr. "Ali Gomaa: Kill them, they stink," *Middle East Monitory*, January 27, 2014.

Osman, Tarek. *Egypt on the Brink: From Nasser to Mubarak*. Lewes, DE: Yale University Press, 2010.

Richards, Alan. "The Political Economy of Dilatory Reform: Egypt in the 1980s." *World Development* 19, no. 12 (1991): 1721–1730.

Rugh, Andrea, B. *Egyptian Advice Columnists: Envisioning the Good Life in an Era of Extremism*. Lewes, DE: DIO Press Inc, 2019.

Sheehan, Edward R. F. "Why Sadat Packed Off the Russians: Egypt Nice Place to Visit from Russia with Love Before the Break." *New York Times*, August 6, 1972.

5
SECTARIANISM'S AMBIGUITY
Lebanon as a Case Study, 1843–1958

Brittney Giardina

Introduction

What does the term "sectarianism" mean? How should it be conceptualized, especially in the context of the Middle East? At the very least, the concept is an elusive one; yet, can it still shed light on historical and political developments? There is no doubt that the term "sectarianism" carries the burden of various definitions, conceptualizations, connotations, and uses. There has been a great deal of scholarly intrigue and ambiguity around this term and related vocabulary, such as "sect" or "sectarian." For instance, Fanar Haddad's 2017 article titled "Sectarianism and its Discontent in Middle Eastern Studies" instigated great terminological and analytical concern. He argues that "the term is too politicized, overused, mired in negativity, and emotionally charged for it to be salvageable. In today's usage, 'sectarianism' leaves too much room for subjective interpretation and personal whim for it to be useful as a category of scholarly inquiry" (Haddad 2017). Essentially, Haddad advocates for the end of the term's use based on its inability to be formally defined or universally used. While Haddad's remarks are highly useful in clarifying the analysis and taking away the ills of sectarianism in one fell swoop, the complete abandonment of this conceptual term in academia does not solve the problem of its widespread use in mass media and politics. Haddad's position brings about many methodological concerns instigated by the term's vagueness: how do we reconcile with ambiguity? Should we still use this term? How do we approach analysis that remains ambiguous?

What follows is an historical case study that points to a variety of understandings of the term "sectarianism." The narrative reveals a deep relation between territorialization and nationalization processes and sectarian identity. I historicize the already heavily explored territorialization and politicalization of sectarian identity in Lebanon from 1843 to 1958. Within this, I adhere to a conceptualization of the term that is both

DOI: 10.4324/9781003329510-6

highly similar to Makdisi (2000) and Hashemi and Postel's proposition of the sectarianization thesis (Hashemi & Postel 2017). Essentially, while analyzing "sectarianization" and the politicization of sectarian identities in the modern age, I denounce any primordial contingencies. Yet, I differ from a simple politicalization perceptive in that I analyze specifically how this was done through territorial intervention and contributed to later nationalistic imaginations. Therefore, my goal here is to show the complex sectarian web of politics, territory, and nationalism while being conscious of the terminological ambiguity at stake. To this end I divide the history into four chronological periods. The first two set the stage for territorialization of identity and proto-nationalist claims. The other two periods deal more directly with formation of nationhood and the solidification of sectarian practices within the political system.

Religious Gerrymandering, Territorial Sectarianization 1843–1860

This first period reveals the clear relationship between sectarian divide and territory, as well as the disconnect between geographical creations and local actualities. As developed later, these developments affected varying visions of Lebanon as a national entity. A startling territorial development came with the European and Ottoman creation of a dual governorship in the Ottoman's Mount Lebanon. Following internal violence of Christians and Druze in 1841, foreign and imperial powers divided Mount Lebanon in 1843 into two districts (one northern and Christian, one southern and mixed) establishing the double *qa'im maqamiya*. Each district was to be ruled by a *qa'im maqam* – the northern district appointed a Christian emir, while the southern a Druze emir, and each *qa'im maqam* was given two wakils or deputies, one Druze, one Christian. Although the northern district's power base was appropriately religiously homogenized, the southern half contained a predominantly Christian population being ruled by a Druze deputy (Traboulsi 2012). This administrative solution to sectarian violence simply augmented the division between the two groups. Aside from the obvious coalescence of sect or communal identities with political ones – as shown through administrative positions based on religious affiliation – political and religious actualities were not fully accredited in this new geographic set up. Mount Lebanon's dual governorship, created and sustained by external forces, disregarded or manipulated internal sectarian or territorial needs, creating political cleavages and differences based on institutional recognition of these newly territorialized sectarian identities.

Essentially, Maronite elites felt that Christians of the south (approximately more than half of the population) (Traboulsi 2012) and under the rule of Druze Amir should be ruled by the northern *qa'im maqam*. Moreover, the Druze felt that it was their right to rule over the whole of Mount Lebanon:

> would the Druze *kaim makam* (sic) administer only to Druze areas, or would his administrative control also cover what in feudal parlance was considered the traditionally Druze part of the country but that now encompassed sizeable

Christian communities? Conversely, would the maronite kaim makam be allowed administrative jurisdiction over Christians in Druze country geographically falling within that of the Druze kaim makamate?

(Farah 2000)

The disparity between local actualities (Druze and Maronite territorial and political claims) and foreign and imperial intent not only reveals the inadequacy of the 1843 decision but also acts as a point of reference against any primordial notions of sectarianism. International powers transformed the apparent immutable meaning of "sect" and "sectarianism" through political and military intervention. What ironicizes this political development is the preceding violence. The violence that "justified" the 1843 decision led to foreign and imperial manipulation of local power arrangements which only led to more violence: "It provided the context for the *Harakat*, a series of commoners' uprisings, *muqata'ji* pre-emptive strikes and civil fighting that lasted from 1841 to 1861, marking the bloody transistion from *muqata'ji* system to peripheral capitalism" (Traboulsi 2012). The economic transition that Fawaz Troubilsi deems "bloody" refers to the end of the *muqata'ji* system and Druze dominance. It is important to note that the decline of Druze supremacy and rise of a Christian (Maronite) one reflects the increased European interest in the region. Moreover, the forced transition from a semi-feudal system to a semi-capitalistic one changed the social structure of the region. It also transformed the sectarian make-up in terms of political efficacy, emphasizing the deep relation between local identity and foreign interference.

Furthermore, "sectarianism" is often equated with sect based violence. Yet as seen here, the picture is not merely homogeneous, monolithic groups fighting each other on the simple basis of difference: "We are sure that the Druze attack us only because they are forced to do so by their *muqata'jis*, even by baton blows. In fact, as long as the leaders enjoy privileges and immunities, Lebanon will never enjoy peace" (Poujade 1867). In this memorandum on behalf of residents of Zahleh (predominantly Christians) to the French consul in 1843, there is a clear attempt to distance the violence from those carrying it out. There are implications here that poke holes in a simple reading of sectarianism as violence between primordial sects. The notion that groups of sects act solely under the influence of community leaders and those actions of the masses are only representative of two things. The first being that "homogenous" religious communities are in fact socially divided and second, that sect violence has more to do with external, top-down political motives than sectarian sentiments or hatreds. Therefore, these events provide evidence against primordial notions of the existence of immutable sects, or sect-violence (or sect-bred violence), as well as revealing the current inability of "sectarianism" to be an all-time explanatory tool. To have a more complex understanding of sect and sectarianism, the inclusion of the territorialization and politicization of identity remains necessary.

Territorial Roots of Lebanese Nationalism 1860–1920

The *Réglement Organique* further crystalized the process of tying local, communal, or sectarian identities to externally designed geographic and international political manipulations (constructions). This was further crystalized as "Mount Lebanon was to be organized into a special Ottoman governorate, or *mutasarrifiyya*. A Christian governor [non-Lebanese, non-Arab Ottoman official] was to head the *mutasarrifiyya*. He would be appointed by and directly responsible to the Sublime Porte" (Akaril 1993). This organization was decided upon by European powers – France, Britain, Austria, Prussia, and Russia. This was justified through the previous violence of 1860 and signified the end of the *muqata'ji* system. Simply put, the *mutasarrifiyya* was marked by external manipulations and the sectarianization of Lebanese evolving political identities. Moreover, during the 1860 war European and Ottoman negotiators spent long hours in Istanbul belaboring every point of the *Règlement*. According to Makdisi, they forced on the people a single public identity, where one's sect defined one's involvement in the public sphere. It also defined a person's ability to be appointed to office, to govern, to collect taxes, as well as to punish. Even to live and exist as a loyal subject (Makdisi 2000). In his analysis Makdisi connects foreign territorial aspirations and creations to increased sectarian mobilization. However, despite this important power dynamic, the *Règlement* did establish some autonomy from Ottoman imperial rule. An autonomy that would prove quite salient in later Lebanese nationalist's claims.

The degree of autonomy experienced in the *mutasarrifiyya* period contributed to what Engin Akarli deems the "Long Peace." Akarli delineates the foreign facilitation of peace and stagnation of elites by discussing how the period from 1860 to 1920 was one of reconciliation and socio-political integration, as the conglomeration of parochial communities on Mount Lebanon moved towards becoming a distinct society. This included having its own distinct political identity, a centralized government, and political traditions (Akarli 1993). More importantly, however, is that later nationalist justifications for Lebanon as a separate, autonomous entity are historically rooted in this political period as a sense of Lebanese identity had emerged among the residents of *mutasarrifiyya*, which manifested in the form of a general political commitment to the privileges that accrued from its autonomous state. Moreover, the hardships Lebanese suffered during the Great War under harsh martial rule eroded the last remnant of respect that existed for Ottoman sovereignty even among Muslims. Subsequently, enhancing the general "…appreciation for self-government. A quasi-nationalistic historical vision even developed, viewing Lebanon as the heir of ancient Phoenicia and as a land where various kin communities peacefully coexisted" (Akarli 1993). Therefore, the establishment of a quasi-self-sufficient political structure in Lebanon, pre-World War I, reinforced if not cultivated nationalistic sentiments. Historical narratives relying on both pre-1861 and post-mustaffariate justifications strengthened these nationalistic notions. Moreover, the boundaries established by foreign powers contributed to a period of autonomy and awareness of a proto-nationalistic feeling.

Later nationalists harken back to this time. Take for instance a request on part of Mount Lebanon to the Honorable Chairman and Members of the Conference on the Limitation of Armaments, Washington D.C.:

> Geographically and socially our country has an integral character. Ever since biblical days it has been regarded as separate from Syria. And when the territories were freed from Turkish rule, as Palestine, Syria, and Mesopotamia, were placed under mandates, Mount Lebanon still stood alone as the country whose legitimate right to autonomy was granted by a Treaty of the European Powers.
> *(Browne 1976)*

There are two notable assertions present here: the idea of a Lebanese "character" and the European bestowal of autonomy. The narrative of geographical and social distinction plays directly into notions of nationalism. Moreover, the treaty referenced refers to the 1861 creation of the *mustafarriate* – further revealing the connection between territorial creation and nationalistic notions. However, despite these internal autonomous developments, the external creation of such autonomy reinforces the salience of intervention. An intervention that tied territory and politics to sect identity and mobilization, which in the long run created varying nationalist notions and narratives. Thus, the connection between territory and identity yielded or at least influenced nationalist narratives to come.

This "long peace" ended with Ottoman entry into World War I, followed by a Sykes-Picot era of European prerogatives that culminated in post-war agreements (e.g., Paris Peace Conference, 1919 and San Remo Conference, 1920) and the formation of the mandate regime. The war and its preceding negotiations created an intense imperialistic environment that would ironically foster local nationalisms: "In a post-World War I period dominated by the right of nations to self-determination, a principal invoked with equal force by Wilson's America and Lenin's Soviet Russia, the legitimization was rooted in the age-old minorities policy, focused on ethnic and religious communities" (Traboulsi 2012). Hegemonizing, European powers had to reconcile their ideological assertions with their colonial interests. They did this through minority groups. The irony comes into play when the nations that were territorially engineered through imperialism and were composed of ethnic and religious communities a part of the "minority policy," began to employ European and Western ideologies to assert their own right to self-rule.

European Domination, Lebanese Mobilization, and Sectarian Solidification

The disintegration of the Ottoman Empire left an historic mark on the political, territorial, and national makeup of the Middle East from imperial collapse to the present. The transition from Ottoman rule to European colonialism and imperialism marked a key development in the creation of territorial imaginations, showing how international intrigue augmented sectarian boundaries. As seen here with Lebanon, as with other modern states evolving through the mandate regime, the members of these new nation-states did not develop organically. Thus, self-actualization and political mobilization were directly influenced by these territorial machinations in a post-Ottoman era, leaving sect-centricity to dominate Lebanese politics or, for that matter, the rest of the French and British mandate in the Middle East. The fact that Lebanon and other mandatory ruled Middle Eastern countries did not "naturally" develop and were instead forced to develop is paramount to understanding the inherent relationship between identity, historical narrative, and sectarianization.

The mandate period only further solidified the connection between these underlying thematic trends in Lebanese politics and history, sectarian and otherwise. The creation of *Le Grand Liban* can then act as the intense hardening of the interaction between external motives, internal mobilization, territory, and nationalization. As noted earlier, the *Réglement Organique* revealed the distance between external territorial aspirations and regional actualities.[1] The creation of *Le Grand Liban*, in the shadow of similar decisions, acts as another piece of evidence for the tangled web that is sectarianism, colonialism, nationalism, and territorialism. The process of drawing Greater Lebanon's borders issued in a series of debates, both on the European and Lebanese sides. There were two main concerns centered around the question of attachment or detachment: isolating Lebanon from the rest of Syria and separating what would be a minority Christian population within the new borders from the proposed Muslim majority (Traboulsi 2012). Moreover these territorial questions corresponded to varying nationalisms – Lebanism, Syrianism, Arabism (Firro 2003) – in support of certain geographical visions.

Jacques Tabet is one example of the interweave between territory and history in relation to certain nationalistic notions. Tabet was a part of a group of Christian intellectuals who felt that "the 'new Syria' they envisaged was to secure, under European, preferably French, protection, the freedom of the Christian population" (Firro 2003: 23). In his 1920 publication *La Syrie,* Tabet draws a strong link between ancient Phoenicia and Syria (or Lebanon) and attempts to historically and ethnographically assert a sort of "Lebaneseness" – apart from the rest of the Arab world and most definitely westward looking:

> La conquête arabe avait groupé, il est vraie, tous ces pays distinctes en un même califat; mais l'étiquette politique que la force impose aux nations, du même qu'elle ne peut changer la nature de leur sol et de leur climat, ne peut pas non plus changer leur âme et leur mentalité; elle tombe d'elle-même lorsque l'arme arabe est brisée. La Syrie, politiquement, ne peut pas être plus arabe qu'elle n'est ottomane. La Syrie est syrienne et phénicienne.
>
> *(Firro 2003: 27)*

There are two elements to Tabet's commentary that work hand in hand to reinforce one another: Arab oppression and Syrian or Phoenician or Lebanese resilience. Strong statements such as *"l'étiquette politique que la force impose aux nations"* or *"lorsque l'arme arabe est brisée"* paint a blatant picture of Arab invasion and domination threatening the heart of Syria – Lebanon. Moreover, Tabet's depiction of this steadfast, unchangeable Lebanese persistence in the face of the caliphate or the Ottomans contributes to the assertion of his brand of Lebanese nationalism. It is one rooted in ancient historical and geographic justifications, with a clear enemy – the Arabs – and an implied ally or savior – the French. When combating the problem of the Arabic language, Tabet introduces the power of the French language: "En réalité la langue arabe reste dans le pays la langue universelle. Elle se trouvera bientôt face à face avec une nouvelle langue: le français" (Firro 2003). Overall, the Maronite, Christian favoritism of the French shows the connection between external territorial dealings with internal, national sentiments–all tied and reinforced by varying conceptions of what Lebanon is in spatial terms.

Briefly, stepping aside from mandate partition and Christian national visions, there are two political documents central to the transition from mandate to independence that must be mentioned: the 1926 Constitution and the 1932 Census. In 1926, France granted Lebanon a written constitution with cooperation of prominent Christian figures, creating a Lebanese Republic riddled with French imagery and influence (i.e.: choice of official language and flag). A Chamber of Deputies took the place of the previous Representative Council, and a Senate was created, both cementing confessional politics. Instead of enacting any semblance of regional autonomy or satisfaction, the document only solidified France's hold and sectarian divide. Moreover, the 1932 census was a large determinate in the political sectarian makeup of the years to come. Mandate Lebanon acts as a culmination point. It blends the imperial hand with the regional voice. It is both an extension of the previous history (the *mutasarrifiyya* and the *Réglement*) and the foundation for coming historical moments. *Le Grand Liban* is the geographical facade of the Lebanese mosaic of sectarian, historical, and national narratives and notions.

Nationalistic Notions 1943–1958

Independence which was arguably the climax of the sectarianization and nationalization processes as they relate to territory in the Lebanese case was materialized through two documents, one written and one verbal agreement (Traboulsi 2019). The first being the revision of the 1926 Constitution and the later called "The National Pact", an agreement between two prominent political figures: Bishara al-Khuri, a Christian, and Riad al-Sulh, a Sunni. The sectarian makeup of the country is embedded in these two nationalistic moments, blurring the lines between nationalism and sectarianism. The amendments to the 1926 constitution not only crystalized Lebanon as a national entity, but also hardened sectarian political practice. Articles imagining the nation, such as the layout of the flag or defining its borders created the notion of a cohesive national identity and acted as the release from mandate hold. Take the clause concerning the flag for example:

Article 5
(As amended by the Constitutional Law of 7 December 1943)
"The Lebanese flag shall be composed of three horizontal stripes, a white stripe between two red ones. The width of the white stripe shall be equal to that of both red stripes. In the centre of and occupying one third of the white stripe is a green cedar tree with its top touching the upper red stripe and its base touching the lower red stripe."

The original Article 5 was:

"The Lebanese flag is composed of three equal vertical stripes, blue, white and red with the cedar in the white stripe."
("The Lebanese Constitution" 1995)

The 1943 amendment to Article 5 does two important things. First, it contributes to the visual imagery of Lebanese nationhood by creating a distinct symbol of nationhood the flag, which was the visual, symbolic separation between countries. Second, it reveals the clear transition from colonial rule to Lebanese independence. The flag goes from harboring blatantly French visual influences to asserting its own aesthetic. Article 1 concerning territory follows the same pattern:

Article 1
(As amended by the Constitutional Law of 9 December 1943)
"Lebanon is an independent, indivisible, and sovereign state. Its frontiers are those which now bound it:
On the North: From the mouth of Nahr Al Kabir along a line following the course of this River to its point of junction with Wadi Khalid opposite Jisr Al-Qamar.
On the East: The summit line separating the Wadi Khalid and Nahr Al-Asi, passing by the villages of Mu'aysara, Harb'ana, Hayt-Ibish-Faysan to the height of the two villages
of Brifa and Matraba. This line follows the northern boundary of the Ba'albak District at the north-eastern and south-eastern directions, thence the eastern boundaries of the districts of Ba'albak, Biqa, Hasbayya, and Rashayya.
On the South: The present southern boundaries of the districts of Sur and Mari'yun
On the West: The Mediterranean."

The original Article 1 was: "Greater Lebanon is an independent and indivisible state. Its frontiers are the present ones which are officially recognized by the Mandatory French Government and by the League Of Nations" ("The Lebanese Constitution" 1995). Similar to Article 5, it moves from French domination to self-assertion. The original clearly stating "officially recognized by the Mandatory French Government" is an obvious reinforcement of colonial power. The revision, while still using some of the introduction, not only departs from any necessary external recognition, but actually delineates the borders instead of simply alluding to them. It is a concrete, detailed self-assertion.

Despite these articles clearly expressing nationhood, the constitution still kept religious pluralism intact by leaving certain articles untouched, such as the distribution of Senate seats delineated in Article 96, unchanged in 1943 but then abrogated in 1947. "According to Articles 22 and 95, the seats of the Senate shall be distributed among the sects as follows: 5 Maronites; 3 Sunnis; 3 Shia, 3 Orthodox; 1 Catholic; 1 Druze; 1 minorities" ("The Lebanese Constitution" 1995). Although this article was eventually repealed, it does display a blatantly sectarian political mindset. One that arguably did not go away in 1947 with its abrogation. The formal, written delineation of Lebanese nationhood stood alongside an informal verbal agreement between two influential political figures. If the constitution did not imply it, the National Pact of 1943 truly put into stone politics along sectarian lines as it confirmed the power sharing formula among the different sects which was already established in Article 95 of the Constitution. This included the 6:5 ratio in political and administrative representation, as well as the distribution of three significant posts of government, namely a Maronite president, a Shia speaker, and a Sunni prime minister (Traboulsi 2019).

By attaching religious and sectarian categories to certain government position, issues related to identity increased in the country. For example, the National Pact facilitated sectarian based politics with the insurance of Christian supremacy. Moreover, the Pact's demographic decision was based on the 1932 census ensuring a fixed Maronite administrative majority based on decade-old demographics. In addition, sectarian identity was used to determine the composition of the cabinet. Maronites and Sunni Muslims were guaranteed two and sometimes three positions and members of other religious groups one position each. Consequently, confessional politics became enshrined as the basis of the Lebanese system. Furthermore, from the outset the Shia population who comprised approximately 20% of the population were underrepresented in the power-sharing structure (Cleveland & Blunt 2018). Sectarian representation became one with political representation at the outset of independence. At a time of national importance, sectarian dynamics came to the forefront, showing the deep connection between the two in the Lebanese case. More importantly, the use of sectarian demographics to reinforce the political at a point of national transition implicates a few different understandings and definitions of sectarianism.

There is the blending of "sectarianism" or *taa'ifia* with the system of confessionalism in a constitutional language. In other words, sectarianism as a political system itself and not just a political system incorporating sect-based actors. On the other hand, this incidence could also show "sectarianism" as "sectarianization" or the process in which sectarian identities become politicized. Moreover, the interaction between al-Khuri and al-Sulh could be seen as sectarianism in so far as it is the simple interaction between figures of distinct religious groups. In short, this one historical moment could account for a variety of "sectarianism"s proving that the term is catch-all in nature. This proves that conceptualizations of the sectarian in relation to politics, territory, nationalism, etc. are necessary to complicate the watered-down term.

Despite the Pact's significance, it was of course not representative of the entire population and thus acted as a window into mandate political schisms, particularly the one between Emile Eddé and Bishara al-Khuri. Georges Naccache – former Prime Minister and then President under the mandate as well as editor of *L'Orient*, spoke out against the Pact with his primary argument being "Un Etat n'est pas la somme de deux impuissances – et deux négations ne feront jamais une nation":

> Le fameux Pacte de novembre – qui est le pacte fondamental de l'indépendance nationale – porte en lui les contradictions qui rendent tout gouvernement impossible. L'expérience nous l'a montré assez cruellement. "Ni Occident ni Arabisation": c'est sur un double refus que la chrétienté et l'islam ont conclu leur alliance. Quelle sorte d'unité peut être tirée d'une telle formule? Ce qu'une moitié des Libanais ne veut pas, on le voit très bien. Ce que ne veut pas l'autre moitié, on le voit également très bien. Mais ce que les deux moitiés veulent en commun, c'est ce qu'on ne voit pas.
>
> *(Naccache 1949)*

Essentially, Naccache is criticizing not the Pact's solidification of sectarian practices, but its seemingly too idealized cooperation between Maronite and Sunni. In his eyes, the alliance is based on denying the essence of the things being aligned. A nation cannot be forged this way. Naccaches's discontent with the Pact is part of the overarching struggle over how to define Lebanon as a nation post-independence, a struggle that was mostly taken up by a Beirut based merchant middle class. This segment of the population was the main driving force behind what was later called "the Merchant Republic" in Lebanon between 1943 and 1958. In other words, according to Shehadi they provided the ideology, skills, and enterprise that helped shape the policy and direction of the country (Shehadi 1987). Here he is drawing the connection between economic and political power, as well as implying a relationship between a commercial/financial oligarchy and ideas of Lebanese nationhood. It is important to note that this influential Beirut based group excluded port cities, further illustrating another way in which territory played directly into the sectarianization and nationalization of Lebanon.

One prominent member of this Merchant Republic is Michel Chiha, the primary author of the 1926 Constitution and owner of the Beirut daily *Le Jour* (1937). While Chiha acknowledges Lebanon's precarious and plural nature, he also recognizes Lebanon and "lebaneseness" as being something distinct:

> Nous dirons pour notre part, avec des arguments plus décisifs encore, que la population du Liban est libanaise, tout simplement, et que reserve faite de Naturalisations très récentes, elle n'est pas plus phénicienne qu'egyptienne, égéenne, assyrienne ou medique, grecque, romaine, byzantine, arabe, avec ou sans consanguinity, ou européenne par les alliances, ou turque par exemple.
>
> *(Chiha 1949)*

Here, in *Liban Aujourd'hui*, he states that Lebanon is Lebanese despite its multi-faceted makeup. It is not more Eastern or Western or Phoenician or Mediterranean. An important underlying notion here is that Lebanon is a distinguishable entity, a central aspect to any nationalism. Moreover, what the Merchant Republic and its consortium members reveal is the emergence of nationalist narratives and discourses. The fact that Lebanon can be characterized as a nation implies defined territorial boundaries, which in this case implicates a sectarian historical narrative. Additionally, the fact that the primary champions of political and economic power, middle class merchant oligarchs, were Lebanese Christians, echoes the past transition of power from Druze to Maronite. Thus, inevitably reflecting the effects of European and Ottoman territorial and political creations.

Conclusion: Nuanced Differences in Conceptualization and Problems in Methodology

Lebanese political history from 1843–1958 perfectly delineates the territorial and sectarian transformation and its effect on nationalism. This historicization differs from other's simple historicization in its intent to understand "sectarianism" conceptually in light of its ambiguity. This history complicates the catch-all term "sectarianism" by dissecting its relation to territory and nationalism, but also by pointing to historical moments of definition (such as National Pact and "sectarianism" as confessionalism or 1860 and "sectarianism" as violence). The above historicization elicits a definition quite similar to that of Usamma Makdisi and highly influenced by the historical narrative present in Fawwaz Traboulsi's analysis. Yet, I differ from Makdisi in the sense that I am defining sectarianism against the backdrop of ambiguity, while he is doing so against the backdrop of certain primordial notions (Makdisi 2000). Moreover, I have expanded upon Makdisi's conceptualization – both, literally, in terms of chronological framework and analytically.

The key historical moments outlined above establish a relationship between sectarianism and nationalism outside of what Makdisi highlights in his work (Makdisi 2000). I build on this by arguing that sectarianism as a practice can incite nationalist sentiments. Therefore, not only does nationalism as a broader paradigm contribute to sectarianism as a discourse, but sectarianism as it relates to territory can produce nationalistic imaginations. In more specific terms, the *mutasarrifiyya* period and decisions such as the *Règlement* began to not only solidify sectarian dynamics territorially, but also laid the groundwork for historical, national ideas during the mandate and independence period (i.e., Jacques Tabet, etc.).

Aside from the adherence to modernity and "sectarianism"'s relationship with nationalism, the framework provided by Hashemi and Postel remains historically salient in the Lebanese case. They introduce the term "sectarianization," implicating certain political themes and historical processes that sectarianism alone cannot. "Sectarianization" is framed and defined as "a process shaped by political actors operating within specific contexts, pursuing political goals that involve popular mobilization around particular (religious) identity markers" (Hashemi & Postel 2017). Moreover, according to Hashemi and Postel other factors also influence the sectarianization process, including class dynamics, fragile states and geopolitical rivalries (Hashemi & Postel 2017). However, overall the term sectarianism is typically void of such reference points and tends to imply a static given and a trans-historical force from the seventh century until today (Hashemi & Postel 2017). This description highlights political motive, constructionist tendencies, and historical context whereas, sectarianism – according to this work – is simply something seen as a monolithic force beginning with the Sunni-Shia divide. Essentially, it is political domination and manipulation that influences sectarianization, instead of belief or religious sentiment.

In relation to the above historization, Lebanese religio-communal identities were "sectarianized" through territorial machinations and political materializations (i.e., the double *qa'im maqamiya* or constitutional sectarian solidifications). Therefore, my definition of the highly ambiguous term "sectarianism," in light of the historical case study presented, is as follows. I argue that sectarianism, at its most fundamental level, is a modern form of identity politics and mobilization where groups and individuals interact with each other and others as part of imagined, homogeneous religious communities to adjust, expand, or maneuver their positions within transforming political and social systems. Sectarianism as a mobilizing tool is the outcome of larger political developments and transforms the meaning of sects. Moreover, sectarianism in its modern sense developed through the formation of what could be termed "nationalistic notions" or the construction of political organisms under the nation-state model and the production of nationalist narratives caused by foreign influence and internal sectarian mobilization. As such, sects and communal identities were themselves transformed by these processes and claimed greater roles in the extended territory, now called national territory. Sect conflict or sect cooperation are part of the sectarianism phenomena, but are not responsible for its formation per se. In short, while sectarianism as a practice can incite nationalist sentiments, nationalism as a broader paradigm particularly at a time of crisis contributes to sectarianism as a discourse, both within certain historic contexts and now.

I am aware that the variance between this understanding of sectarianism alongside other instrumental or constructivist notions is more semantic than anything. However, that is exactly my point. By historicizing the concept of sectarian identities within Lebanese political history from 1843 to 1958, a viable explanatory definition of "sectarianism" that is historically sympathetic could be extracted. Yet, despite this viability there is still a fundamental problem with my current methodology that I mentioned earlier. It is only truly effective in regards to specific sectarian narratives or perspectives. Consequently, I am proving the need for its conceptualization versus adopting it to read the history. However, this nuance is important in terms of historical sympathy. To further complicate this logic, while the definition and corresponding historical context validates pre-existing top-down approaches such as Makdisi (2000) or the "sectarianization" thesis of Hashemi and Postel (2017) the issue of the cultural reality, the fact that these identities are identities also remains a valid factor. How do we explain sectarian identities not only by how they are conjured up, but by how they are experienced as well?

Should we adhere to this understanding of "sectarianism" if it does not account for what could be the so-called authentic form of sectarian identities? Are we invalidating these identities by solely tracing their political and authoritarian origins?

The question then becomes: does the term "sectarianism" need to account for all of these facets, or do new explanatory concepts need to be introduced alongside it? Should the burden of all sectarian relations fall on this one word? Is that not the initial problem? Would abandonment be more effective then? Or does the reality of "sectarianism"'s wide use remain salient enough? It seems that we must find a balance between the virtues and hindrances of ambiguity, between complete abandonment and highly contextual definitions, as well as between the construction and the essence of sectarian identities.

Note

1 Greater Lebanon was created by annexing the coastal cities of Tripoli, Tyre, Sidon and Beirut. Additionally, France removed the Fertile Biqa Valley from Syrian jurisdiction and placed it within the frontiers of the Lebanese state.

Bibliography

Akarli, Engin Deniz. *The Long Peace: Ottoman Lebanon, 1861–1920*. Berkeley: University of California Press, 1993.

Browne, Walter. *The Political History of Lebanon, 1920–1950*. Vol. 1. Salisbury, North: Documentary Publications, 1976.

Bunt, Martin and William L. Cleveland. *A History of the Modern Middle East*. New York: Routledge, 2018.

Chiha, Michel. *Liban d'aujourd'hui: 1942*. Beirut: Editions du Trident, 1949.

Farah, Caesar E. *The Politics of Interventionism in Ottoman Lebanon, 1830–1861*. Oxford: Centre for Lebanese Studies, 2000.

Firro, Kais. *Inventing Lebanon: Nationalism and the State Under the Mandate*. London: I.B. Tauris, 2003.

Haddad, Fanar. "'Sectarianism' and Its Discontents in the Study of the Middle East." *The MiddleEast Journal* 71, no. 3 (2017): 363–382.

Hashemi, Nader and Danny Postel, *Sectarianization: Mapping the New Politics of the Middle East*. New York: Oxford University Press, 2017.

"The Lebanese Constitution." *Arab Law Quarterly* 12, no. 2 (1997): 224–261.

Makdisi, Ussama Samir. *The Culture of Sectarianism: Community, History, and Violence in Nineteenth-Century Ottoman Lebanon*. Berkeley, CA: University of California Press, 2000.

Naccache, Georges. *L'Orient*, May 10, 1949.

Poujade, Eugen. *Le Liban et la Syrie, 1845–1860*. Paris: A. Bourdilliat et cie, 1867.

Shehadi, Nadim. *The Idea of Lebanon: Economy and State in the Cénacle Libanais 1946–54*. Beirut: Centre for Lebanese Studies, 1987.

Traboulsi, Fawwaz. *A History of Modern Lebanon*, 2nd ed. London: Pluto Press, 2012.

6
FALLING TOGETHER

Identity and the Military in Fragmented Societies

Dylan Maguire

Introduction

Establishing linkages between identity and security is not difficult. The implications for socially constructed identities on power dynamics in fragmented societies between and within national, ethnic, and sectarian units remain salient. This chapter draws from several bodies of literature to link nationalism with ethnicity and sectarianism and test their impact on security institutions prior to and following civil war. It analyzes power-sharing dynamics within consociational systems of government to measure how elites reform military institutions to reflect new interpretations of security priorities. Institutional analysis is a valuable tool for examining power-sharing dynamics, as well as evaluating elite priorities. Decisions regarding the structure of institutions are consciously made to produce preferred outcomes. The process of state formation is a series of decisions regarding the structure of institutions. Nation-building can also be explored in this manner. While the boundaries of identity are far more elastic than those of institutions, formal structures reflect their creators' interpretations of identity. For example, military institutions are structures formed, in part, to defend an interpretation of identity, be it national, ethnic, or religious. Moreover, military institutions are a unique unit of analysis for examining elite preferences at the nexus between identity and security.

Applying this model of institutional analysis, this chapter examines two cases by comparing military institutional policy before and after conflict: (1) the Lebanese Armed Forces prior to the 1975–1990 Civil War and following the National Reconciliation Accord, or Ta'if Agreement and (2) the Iraqi Security Forces prior to the 2003 invasion and following the implementation of the 2005 constitution. In doing so, this chapter contributes to the understanding of how several national, ethnic, or sectarian groups can achieve balance within military institutions and serve inclusive state interests.

The chapter proceeds as follows. The first section explores the extensive literature on national-identity formation and links it to ethnicity and sectarianism. Like nationalism, sectarianism is socially constructed to reflect a specific power distribution, which carries over into institution building. The second section applies findings from the literature on nationalism, ethnicity, and sectarianism to the analysis of military institutions by focusing on five issue areas where these concepts can have measurable impact: (1) recruitment, (2) promotion, (3) organization, (4) deployment, and (5) civil-military relations. By focusing on these areas the chapter develops a set of criteria to apply in the case studies. The third section uses the comparative approach to analyze these criteria in the cases of Lebanon and Iraq. The case studies first establish a baseline of inter-group dynamics prior to conflict and its institutional impact on the two militaries. It then examines the power-sharing agreements established after conflict. Finally, the chapter analyzes the observed changes in the two militaries. The conclusion links the discussion of identity and security with the analysis of militaries in fragmented societies and makes a recommendation for future research.

Identity

Nationalism

The literature on national identity formation reflects two major themes: (1) the socially constructed nature of nationalism and (2) the situational power dynamics of inter- and intragroup relations. The interaction of these two themes form the basis of political identity and are used to conceptualize, establish, and maintain state power. That power is in turn used to create the political environment that nationalism helps to navigate. Neither one is primary but exist in a mutually supportive relationship. Causal theories positing the nation's creation of the state or the state's creation of the nation are false. Rather, the simultaneous occurrence of these two processes produce both political and ideational units that may map onto one another, but often do not (Danforth 1993). The social construction of "imagined communities" builds on commonalities between far flung groups to establish shared narratives (Anderson 1991). These commonalities can be of a religious, cultural, ethnic, or racial nature and are used to produce the "social-cultural artifact" that is the nation (Marashi 2008).

The epistemic quality of this shared narrative transcends common ideology and is found at the heart of an individual's loyalty to the group, it is a "state of mind, an act of consciousness" (Shelef 2010). Subconscious interpretations of this commonality are inherent inputs in a national leaders' decision-making processes. National leaders value centripetal forces that maintain group cohesiveness and secure collective survival while reinforcing their own advancement. Political and national boundaries are often at odds, with many nationalisms vying for control over the same territory or populace. By defining a national unit as inherent to a physical space other potential national units must be displaced, dominated, or assimilated

(Gellner 1983). Nationalism seeks to create homogeneous communities within political boundaries. When these efforts are not entirely successful, "sub-national" units may emerge that exist under the control of another (Anderson 1991). The relational aspects of control produce categories of "power-holders and the rest" where national groups seek to concentrate power within their own group at the expense of potential challengers (Gellner 1983). Power-holders fear the rise of counter-nationalisms from the powerless subnational units and combine "loyalty to the state with membership in the nation" producing hard national boundaries (Danforth 1993). The retention of power is cloaked in narratives of stability to generate compliance from those in the dominant nationality and those sub-national groups viewed as potential allies.

National and sub-national units are led by elites with vested interests in identity formation and maintenance for group mobilization. These efforts, while fed by genuine, popular nationalist enthusiasm, are scripted by elites who seek to maintain their position within their national group and either retain control or change their position relative to a more dominant national group (Anderson 1991). Intra-group power dynamics involve elite manipulation of shared identity to produce group solidarity and to define the group in relation to others, only after they "reject a national other, can they define and create a national self" (Danforth 1993). The social construction of characteristics that shape intra- and inter-group power dynamics is found outside of the literature on nationalism where scholars have observed similar mechanisms at work.

Ethnicity, Sectarianism, and Confessionalism

Described as a set of "cultural characteristics" that are shared within a group, ethnicity is invested with social value and taught to younger generations (Enloe 1980b: 12). Ethnicity is instrumentally used by elites in shaping society to benefit power-holders in achieving four goals: (1) to ensure desirable divisions of labor in society and adequate labor supplies for sensitive security positions, (2) to prevent alliances between other sectors of society that may form along nonethnic axis, (3) to produce positive group cohesion using narratives that are not based on fear, and (4) to build social units whose reactions to political stimuli and policy making are somewhat predictable (Enloe 1980b). Much like nationalism, ethnicity contains ideational qualities that are not centered on power politics. However, ethnic elites, especially those facing domestic security challenges, see societal ethnic cleavages as exploitable opportunities. Ethnic cleavages serve as ordering principles for interpreting domestic security concerns. This perspective produces division between "national" and "state" security, with the former representing the security of a particular group and the later representing the security of institutions and borders. When one ethnic group dominates a heterogeneous society its interpretation of national security will be superimposed onto state security concerns. Nondominant ethnic groups can be left out of national security calculations, or worse, be portrayed as possible state security threats. Dominant ethnic elites design security institutions to best satisfy their national security concerns while maintaining the inter-ethnic cleavages that best suit their political needs (Enloe 1980a).

Religious cleavages resemble ethnic cleavages in many ways. In his discussion of sectarianism, or ta'ifiyya in Arabic, and its mobilization, Fanar Haddad identifies "competition for economic benefit and state patronage" as drivers for hardening boundaries between in- and out-groups. When state policy is perceived to be linked to sectarian discourses, groups develop narratives that reflect their relationship to the state (Haddad 2011). If a group benefits from its relationship with the state it will develop narratives that reinforce an in-group identity (Haddad 2011). If, however, a group perceives state policy as restricting it to peripheral status narratives of discrimination and victimhood will develop and consolidate around an out-group identity (Hechter 1975). Haddad views sectarianism as a non-discrete variable with three broad categories: assertive, passive, and banal sectarianism. Changes in the political climate can move sectarianism's salience one way or the other along a continuum. With heightened political tension, sectarian identity can become more politically assertive as an attribute of group identity (Haddad 2011).

Confessionalism is the institutionalization of sectarianism in government. This can take many forms but most commonly includes the mapping of "multi-communalism" onto "politico-administrative structures." These religious communities are composed of individuals who identify with a particular organization, religious institution, or "way of communal thinking" (Beydoun 2003). In turn, these communities make up the critical units for managing society and building a coherent form of government. However, while these units take the form of political blocs imbued with the power their members have invested in them, the religious identity of those individuals remains subjective. The political blocs, and the elites who rise to control them, have an interest in defining what identity those blocs maintain and thus attempt to manage the beliefs of their members. Security institutions provide one such mechanism.

Security Elite Considerations

Ethnic elites project their national security concerns onto fragmented societies through state security maps which in turn are used to manage security institutions. These security maps contain three broad categories for conceptualizing groups and for how groups conceptualize themselves in relation to dominant elites. The core group is politically acceptable to dominant elites and has easy access to command positions within security institutions. This group views itself as capable of full participation in all aspects of the political and security apparatus. The middle category includes groups that do not share ethnic ties with the core, but are not considered security threats. These groups are able to join security institutions although most likely not in positions of high command and view themselves as secure enough to lobby for increased participation in the political and security apparatus with real potential for upward mobility. Peripheral groups have limited access to the security apparatus and are most likely seen by dominant elites as politically unreliable (Peled 1998). They are barred access to all but the lowest positions in the security apparatus and view themselves as disconnected from dominant sectors of society (Enloe 1980a). When groups are excluded from the security apparatus they are more likely to fear it as a potential threat, which in turn may increase "ethnic self-consciousness and collective interest" (Enloe 1980a). As this cycle continues that interest becomes politicized and ethnic groups may seek violent remedies. Causal theories of civil war are varied. Fearon argues that state weakness, poverty, population size, and instability are strong indicators for civil war. He holds these structural factors stronger predictors than ethnic or religious grievances (Fearon & Laitin 2003). Kalyvas finds that micro cleavages at the local level are better predictors than macro-structural indicators (Kalyvas 2001). Mueller asserts that civil wars are prosecuted by criminal bands that use identity in an instrumental way to challenge authority figures and redistribute power and wealth (Mueller 2000). However, Collier and Hoeffler maintain that "ethnic dominance" when proxied as a political grievance is one of the strongest predictors of civil war (Collier & Hoeffler 2004). Applying the international relations theory of the security dilemma onto ethnic power dynamics, Sisk argues that ethnic boundaries harden as grievances increase and that once a cycle of violence commences it is very difficult for identity lines not to take a militarized form (Sisk 2013).

Civil war termination is an equally contested subject. However, most theories, besides those viewing total victory as the only real strategy for termination, advance power-sharing formulas between competing elites as essential. Power-sharing must take place at all levels and include permanent arrangements for the distribution of state resources. These grand power sharing bargains can only last when parties to the deal fear the costs of failure more than any benefits they may gain from continued conflict (Sisk 2013). Security institutions play a prominent role in these grand bargains. In many cases, security forces participated in the conflicts or, if they remained passive, are viewed as weak by combatants. Security and access to security institutions must be redistributed to produce lasting conflict resolution, a bitter pill to swallow for elites and privileged groups grown accustomed to their status (Sisk 2013). Failure to include previously peripheralized groups into security institutions poses a major threat to the longevity of grand power-sharing bargains. Peled notes that states can develop "ethnic military manpower policies" that seek to address the systems of inclusion and exclusion that form the basis of state security maps by reforming recruitment and deployment policies (Peled 1998).

Consociationalism

Grand power-sharing bargains in fragmented societies often take the form of consociational or centrifugal democracies, a confessional system of government advanced by Arendt Lijphart for managing politicized sectarian groups in the Netherlands. He identifies elite behavior as the primary variable for stabilizing institutions in societies where political culture is fractured along identity cleavages and political sub-cultures. In systems of government where all decisions are viewed as zero-sum games, grand coalition cabinets controlled by a "cartel of elites" must negotiate important policies to ensure buy-in from all groups. Lijphart notes four key features for successful power-sharing: (1) elite ability to accommodate divergent interests and sub-cultures, (2) elite ability to work with rival elites, (3) elite fear of further political discord and interest in maintaining stability, and (4) sub-culture dynamics. This last feature stresses the importance of sub-culture cohesion and the ability of elites to control their groups and act as united political blocs (Lijphart 1969). Critiques of Lijphart's theory note that power-sharing along ethnic or sectarian lines risks creating sources of conflict into the new political order (Sisk 2013). This framework also tends to produce political deadlock as every party to the agreement has the power of veto over decision-making processes. Additionally, this system of confessional voting entrenches group boundaries by raising barriers to cross-confessional political organizations and produces elite oligarchs whose standing in their respective groups is solidified by their near guaranteed access to state resources (Sisk 2013).

Military Institutions

Militaries are neo-traditional by nature due to their hierarchical and hyper-masculine culture making power-sharing arrangements especially difficult to manage. Regardless of religious or political identity, officers and security elites seek to legitimate their own authority with historical and national narratives (Janowitz 1977). When attempting to accommodate multiple national, ethnic, or sectarian narratives in a military institution, advocates find that without a unitary narrative legitimation and decision-making can prove problematic. In analyzing the ethnic or sectarian dynamics of a military the literature suggests four issue areas for analysis: (1) what are the institutional patterns of recruitment from ethnic or sectarian units, (2) does the internal organization of the military reflect ethnic or sectarian biases, (3) are ethnic or sectarian concerns a factor when deploying the military, and (4) how does the ethnic or sectarian composition of the military affects its relationship with the civilian government (Enloe 1980b). To these four issue areas, this analysis will add a fifth, that of the institutional patterns of officer promotion between and among ethnic or sectarian groups.

Recruitment

Recruitment patterns go to the very heart of the ethnic security dilemma. As the military is a critical component of any political order, inclusion and membership in its ranks reflects the institutional trust that governing elites place in particular communities. Recruitment patterns are often legacies of colonial authority in developing states, with certain "martial races," or more trusted minorities, recruited in higher numbers to offset colonial suspicion of restless majorities. This created imbalance in military recruitment in post-colonial states has implications for inter-communal dynamics. If, following civil wars, the internal composition of the military does not reflect the grand political bargain it is highly likely the military will continue to employ state security maps that prioritize identity over other more salient factors. Additionally, the military will remain an essentially ethnic or sectarian force in the eyes of excluded groups (Enloe 1980b).

Promotion

Officer corps demographics are commonly used as a metric for equality in promotional patterns. Officers are products of military academies established by security elites to teach dominant interpretations of nationalism and institutional identity and are thus representations of accepted ethnic and sectarian qualities (Janowitz 1977). Selection of officers for senior command or for critical units are also a significant indicator for determining who is trusted by the security elite. In militaries employing state security maps to determine leadership roles, "individuals from the same religious, tribal, ethnic, or regional group" will be chosen due to their political reliability (Brooks 1998). If officers from one group are promoted at a faster rate or in greater numbers than those from other groups these effects will be exaggerated as the command-and-control of the military will continue to reflect these imbalances over time. Even when merit is used as the objective measure for promotion, it can often mask preferences for over-representation of some groups and under-representation of others (Enloe 1980b).

Organization

National security tasks can take the form of responses to external or internal threats. Internal security considerations take precedence in discussions concerning militaries in fragmented societies. The organization of units with the expressed purpose of domestic security will reflect the security elite's views of the political reliability of certain groups. A common indicator for the use of state security maps in ordering organizational preferences is if special units are homogeneous or heavily weighted towards one ethnic or sectarian group. Likewise, state security maps are in use if preferred units receive higher quality supplies or equipment than others deemed less politically reliable.

Deployment

Observing where militaries are deployed and if ethnic or sectarian factors are at play is another good indicator for measuring the use of ethnic security maps. These types of deployments take two primary forms. One, if ethnically mixed or ethnically homogeneous units are only deployed in areas or situations where their commanders feel they will remain politically reliable. Two, if militaries are deployed to counter perceived security threats in ethnically or religiously homogeneous regions. This last type can produce problematic inter-communal dynamics as the military's "image" remains tainted in the eyes of communities who feel they are being policed by outsiders (Enloe 1980b).

Civilian-Military Relations

As democracies, consociational systems of government are assumed to value civilian control over the military. As with other issue areas, if ethnic or sectarian factors inhibit relations between civilian and military elites state security maps may be at play with security elites viewing the civilian leadership itself as a potential threat or as illegitimate. If neo-traditionalist militaries refuse deployment or reform due to conflicts of interest with the civilian government, power-sharing dynamics among ethnic elites may breakdown.

Case Study: Lebanese Armed Forces and the 1989 National Reconciliation Accord

Sectarian Politics in a Divided Society

Lebanon is one such fragmented society with a population composed of both Christians and Muslims. These communities are each further subdivided into smaller sectarian groups, which form the socio-political units of analysis. The Christian community is composed of Maronite Catholics ("Maronite"), Roman Catholics ("Catholic"), Greek Orthodox ("Orthodox"), and Armenian Christians ("Armenian"). The Muslim community is composed of Sunni and Shia. Smaller but important religious sects include the Druze and the 'Alawi. Lebanese politico-religious institutional legacies hark back to the Ottoman Era when what is now Lebanon was part of a small, but influential, district of the empire. For most of the Ottoman period, the Sultan and his representatives allowed the local aristocracy to retain significant power in local politics. These wealthy landowning families maintained strong familial ties to the religious authorities lending the local political leadership legitimacy. Constantinople, the imperial capital, appointed an Ottoman official to oversee its imperial possession, but drew the bureaucratic class, including military officers, from local non-aristocratic social groups to offset the political power of the local aristocracy (Janowitz 1977). Following the Ottoman Empire's collapse and the start of the French mandate, colonial authorities, seeking to undermine any vestiges of Ottoman influence, empowered minority groups who were viewed as more politically reliable. This strategy was reflected in the locally raised colonial military force where French military officials displayed a preference for enlisted personnel and native officers from minority groups inhabiting the rural areas outside of major cities (Janowitz 1977). These recruitment preferences reflected the state security map employed by the French. When one social group was seen as agitating against colonial authority, military officials would recruit from that group's competitor. As Arab nationalism grew in popularity among Sunnis and to a lesser extent Orthodox, the French decreased their recruitment in these communities and increased recruitment among Christians, especially Maronites (Barak 2009).

Post-Colonial Power-Sharing

After Lebanese independence in 1943, the major religious groups reached an agreement known as the National Pact in which the confessional nature of politics was enshrined in prescribed roles for each community (Lijphart 1969). Under the agreement, the president was a Maronite, the prime minister a Sunni, the speaker of parliament a Shia, the deputy to the speaker and the deputy to the prime minister both Orthodox, the commander of the Armed Forces was a Maronite, and the chief-of-staff of the Armed Forces was a Catholic (until 1959 when a Druze was appointed). Additionally, according to the 1932 census, undertaken by the French, Christians held a slight majority with 51% of the population. Thus, parliamentary seats were reserved along a quota system in a 6:5 ratio in favor of the Christian community. Parliamentary elections were held on a regional basis where elites from each confessional group dominated the local political scene. This ensured that the cartel of elites was well situated to maintain their hold on national institutions and that the balance of power among the confessional groups would remain stable according to the agreed upon division-of-power (Barak 2009). However, confessional elites from each group faced political competition from within their groups as well. The hyper-local nature of politics allowed elites to use their patronage networks to shut out potential challengers and control intra-group politics by emphasizing inter-group competition (Beydoun 2003).

Lebanese Armed Forces Pre-Civil War

Recruitment

In the period immediately following independence, the Armed Forces remained largely removed from politics despite a significant presence of Christians, especially Maronites, within its ranks and officer corps. While conscription was the norm for military recruitment in most post-colonial states in the region, Lebanon's senior military leadership was wary of opening the institution and changing its sectarian balance. In 1949, Chief-of-Staff Tawfiq Salem, a Catholic, cautioned the government from enacting a universal military service law due to concerns that the army's lower ranks would fill with Assyrians, Muslims, and Druze (Barak 2009). Despite these concerns, the period 1945–1975 saw increased Muslim, especially Shia, participation in the army's lower ranks due to the unpopularity of enlisted life among Christian youth (Barak 2009). However, the officer corps remained dominated by Christians, largely Maronite, with perhaps 75% coming from these communities (Enloe 1980b). By 1974, Christian dominance in the army had become a salient issue in the Muslim community. The Lebanese National Movement, a pan-Muslim opposition group made accusations that the Lebanese Army was a "Christian army" serving narrow sectarian goals (Barak 2009).

Promotion

Averages over the 17-year period 1958–1975 show that while all the sects were represented in the officer corps, Maronites held a full third of all positions. Christians comprised 55% of the officer corps overall, a full 35% of that was Maronites, with Catholics making up 10%, and Orthodox consisting of 9%. Muslims totaled 45% of the officer corps but the breakdowns were far more even, with 15% Sunni, 15% Shia, and 15% Druze. Close family networks linked the political and military establishments. Appointments and promotions for senior positions within the military followed from communal leadership preferences (Barak 2009: 30). Thus, with Maronites firmly at the helm of the state, senior military posts remained the almost exclusive right of the Christian community. The army commander and the head of military intelligence were both Maronites and the chief-of-staff was a Catholic until 1959 when Muslim pressure forced the government to appoint a Druze (Barak 2009). These senior posts were filled according to seniority, not merit, with the longest serving Maronite officer replacing his predecessor in roles reserved for Maronites. In addition to holding the army's most senior leadership positions, Maronites also commanded many of the most important combat units, including the artillery corps, the armored corps, and the Republican Guard. Maronites commanded the Military Academy were all officers received their indoctrination and military training. After 1970, pressure from the Muslim community forced senior army leadership to attempt sectarian parity among battalion level commander, however, it was never reached due to a shortage of Muslim officers (Barak 2009).

Organization

Even with its officer corps firmly controlled by Maronites, the Armed Forces' first Commander-in-Chief, and later president, Fuad Chehab instilled an ethic of non-intervention in domestic politics commonly referred to as Chehabism (Gaub 2014). Under his command, the army continued to reflect the preferred sectarian makeup of the Maronite dominated state but was not used as an instrument for changing the delicate inter-communal balance of power. However, at brigade level, the army consisted of homogenous sectarian units with officers of the same sect commanding (Gaub 2014). This organizational structure facilitated the wedding of specific units to particular regions as enlisted personnel often served in the region where they came from and among those who shared their sectarian identity.

Deployment

Despite Chehab keeping the army separate from sectarian power struggles the introduction of a new element to the political scene drastically changed the balance of power. Leading up to its expulsion from Jordan during "Black September," the Palestinian Liberation Organization, supported by its regional ally Syria, moved its base of operations to the Lebanese-Syrian-Israeli border. This new political actor, one with military training, access to military hardware, and the zeal to fight, challenged the Maronite dominated Armed Forces and alarmed Christian elites. Muslim elites, however, sympathized with the Palestinians' plight and demanded that the Armed Forces prioritize the defense of Lebanon's sovereign territory against increasing violations by the Israeli Defense Forces (Enloe 1980b).

The Palestinians were supported not just by their Sunni kin in the Lebanese community but also by the Shia and Druze communities. Furthermore, non-sectarian opposition movements such as the Communist Action Organization also supported their fight against the perceived threat of western forces. However, Christian elites, especially the Maronites, were deeply suspicious of the Palestinians and their Syrian patrons. Despite the steady increase of Muslim inclusion within the enlisted ranks of the armed forces, the Maronite-dominated officer corps was deeply apprehensive towards the new Palestinian population, which it saw as aggressive. In turn, the Palestinian resistance, fearful of Israeli incursions, began to openly carry arms and test the armed forces. Events came to a head and the Armed Forces deployed to counter the rising power in the Palestinian refugee camps (Barak 2009). With the election of Suleiman Frangieh, a Maronite leader, for president in 1970, the Christian dominated armed forces were sent to put down the ascendant Palestinians. His tough talk concerning restoring Lebanese sovereignty vis-à-vis the Palestinian guerrillas won him the election but it was not enough to hold the Armed Forces, riven by sectarian cleavages, together. The armed forces' deployment to the camps caused standoffs between army units and the Palestinian guerrillas. Army units began to arrest Palestinians they found carrying arms and the guerrillas responded by taking Lebanese soldiers as hostages. When the armed forces issued an ultimatum demanding their soldiers back and it went unanswered they attacked the refugee camps with artillery and airstrikes (Barak 2009). These battles split the armed forces in two. Many Muslim enlisted personnel and junior officers were sympathetic towards the Palestinians while many of the junior Christian officer's thought that their senior leadership were being "hesitant" in dealing with the Palestinian threat (Barak 2009).

Civil-Military Relations

Chehabism, the ethic of non-interference by the military in sectarian power politics, was important in that it affirmed the armed forces as a national institution. Chehab's view that the army was not "above the government" added to the political elite's feelings of security. However, once Chehab became president the military became his main constituency, blurring the lines between civilian government and the military. As the military took a more active role in government the sectarian cleavages in its own ranks were politicized and opened to exogenous shocks (Barak 2009). Chehab's presidency and that of his successor, Charles Helou, are commonly looked back on as times of stability but this memory hides the fact that the commander turned president contributed to the process that eventually led to civil war (Barak 2009).

National Reconciliation Accord (Ta'if Accord) 1989

Following a bitter 15-year civil war that involved almost all of Lebanon's immediate neighbors and many other regional actors, a power-sharing agreement was reached during negotiations at Ta'if, Saudi Arabia in September 1989. The agreement, commonly known as the Ta'if Accord, was a renegotiation of the basic principles of the 1943 National Pact that had institutionalized Christian dominance. Under Ta'if, the president remained a Maronite, the prime minister remained a Sunni, and the speaker of parliament remained a Shia; however, executive power was removed from the office of the president and transferred to the cabinet, chaired by the prime minister. The term of the Shia speaker of parliament was also extended to four years establishing a multi-communal troika that has come to be called the "three presidents" (Baramy 2014). The quota for seats in parliament was also renegotiated with the old 6:5 split abolished in favor of an equal split between Christians and Muslims. This even split was further subdivided between the "denominations of each sect," and the number of districts was increased, ensuring representation in parliament for every community, no matter how small.

These last measures ensured the political dominance of the cartel of elites within and among the different sects. The new division of power was accompanied by a commitment to abolish "political sectarianism." The agreement charged parliament with adopting "proper measures" to achieve this task and appointing a council, including the president, prime minister, and speaker, to examine and propose the means capable of abolishing sectarianism. The agreement stipulated that sect would no longer be denominated on identity cards. However, the confessional affairs of each sect remained firmly enshrined in the agreement. In terms of security reforms, the Maronite president remained the head of the Civilian Supreme Defense Council but the Sunni Prime Minister became his deputy. Sectarian representation in standard security sector employment, including in the Armed Forces, was abolished with "top-level jobs and equivalent jobs" shared equally between Christians and Muslims. The internal security forces, not the Armed Forces, were charged with domestic security and their ranks were opened to all Lebanese without exception. The Armed Forces were charged with defense of the homeland and with the protection of public order but only if the internal security forces were incapable of providing adequate security. The agreement emphasized that the armed forces' primary concern was the threat posed to Lebanon by "Israeli aggression" and that the armed forces would deploy to border areas adjacent to Israel to provide for the return of security and stability. With this new emphasis, the armed forces began a period of reorganization.

Lebanese Armed Forces Post-Civil War

Recruitment

Following the war, the government passed a national military conscription law called the Flag Service Law. This law attempted to shift the demographic balance within the rank and file to more appropriately represent the country's population and to promote the "socialization and intermingling" of different sects in a national institution (Baramay 2014). Still, the armed forces were forced to recruit Christians as Maronites avoided their military service due to the perception that it was a "crippled institution" (Nerguizian 2015). Muslim draftees, especially rural Sunnis, enthusiastically participated viewing service as an employment opportunity. Conscription was repealed in 2005 and the Armed Forces now rely on a system of contractual volunteers, with Sunnis as a majority (Knudsen 2014). The armed forces' attempted to recruit Christians and Muslims into the officer corps in near equal numbers ignoring the demographic shifts in the country where the Muslim population is increasing and the Christian population is decreasing in relative terms. A multi-confessional council, appointed by the government, monitors the sectarian composition of the Armed Forces (Gaub 2014).

Promotion

The period 1990–2004 saw a small, but significant, decrease in the number of Christian officers relative to the pre-war years and is a testament to the multi-confessional council's management of the officer corps composition Christians in this period account for 47% of the officer corps, with 30% of the total Maronite, 8% Catholic, and 9% Orthodox. Muslims during this period accounted for 53% of officers, with 16% Sunni, 27% Shia, and 10% Druze. In 2010, the number of Christian officers again reached near half of the total with 49% , but the number of Maronite officers decreased to 29% and the number of Orthodox officers increased to 11% . The number of Muslim officers remained steady at near half but Sunni officers increased to 22% of the total and Druze officers decreased to 7%. Fluctuations are most likely attributed to changing demographics in the country. Implementation of the power-sharing agreement was especially relevant in terms of assigning "top-level jobs." The commander of the armed forces remained a Maronite and his Chief-of-Staff is a Druze. However, their deputies are now subject to sectarian quotas as well. The deputy chief-of-staff for personnel was now Sunni, the deputy chief-of-staff for operations Shia, and the deputy chief-of-staff for logistics and Deputy Chief-of-Staff for planning were Christians, but not always Maronites. In turn, military intelligence positions were also commonly seen as reserved for different sects with the director of military intelligence slot usually held by a Maronite and his deputy coming from the Shia community (Nerguizian 2015).

Organization

Integration had the defined goal of once again creating a national institution not beholden to the sectarian cleavages that dominated politics. Immediately following the civil war, units of the armed forces remained divided along sectarian lines with the Christian units taking orders from the commander of the Armed Forces, a Maronite, and the Muslim units taking orders from the prime minister, a Sunni (Barak 2009). With the implementation of the power-sharing agreement this division slowly disappeared, and the armed forces undertook a process of reorganization that saw units integrated along a non-sectarian and non-regional basis (Gaub 2014). This process again involved the multi-communal council. Two processes, one of integrating units while, two, maintaining sectarian quotas for unit composition. This reflected the delicate balance that the armed forces sought to achieve and maintain. At the brigade level, the armed forces' leadership sought to reach a ratio of 60:40 between Muslims and Christians. At the battalion level, it sought to reach a ratio of between 65:70 and 35:30. A 50:50 split was sought for special units such as the commando regiments, special forces, and Republican Guard. Special units were also assigned officers on a sectarian basis with the Ranger Regiment and Air Assault Regiment commanded by Maronites and the Navy Commando Regiment commanded by a Sunni. However, conventional units' officers were not assigned by sect (Nerguizian 2015).

Deployment

The armed forces remained "hesitant to take action" and were "extremely risk adverse" due to a complex and fragile sectarian composition despite reorganization and institutionalized balancing between the sects (Barany 2014). Rotation policies were enacted to break the ties between particular units and regions of the country not only to have units serve in other parts of the country but to severe local politicians influence over unit commanders. Six-month tours of duty were enacted, after which units rotated to different duty stations (Barany 2014). The power-sharing agreement's stipulation that the majority of the armed forces slowly evolved as sub-state security providers, namely Hizbollah who proved more adept at providing a credible deterrent along the southern border (Knudsen 2014). The Armed Forces now concentrated the bulk of their manpower on providing security along the Lebanese-Syrian border and managing heightened Sunni-Shia and Sunni-'Alawi tensions (Nerguizian 2015).

Civil-Military Relations

The armed forces' relationship with the government and society was strong, but its ability to carry out its mandate was questionable given the internal pull of political, sectoral, and regional loyalties (Barany 2014). The power-sharing agreement that terminated the civil war was made possible by the combatants' realization that they would never be able to achieve their maximalist goals. Prior to this realization, Christian factions sought to reimpose the traditional order, while Muslim factions sought a complete reordering of society. Power-sharing was a compromise between these two irreconcilable positions (Barak 2009). The armed forces reflect this inter-elite grand bargain. It is an institution that serves an inclusive idea of the nation, but is also beholden to sectarian demands that limit its effectiveness and representative attributes.

Case Study: Iraqi Security Forces and the 2005 Constitution

Cross-cutting Ethno-sectarian Cleavages

Iraq is another such fragmented society with a population divided into three major identities, two on a sectarian basis and one by ethnicity. The vast majority of the country is Arab-Muslim split between a Shia majority and a Sunni minority. Ethnic Kurds are another important minority, who while also predominantly Sunni mostly identify first as Kurds. For the purposes of this study the socio-political units of analysis are the Arab-Sunnis ("Sunni"), the Arab-Shia (Shia), and the Kurdish-Sunnis ("Kurds"). Smaller but important religious sects include a variety of Christian denominations and other religious minorities such as the Yezidis. The modern state of Iraq was cobbled together by the British from the Ottoman administrative districts, or vilayets, of Baghdad, Mosul, and Basra. During the late stages of Ottoman rule notable urban families in each of these districts increased their landholdings in rural areas and solidified their control over the peasantry. Ottoman bureaucratic reforms welcomed this urban class into local administrative roles and the officer corps translating its economic holdings into political power (Eppel 1998: 229). When Faisal took the throne as King of Iraq in 1921 at the behest of the British these urban administrators and officers formed the core of the new bureaucracy and military.

The British alliance with the Sharifians during World War I led Faisal first to Damascus and finally to Baghdad. With him he brought Sunni officers from middle-class Syrian and Palestinian families some of whom were steeped in the emerging trend of Arab nationalism (Eppel 1998). British administrators relied on their networks of urban notable families to counter the growing threat of Arab nationalism while Faisal tried to balance his need for British military power with his desire to build a strong centralized Iraqi state. His fledgling Iraqi army was staffed with officers who shared his vision and saw a prominent role for their institution and its ability to offset the political clout of the established Shia urban notables and landlords (Dawisha 2009). Faisal and his coalition of British administrators and mainly Sunni officers concentrated state power in Baghdad and fought successive rebellions led by Shia and Kurdish tribal leaders resisting encroachment on their traditional privileges (Dawisha 2009).

Sectarianism Under Ba'ath Rule

The overthrow of the monarchy in 1958 saw a progression of military governments led by generals whose institutional lineage was rooted in an officer class committed to state centralization. It is beyond the scope of this chapter to cover the full breath of Iraqi history, however, Saddam Hussein – while not from the officer class – also focused the policies of the Ba'ath Party on continued state centralization. His rule of Iraq was inspired by Joseph Stalin (Woods et al 2011). His totalitarian-authoritarian style of government was deeply paranoid of all foreign and domestic threats. This paranoia was well deserved. Iraq, since its independence from the British, had suffered countless coups and coup attempts. Challengers, especially those rising out of the military, were the greatest internal threat to Saddam's rule. Therefore, he relied on a system of patronage that favored loyalty above all else. Saddam relied primarily on the Sunni minority for the most sensitive security positions although some high-ranking officers were from the Shia majority and Kurdish minority.

Saddam also feared elements from within the Sunni community and favored the tribes from around his birthplace of Tikrit when staffing the units that handled his personnel protection (Jaber & Dawod 2003). Events would further solidify Saddam's paranoia as well as institutional predisposition to Sunni officers. Iraq's propaganda machine during the Iran-Iraq war would increasingly use narratives of Arab versus Persian primordial conflict to sustain the war effort. This implicitly highlighted much of the Iraqi Shia population as a potential fifth column in the minds of the Sunni dominated officer corps; a tendency that was further solidified in 1991 when Shia and Kurdish rebellions broke out after the military's defeat. Sectarianism, while not the only cleavage dividing Iraq under Saddam's rule, was a fact of social life in a state ruled by a dictator who patronized a sectarian minority in order to maintain his power over the Iraqi army pre-2003.

Recruitment

Recruitment for enlisted personnel in the Iraq army relied heavily on Shia and Kurdish conscripts. During the Iran-Iraq War these soldiers played a pivotal role in providing the regime with sufficient forces to wage war on multiple fronts. However, following the war, Saddam demobilized many of the conscript units and strengthened Sunni combat and special units. The allied tribes in the Sunni heartland in the north and west of the country provided the bulk of the soldiers for the Republican Guard and Special Republican Guard, two praetorian units kept outside the command structure of the regular army as a coup-proofing strategy (Brooks 1998). When these special units faced Shia and Kurdish insurrections following the 1991 Gulf War they remained politically reliable and defended their "privileged status" in Saddam's political order (al-Marashi & Salama 2008).

Promotion

Promotional patterns in the Iraqi army relied almost exclusively on personal loyalty. Men with no military qualifications were often found in senior command due to their familial or personal relationships with the dictator (Baram 2002). Briefly, during the Iran-Iraq War, Saddam allowed merit-based promotions to be introduced when the war effort was suffering from a lack of officers with military expertise in key positions. However, this practice was quickly stopped following the war's end when most successful generals were put under house arrest as Saddam feared their skill and popularity. Promotion in the Republican Guard and Special Republican Guard was based on a combination of merit and political reliability. These overwhelmingly Sunni units were led by officers often from the same Tikrit based Abu Nimr clan as Saddam. Specifically used for regime protection, these units were stationed at all presidential residences and their officers had personal contact with Saddam (Talmadge 2015).

Organization

The Iraqi Army was organized in the Soviet manner with large conscript infantry formations supported by heavy weapons units and a special emphasis on armored strike forces. It was not well integrated, with little communication between elements even within the same unit. This was mainly due to Saddam's fear that well-organized units in communication with each other were more likely to stage a successful coup. Further coup-proofing strategies including giving preferential treatment to high-ranking regular army officers and Republican Guard and Special Republican Guard (International Crisis Group Report 2003). These rewards included the most modern equipment, new housing, the best healthcare, and regular salary increases and gifts (Baram 2002). Praetorian units were considered to be Saddam's private army and were allowed leeway in many aspects of military life that the regular army was not. For instance, during the height of the sanction's regime when the army went without pay for years, these special units not only were paid regularly, but were allowed to shop in markets reserved for the highest-level regime officials.

Deployment

Deployments were subject to the whims of the dictator and his perceived threat environment. While Shia and Kurdish conscript units were used as cannon fodder in the war against Iran, Republican Guard units were used as elite shock troops in critical battles. Following the war, the Republican Guard was deployed to suppress a Shia revolt in the south and a Kurdish revolt in the north. Saddam again sent the Republican Guard to Kurdish-held territory to put down further foreign sponsored Kurdish rebellions (Baram 2002). During periods of relative calm, Saddam used Kurdish conscripts in Shia regions as a strategy to keep his Sunni dominated regime's ethnic and sectarian competitors busy fighting each other (Enloe 1980a).

Civil-Military Relations

Relations between Saddam's civilian regime and the military were complex. Saddam, while fancying himself a military man, had no military education having been rejected from the military academy in his youth. This black mark on his record forced him to treat many career military officers poorly (Woods et al 2011). Saddam's habit of belittling officers in front of each other created unrest within the officer corps that only served to fuel his suspicion of coups. However, at key moments, such as following the 1991 Gulf War, Saddam provided increased benefits to the officer corps to buy their loyalty during times of regime instability (Brooks 1998). Saddam's relations with the officers in the Republican Guard and the Special Republican Guard were far better due to their privileged position within the security apparatus.

The 2005 Constitution

The 2005 Constitution was an attempt to correct the wrongs committed under Saddam's authoritarian dictatorship and establish a power-sharing agreement that would allow all the major communities a place in political life. Parties during the negotiation included local sectarian elites who had survived the dictatorship but also included many long-time political exiles with powerful foreign supporters but with little constituency in the country (Al-Ali 2014). The post-negotiations government reflected the informal division of power among ethno-sectarian elites. The Shia, as the dominant demographic population claimed the powerful prime minister post with Kurdish and Sunni deputies. The Kurds, as the minority kingmakers, took the presidency with Shia and Sunni deputies. The Sunnis accepted the speaker of the assembly position with Shia and Kurdish deputies. Following this trend, ministerial posts in the cabinet were assigned along ethno-sectarian lines with each major group and some minor groups jockeying for positions that reflected the informally agreed upon balance-of-power (Dawisha 2009). Article three stipulates that "Iraq is a country of multiple nationalities, religions, and sects." This formal recognition of the heterogeneity of its population was a far cry from the brutal manner in which the previous regime had dealt with the complex Iraqi social fabric. This new discourse was further strengthened in Article 4, where Arabic and Kurdish, were named as the "two official languages of Iraq" with all government documents and official conferences held in both. However, this new found equality came with a significant caveat. The fifth clause of Article 18 stipulates that "Iraqi citizenship shall not be granted for the purposes of the policy of population settlement that disrupts the demographic composition of Iraq." While population transfers had been an issue in the past, especially around Kirkuk, this article firmly locks in place Iraq's current demographic balance giving sectarian cleavages newfound salience. The first clause of Article seven added to the de-Ba'athification already underway by stipulating that "any entity or program that adopts, incites, facilitates, glorifies, promotes, or justifies racism or terrorism...

especially the Saddamist Ba'ath in Iraq and its symbols...shall be prohibited" (al-Marashi & Salama 2008). While the text of this clause is clearly meant to hinder any future sympathy towards the Ba'ath Party, its spirit could also aid those who sought to permanently freeze out not only all former Ba'ath Party members but also Sunnis entirely. For many Sunnis, the Ba'ath Party had been their only form of political participation and to bury it completely would be to hide their own experience and memory.

Article nine deals exclusively with the security forces. The first clause, subsection A, states "the Iraqi armed forces and security services will be composed of the components of the Iraqi people with due consideration given to their balance and representation without discrimination or exclusion." The security forces, ideally, would reflect the larger power-sharing agreement reached between the three major negotiating partners. Sectarian and ethnic considerations would play a major role in establishing and maintaining units within the Security Forces. Subsection B states that "the formation of military militias outside the framework of the armed forces is prohibited." This subsection would prove especially problematic as militias increasing inserted themselves into security operations. This issue of multiple forces was compounded by Article 121, fifth clause, which states that "the regional government shall be responsible for...the establishment and organization of the internal security forces for the region such as police, security forces, and guards of the region." The clause relates specifically to the Kurdish Regional Government's Peshmerga forces, which constitute an autonomous force almost completely outside the central chain of command.

Iraqi Security Forces Post-2005

Recruitment

The Coalition Provisional Authority issued Order #2 shortly after the overthrow of the regime ending conscription, dissolving all security institutions, and effectively ending Sunni domination of the security apparatus. Recruitment into the new Iraqi 96 Security Forces was largely handled by powerful intermediaries such as political party leaders, tribal chiefs, and provincial officials for ostensible vetting. In reality this recruitment approach encouraged identity based patronage networks to grow in the ranks (International Crisis Group Report 2003). Militia units from the Mahdi Army and the Badr Corps, armed wings of important Shia political organizations, were "reintegrated" into the new security apparatus in mass (Ucko 2008). Many non-militia recruits were Shia from the south who had served in the army during the Iran-Iraq War and been demobilized at the war's end (Rayburn 2014).

The new security forces faced many recruitment challenges among the Sunni and Kurdish segments of the population. Sunni recruits faced stiff de-Ba'athification vetting requirements and graduating from Shia-controlled boot camps also proved difficult. Young Sunni men became increasingly reluctant to leave their home provinces as the government sought to implement Shia maximalist policies with a corresponding deterioration in the security situation in Sunni areas (Ucko 2008). Kurds joined national units established by the central government but the Kurdish Regional Government refused to form multi-ethnic units and instead formed Kurdish only units that remained within their regional chain-of-command (al-Marashi & Salama 2008).

Promotion

Promotional patterns in the reorganized Security Forces continued to serve as a patronage system. Commands outside of the Kurdish controlled north were distributed on a largely sectarian basis (Republic of Iraq 2003a). De-Ba'athification immediately stripped all Sunni officers of their previous ranks and blacklisted officers above the rank of colonel. While the security forces' chain-of-command was constitutionally set up to flow through the Ministry of Defense, a separate chain of command ran directly through the prime minister's office reporting to the national security advisor. This chain of command was staffed by officers loyal to Shia political organizations and affiliated militias and focused many of its efforts on controlling appointments within the security services (Gaub 2014). Shia officers seen as aggressively pursuing Sunni resistance were rewarded while any officer that sought to rein in Shia militias was forced out (Dawisha 2009). The Ministry of Defense was staffed with many very capable officers with combat experience and institutional knowledge gained during service in the Iran-Iraq War. While de-Ba'athification took its toll some Sunni officers were brought back as their military experience was needed to address current security concerns.

Organization

The deteriorating security situation following the decision to dissolve all security institutions led to evolving projections of the size of the new Iraqi army. However, unlike the previous emphasis on large, conscripted infantry units and armored strike forces the new army consisted of mainly light infantry units (International Crisis Group Report 2003). The decision to organize along smaller more tactically mobile units in part stemmed from the internal nature of the security threat but was also significantly influenced by both domestic and foreign fears of an overly strong military. Sectarian quotas for unit composition and organization were not formalized, however, Article 9 was frequently referenced when making ethno-sectarian driven political appointments or stripping officers of their commands (Gaub 2014). Constitutional claims to "balance and representation" hid the fact that significant resistance to units composed of multiple ethno-sectarian groups produced relatively homogenous units (al-Marashi & Salama 2008: 49). This improved unit security as it protected against so-called "insider attacks" but it did little to remove the perception of Shia dominance and Kurdish irredentism. In fact, many Kurdish units seconded to the Iraqi Army flew the Kurdish flag and wore patches denoting their militia affiliation.

Deployment

Deployment patterns reflecting new state security maps became evident as Shia government security operations and Sunni resistance spiraled out of control (Dawisha 2009). In one such operation, Ministry of Interior troops, including many Badr Corps members, surrounded the Sunni Adhamiyah neighborhood in Baghdad in an attempt to push residences west across the river and away from the predominately Shia east. This type of operation became common as operations were undertaken to "passify" Sunni resistance in neighborhoods in Baghdad and the "Sunni Triangle," the area between the cities of Baghdad, Ramadi, and Tikrit. Sunni recruits in units deployed to these areas often refused to participate in operations adding to the Shia dominated government's biased suspicion of them as unreliable (Gaub 2014). Meanwhile, powerful Kurdish political party leaders refused to allow Arab units to deploy in Kurdish dominated areas and allowed minimal deployments of Peshmerga units outside these same areas with the notable exception of the prestigious posting of guards outside the Iraqi Parliament.

Civil-Military Relations

Civil-military relations following the signing of the 2005 constitution largely came to reflect the new balance of power within the government. While the Security Forces nominally served the state and all of the Iraqi people, their use as an arm of Shia maximalist polices began to make Sunnis feel as if there were again under occupation from their fellow countrymen. For example, in 2011 Prime Minster Nouri al-Maliki signed an arrest warrant for Sunni Vice-President Tariq al-Hashemi for membership in a terrorist organization. al-Hashemi fled to the Kurdish region where the Kurdish Regional President Masoud al-Barzani granted him asylum. The security forces were tasked with tracking down al-Hashemi and when they couldn't arrest him they arrested a number of his bodyguards and family members, and tried them all, including al-Hashemi who they tried in absentia. The politicization of the Security Forces and their use against officials colored the line between civilian political battles and the Security Forces as a state institution. Despite these challenges, the reconstituted security forces were seen in a mostly positive light by a majority of Iraqi citizens with 73% having a favourable opinion of the army in 2009 (The International Republican Institute 2009).

Conclusion

Socially constructed identities – be they national, ethnic, or religious – have profound effects on inter-group power dynamics in fragmented societies. The politicization of these differences and their exploitation by elites serve both individual and group objectives. Elites seek to amass and guard their power both in relation to other sectarian groups and against ingroup challengers. Sectarian narratives are used to produce in-group cohesion and reinforce elite dominance. Lijphart's "cartel of elites" is an apt description of this phenomenon. Elites from different sects appear to have more in common with each other than with their sectarian brethren. Their manipulation of sectarian narratives not only aids them in maintaining in-group power but also aids other sectarian elites who use them as foils for counter-narratives. Sectarian counter-narratives constructed with discrimination and victimhood as inputs are the direct by-products of state security maps. Observations of the implementation of state security maps illuminates the dichotomy between national security and state security in such fragmented societies. Any post-civil war power-sharing agreement must strive to make reconstituted Armed Forces a national institution. Such an agreement must reflect an inter-elite consensus on state security priorities.

Armed forces that represent an inclusive interpretation of the nation, not a narrow interpretation of sectarian security, will not employ state security maps that view other sects as potential challengers. In doing so alternative interpretations of security can take hold. Herein lies both the promise of peace and the potential threat of indecision. The power-sharing agreement reached at Ta'if produced a durable peace. However, the critiques of consociationalism suggest that its constraints on decision-making produce never ending negotiations over issues that participants can find no compromise on. The Lebanese armed forces face similar difficulties. During times of peace, it functions as a symbol of national unity and pride but if Lebanon was ever to face war the armed forces' ability to protect the nation and not succumb to the sectarian cleavages highlighted above are doubtful. Elites maintain their monopoly on intra-sect power and the cartel of elites continues to negotiate every minutia of governance. Yet, this imperfect system is preferable to continued civil war. The politicization of identity in Iraq is the result of two interrelated processes. The first is the brutal dictatorship of Saddam Hussein that turned identity into a means to control large numbers of people through fear. Non-Sunnis were made to feel as outsiders in their own country and special coup-proofing units kidnapped, tortured, and killed all resisters. State security maps caste wide nets of suspicion over all communities, Shia, Kurdish, and Sunni alike. The second process was the power grab made by Shia and Kurdish sectarian elites following the downfall of the regime. These elites used their own state security maps to sanction Sunni populations while providing increasing security for target populations, namely in the Shia south and Kurdish north. This created a backlash among Sunnis, especially elites in the previous regime, who saw their collective access to resources and security quickly erode. Both processes produced fear in competing communities forcing successive cycles of violence.

Interestingly, the rise of Sunni resistance organizations, Kurdish regional militias, and Shia extra-governmental militias provides an interesting avenue for further research. If state militaries use security maps in order to identify ethnic and sectarian groups that are considered political reliable while also categorizing other groups as politically unreliable, then resistance organizations and militias perform similar analyses. Future research using this same theoretical paradigm and methodology could examine how and in what ways non-state actors use security maps to categorize ethnic and sectarian groups that fall into their area of operations. This could provide insights both in the cases of Lebanon and Iraq, where militias work with the security forces, but also in states where militias exist completely separate from state institutions and are the largest organizers of violence. The elastic boundaries of identity and the hard boundaries of security provide an interesting framework for analyzing inter-group dynamics in fragmented societies. National, ethnic, and sectarian identities provide rallying points for threatened and dominant communities alike. Security institutions are just one unit of analysis for measuring these dynamics but they exhibit the hard truth of the struggle between different identity groups inhabiting a single political unit.

Bibliography

al-Ali, Ziad. *The Struggle for Iraq's Future: How Corruption, Incompetence, and Sectarianism Have Undermined Democracy*. New Haven: Yale University Press, 2014.

al-Marashi, Ibrahim and Sammy Salama. *Iraq's Armed Forces: An Analytical History*. London: Routledge, 2008.

Anderson, Benedict. *Imagined Communities*. New York: Verso, 1991.

Baram, Amatzia. "Saddam Husayn, the Ba'ath Regime, and the Iraqi Officer Corps," in *Armed Forces in the Middle East: Politics and Strategy*, edited by Barry Rubin and Thomas A. Keaney, 206–230. London: Frank Cass, 2002.

Barak, Oren. *The Lebanese Army: A National Institution in a Divided Society*. Albany: State University of New York Press, 2009.

Barak, Oren. "Towards a Representative Military? The Transformation of the Lebanese Officer Corps Since 1945."*Middle East Journal* 60, no. 1 (Winter 2006): 75–93.

Barany, Zoltan. "Building National Armies after Civil War: Lessons from Bosnia, El Salvador, and Lebanon." *Political Science Quarterly* 129, no. 2 (2014): 211–238.

Beydoun, Ahmad. "A Note on Confessionalism," In *Lebanon in Limbo: Post-war Society and Statein anUncertain Regional Environment*, edited by Theodor Hanf and Nawaf Salam, 75–86. Baden-Baden: Nomos Verlagsgesellschaft, 2003.

Brooks, Risa. *Political-Military Relations and the Stability of Arab Regimes*. New York: Oxford University Press, 1998.

Collier, Paul and Anke Hoeffler. "Greed and Grievance in Civil War." *Oxford Economic Papers* 56 , no. 4 (2004): 563–595.

Cronin, Stephanie. *Armies and State-building in the Modern Middle East*. London: I.B. Tauris, 2014.

Danforth, Loring M. *The Macedonian Conflict: Ethnic Nationalism in a Transnational World*. Princeton: Princeton University Press, 1995.

Dawisha, Adeed. *Iraq: A Political History From Independence to Occupation*. Princeton: Princeton University Press, 2009.

Enloe, Cynthia H. *Ethnic Soldiers: State Security in Divided Societies*. Athens: University of Georgia Press, 1980a.

Enloe, Cynthia H. *Policy, Military, and Ethnicity: Foundations of State Power*. New Brunswick: Transaction Books, 1980b.

Eppel, Michael. "The Elite, the Effendiyya, and the Growth of Nationalism and Pan-Arabism in Hashemite Iraq, 1921–1958," *International Journal of Middle East Studies* 30, no. 2 (May, 1998): 227–250.

Fearon, James D., and David D. Laitin. "Ethnicity, Insurgency, and Civil War," *American Political Science Review* 97, no. 1 (February 2003): 75–90.

Gaub, Florence. "Arab Armies: Agents of Change?" Chaillot Paper no. 131, European Union Institute for Security Studies, March 2014.
Gellner, Ernest. *Nations and Nationalism*. Ithaca: Cornell University Press, 1983.
Haddad, Fanar. *Sectarianism in Iraq: Antagonistic Visions of Unity*. London: C. Hurst & Co., 2011.
Hechter, Michael. *Internal Colonialism: The Celtic Fringe in British National Development*. Berkley: University of California Press, 1975.
International Republican Institute Survey of Iraqi Public Opinion. The International Republican Institute, 2009. https://www.iri.org/wp-content/uploads/2010/08/201020August203020 Survey20of20Iraqi20Public20Opinion20November2023-December203120200928129.pdf.
International Crisis Group Report2003: 13.
Jaber, Faleh A. and Hosham Dawod. *Tribes and Power: Nationalism and Ethnicity in theMiddle East*. London: Saqi Books, 2003.
Janowitz, Morris. *Military Institutions and Coercion in the Developing Nations*. Chicago: University of Chicago Press, 1977.
Kalyvas, Stathis N. "New and Old Civil Wars: A Valid Distinction?" *World Politics* 54, no. 1 (October 2001): 99–118.
Knudsen, Are J. "Lebanese Armed Forces: A United Army for a Divided Country." *Insight* no. 9, Chr. Michelson Institute, November 2014.
Lijphart, Arendt. "Consociational Democracy," *World Politics* 21, no. 2 (January 1969): 207–225.
Marashi, Afshin. *Nationalizing Iran: Culture, Power, & the State, 1870–1940*. Seattle: University of Washington Press, 2008.
Mueller, John. "The Banality of Ethnic War," *International Security* 25, no. 1 (Summer 2000): 42–70.
Nerguizian, Aram. "Between Sectarianism and Military Development: The Paradox of the Lebanese Armed Forces," in *The Politics of Sectarianism in Postwar Lebanon*, edited by Bassel F. Salloukh, Rabie Barakat, Jinan S. al-Habbal, Lara W. Kattab, and Shoghig Mikaelian, 108–135. Northampton: Pluto Press, 2015.
Peled, Alon. *A Question of Loyalty: Military Manpower Policy in Multiethnic States*. Ithaca: Cornell University Press, 1998.
Rayburn, Joel. *Iraq After America: Strongmen, Sectarians, Resistance*. Stanford: Hoover Institution Press, 2014.
Shelef, Nadav. *Evolving Nationalism: Homeland, Identity, and Religion in Israel, 1925–2005*. Ithaca: Cornell University Press, 2010.
Sisk, Timothy D. "Power-Sharing in Civil War: Puzzles of Peacemaking and Peacebuilding," *Civil Wars* 15, no. 1 (2013): 7–20.
Talmadge, Caitlin. *The Dictator's Army: Battlefield Effectiveness in Authoritarian Regimes*. Ithaca: Cornell University Press, 2015.
Ucko, David. "Militias, Tribes, and Insurgents: The Challenge of Political Reintegration in Iraq," *Conflict, Security & Development* 8, no. 3 (October 2008): 341–372.
Woods, Kevin M., Williamson Murray, Elizabeth A. Nathan, Laila Sabara, and Ana M. Venagas. "Saddam's Generals: Perspectives of the Iran-Iraq War." Institute for Defense Analyses, 2011.

7
ACCIDENTALLY ACCELERATING SECTARIANISM[1]

Elections and the U.S. Role in the Iraqi Civil War

Frank Sobchak

Introduction

The conventional wisdom that explains Iraq's descent into sectarian conflict follows a narrative that the U.S. invasion removed barriers to intercommunal violence held in check by the authoritarian government of Saddam Hussein, leaving behind sectarian tinder waiting to catch fire. When Al-Qaeda in Iraq extremists blew up the Shia religious shrine in Samarra in 2006, those pent-up sectarian tensions quickly ignited into a broad civil war. But such a narrative is too simplistic and ignores the actions that the U.S. took as an occupying force in the nearly three years between the invasion and the onset of civil war.

As early as the first few months into the occupation, U.S. commanders and political officials began making decisions that affected the distribution of political power in post-occupation Iraq. Those decisions, principally about the conduct of the first democratically held elections in the country's history, exacerbated tensions between Iraq's different ethnic and sectarian groups. By providing new grounds for competition without sufficient time for reconciliation, the elections unwittingly accelerated sectarian violence that grew into civil war. While the role of other actors in Iraq's downward spiral should not be minimized, there is much to be learned from American decisions about Iraq's elections and their part in the country's sectarian nightmare.

Initial Electoral Decisions

American planners originally envisioned being able to hand over a functional Iraqi state to either expatriate or domestic leaders, and as a result little planning had been put towards post-regime change elections. But as it became clear that neither contingency would transpire in the months after the fall of Saddam Hussein, the holding of elections and writing of a new Iraqi constitution became critical topics

DOI: 10.4324/9781003329510-8

of debate for senior U.S. officials. Indeed, American military doctrine considered holding elections a critical component of establishing long-term stability. Initially, senior U.S. leaders preferred that caucuses, with members selected by coalition authorities, choose the Iraqi representatives who would write a new constitution. But those plans immediately came into conflict with the desires of Iraqis who pressed for more agency in the process and a more rapid return of sovereignty. Less than three months after coalition forces invaded in March 2003, Iraq's senior Shia cleric, Grand Ayatollah Ali Sistani, issued a fatwa, or religious decree, requiring that the new constitution be written by a group that was directly elected by Iraqis. Other Iraqi leaders joined the chorus resisting coalition plans, and SCIRI (The Supreme Council for the Islamic Revolution in Iraq) leader Abdul Aziz al-Hakim requested that the UN intercede and mediate a solution. Veteran UN diplomat Lakhdar Brahimi was dispatched to Iraq and in short order formulated a compromise under which an Iraqi Interim Government would serve until nationwide elections in January 2005 for an Iraqi Parliament that would form a transitional government. That transitional government would then draft a constitution, thereby meeting Sistani's demands, albeit at a slower pace.

U.S. officials decided that the January 2005 election would be a nationwide competition of national parties for a proportional electoral share, rather than individual politicians vying for regional positions responsible to a local electorate. This decision had far-reaching consequences because the proportional system favored larger, better-funded parties such as those receiving significant assistance from Iran, and it would amplify the impact of an election boycott by religious or ethnic groups (Diamond 2005). The election format reflected the end of an intense debate amongst U.S. senior leaders. Many military leaders had hoped democratic processes could be constructed slowly and at the grassroots level, with local and regional elections before moving on to a national ballot. Indeed, one early draft plan did not schedule the first national elections until after six years of building democratic structures from the bottom up. But intense pressure from Iraqi Shia leaders and the international community insisting that the U.S. fulfill its promises of bringing democracy to Iraq, meant that long delays were not viable. The impending U.S. national election scheduled for November 2004, and the George W. Bush administration's desire to show progress in Iraq, provided further impetus for an accelerated electoral timetable.

Warnings Unheeded

As the January 2005 election approached, various Sunni politicians, including Iraqi Interim President Ghazi al-Yawar, pleaded with coalition officials to postpone the election. If Sunni Arabs boycotted, they would have little say in the composition of the new Iraqi constitution, a dangerous result with potentially permanent consequences. "This election has a unique role of drafting a constitution," Yawar told reporters. "How can you draft a constitution unless all ethnicities, sects, religions, and political ideologies are included?" (McCarthy 2005). Interim Prime Minister

Ayad Allawi, a secular Shia, added his voice to the calls for a delay. Allawi was particularly worried that the brutal battle of Fallujah, which had concluded a mere six weeks before the elections, would deter Sunnis from voting (Rayburn et al. 2019; Allawi 2007). Further complicating the personal choices of many Sunnis, the extremist group Al-Qaeda in Iraq declared that anyone found voting would be summarily put to death. Despite the dangers and entreaties of Sunni leaders, coalition officials decided to hold the elections as scheduled. In a joint letter to Allawi on November 29, the U.S. senior diplomatic and military leaders in Iraq emphasized that "a decision to delay the election will unavoidably be understood by everyone as military success for the insurgency and a counterbalance to the success of the battle for Fallujah."[2]

The Vote and the Boycott

Several assessments from the intelligence community had projected that the elections would not even transpire due to insurgent threats, Sunni boycotts, and logistical challenges.[3] But despite 108 attacks on election day against polling stations, approximately 8.5 million Iraqis voted, a 58% turnout: a statistic in line with U.S. historical averages (Katzman 2005).[4] The United Iraqi Alliance (UIA), a Shia Islamist conglomerate that had the support of Grand Ayatollah Sistani, had clearly won, with 140 seats and 58% of the popular vote, but as Allawi, Interim President Ghazi al-Yawar, and other Sunni leaders had expected, millions of Sunni Arabs boycotted the election (Katzman 2006).

The U.S. strategy of clearing out insurgent strongholds allowed the elections to take place, but it failed to create an environment that encouraged Sunnis to vote. In Ninawa, only 17% of the population voted, most of whom were Kurdish (Mozaffar 2006). Across all of Sunni-majority Anbar, only 16,682 Iraqis voted, about 2% of registered voters (Estes 2009). Sunnis did not vote for a variety of reasons. Many were intimidated by insurgent threats or the potential for danger at polling sites. Still others were swayed by calls for a boycott from tribal leaders who feared elections would upend their traditional standing and influence.[5] Some, believing wild conspiracy theories, chose not to participate because they thought Sunnis were a majority of the population and would still win without their individual ballots.

To Sunni leaders the impact of the election debacle was clear. The boycott guaranteed the election spoils would go to Shia Islamist and Kurdish nationalist parties who aimed to ensure Sunnis would never again be a threat to their interests. Of 275 seats in the transitional national assembly that would write the constitution, Sunni Arabs earned only 16 seats, a striking underrepresentation.[6] Estimated to be 20% of Iraq's population, Sunni Arabs instead would hold just 5% of the seats in the legislature. The combined seats of Turkomans and Christians equaled the Sunni representation, even though both groups together made up less than 5% of Iraq's population. For many Sunnis, instead of a unifying moment of pride for the Iraqi nation, the election prepared the ground for future sectarian conflict and became an excuse to continue fighting. For Shia extremists, the election served as a vehicle to capture the machinery of government and implement their sectarian agendas.

Most American officials overlooked those problems and instead exuded nearly unbridled optimism – that the elections had, "locked in irreversible momentum" that gave the Iraqis "an alternative to the insurgency" (Batiste & Daniels 2005). Some military officers commented that the successful election reminded them of the joy felt by an earlier generation during the World War II liberation of Europe, with one observing it was, "the single most professionally inspirational day of my life."[7] But just four days after the elections, the U.S. Ambassador to Iraq John Negroponte gave General George W. Casey, the military commander, a September 1967 clipping from *The New York Times*. In the congratulatory atmosphere, the article was a warning. "U.S. Encouraged by Vietnam Vote," the *Times* headline read. "Officials cite 83 percent turnout despite Vietcong terror. United States officials were surprised and heartened today at the size of turnout in South Vietnam's presidential election despite a Vietcong terrorist campaign to disrupt the voting" (Grose 1967). While history had not repeated itself, it had echoed.

The Ja'afari Government and the Mada'in Omen

On April 7, 2005, Da'wa Party leader and member of the UIA electoral block Ibrahim al-Ja'afari was named as Prime Minister designate. Ja'afari's appointment marked the end of the Iraqi Interim Government and the beginning of the Iraqi Transitional Government, which principally existed to draft a national constitution. For the first time in its modern history, Iraq was about to come under Shia political control, an opportunity that Iraq's Shia leaders did not intend to squander. The period of Ja'afari's government formation in 2004 was ominous and fraught with sectarian tension. On April 16, clouded reporting indicated that Sunni militants had taken as many as 150 Shia hostages in the mixed-sect town of Mada'in, 16 kilometers south of Baghdad, threatening to execute them if the remaining Shia did not flee immediately. Iraqi politicians reacted to the murky information by forming sectarian blocks and issuing statements that enflamed tensions. National Security Minister Qasem Daoud, a Shia politician close to Grand Ayatollah Ali Sistani, bombastically argued that the incident was "an attempt to drag this country into civil war," while other parliamentarians described it as "a kind of ethnic purge" (Worth 2005).

Three battalions of the Iraqi Army were ordered to retake the town and prepared for intense Fallujah-type house-to-house combat. As Iraqi troops entered the town, they found no insurgents or hostages and many townspeople were surprised by the drama, reporting that there had been no sectarian violence at all. After the incident, Sunni and Shia politicians created alternate realities of what had happened. Sunnis claimed it had been a conspiracy created as a pretext for "striking the Sunni areas around Baghdad as a preface to sparking riots and fights between the two sects" (Worth 2005; Mizbana 2005; Salman & McDonnell 2005). Shia politicians claimed the event had transpired as reported, but that hostages had been killed and dumped in the Tigris to conceal the massacre. Events in Mada'in and how both sides interpreted them illustrated that tensions in Iraq had become acute, where a solitary instance of sectarianism, or even a rumor of one, was enough to create a national-level crisis and talk of civil war. After the incident, rather than defusing tensions by ordering a joint investigation to reveal what actually happened, Sunni and Shia politicians created opposing narratives of what occurred, complete with their own "facts" that they exploited for personal and political gain.

Such difficult times begged for a leader of the stature of Nelson Mandela or Martin Luther King, Jr., one with strength of will to renounce calls for violence and vengeance in favor of negotiation and reconciliation. Instead, Ibrahim al-Ja'afari was chosen to lead a wounded and smoldering Iraq. When he formed his government in April 2005, Shia leaders controlled the most powerful ministries in an imbalanced distribution that reflected election results and the Sunni boycott but not demographics. Shia ministers controlled 16 agencies, Kurds 8, Sunnis 6, Christians 2, and Turkmen 1. Some of those ministers would soon use their electoral victory to implement a campaign of sectarian violence. The unintended results of American decisions about Iraq's elections and the Sunni boycott were beginning to come to fruition.

Bayan Jabr and the Interior Ministry

The most dangerous sectarian posting was Bayan Jabr, a SCIRI politician with ties to the notorious Badr Corps militia, as the interior minister. In short order, Jabr purged national police forces of 300 Sunni officers, labeling them "criminals," and exchanging them with Shia candidates, mostly members of the Badr Corps. Jabr also hired 15,000 new recruits, the majority of whom were Shia, as a way to further dilute Sunni influence (Moss 2006).[8] As the organization's demographics shifted, becoming majority Shia, Jabr's police began a campaign of extrajudicial violence and intimidation in Sunni neighborhoods under the guise of pursuing insurgents and terrorists. As the sectarian takeover of interior ministry forces progressed, reports became more common from Sunni neighborhoods that "gunmen in police uniforms routinely abducted people from their homes, cars, and – in one particularly flagrant case – hospital beds" (Perito 2011).

The Rise of Sectarian Violence

Partially as a response to the formation of the Ja'afari government and violence from Jabr's ministry, sectarian elements crept into Baghdad's mixed sect neighborhoods seeking to defend their confessionals and cleanse them of rivals. The Sunni extremist group Al-Qaeda in Iraq (AQI) aimed to intimidate Shia living in Baghdad and overthrow the first Shia Iraqi government in the nation's modern history. To highlight this objective, AQI's leader, Abu Musab Zarqawi, named the units responsible for those objectives the Umar Brigades in July 2005. They were so named to recall the success of the second caliph, Umar, a Sunni who had conquered Persia and spread Islam through South Asia. Virulently sectarian, they targeted Badr Corps leaders and Shia civilians in Baghdad and other provinces, successfully assassinating Badr commanders Kharry al-Amri and Adel Khosk Khabar. The brigades were extremely effective in employing social media and other techniques to stoke Sunni fears and paint Zarqawi as the defender of Iraq's Sunni population, which, given the excesses of Jabr's Interior Ministry, were not difficult tasks.[9]

Shia militias such as Jaysh al-Mahdi (JAM) and Badr responded to AQI's violence with their own attacks and began a campaign to ethnically "cleanse" mixed neighborhoods in Baghdad of Sunnis. Often, these sectarian elements first threatened civilians to pressure them to move. If that failed, they quickly shifted to violence. One resident of the primarily Sunni neighborhood of Ameriyah described how the initial phases of the conflict began:

> In 2005, we began to see how insurgents, Al-Qaeda, were taking root in the gangs roaming Ameriya. The first sign that Al-Qaeda was moving into our area was the graffiti... Then one of the mosques in the area known for its sectarian leanings became a gathering point for those of the Al-Qaeda mindset. That was when this new ideology began emerging in the neighborhood. People started saying that Shi'ites were infidels. Many of my Shi'ite neighbors fled then.
> (Kukis 2011)

Shia militias used strikingly similar tactics in other mixed neighborhoods of Baghdad and north Babil. Saman Dlawer Hussein, a Sunni who lived between the Baghdad neighborhoods of Mansour and Washash, described how the Jaysh al-Mahdi militia moved in:

> Everything started to change for the worse ... around the beginning of 2005... The troubles started with three suicide car bombs in Washash ... then we started to hear stories about how the Mahdi Army was forcing Sunni families to leave Washash. There was no killing during this time that we knew of, no murdering of Sunni families. Sunnis were being made to leave Washash under threat, but widespread murders were not happening yet... As the neighborhoods around Baghdad split along sectarian lines, it became difficult to move around the city because of the checkpoints set up by insurgents and militias... A lot of my classmates began dying in their neighborhoods.
> (Kukis 2011)

As Iraq's civil war simmered, the duly elected government representatives responsible for keeping the peace and preventing sectarian strife, Bayan Jabr's Ministry of the Interior, responded aggressively to Sunni attacks but generally ignored Shia sponsored violence.

Al-Qaeda in Iraq's Car-Bomb Offensive

To this intensely toxic sectarian environment, AQI added a massive car bomb campaign that targeted Shia political officials and civilians in Baghdad. Determined to incite civil war, Zarqawi employed tactics significantly different from the more secular Sunni resistance organizations in the degree of nihilistic violence, which aimed to murder as many innocents as possible. As Zarqawi and Al-Qaeda in Iraq became the dominant force in the Sunni resistance, the focus shifted from expelling the "occupying forces," to killing fellow Iraqis, specifically Shia. Zarqawi viewed the Shia as apostates and believed that starting an apocalyptic sectarian civil war in Iraq and beyond was the most effective way to bring the Sunni-Shia conflict to fruition. Years later, while being held as coalition prisoners, some of AQI's senior leaders described Zarqawi's desire to incite a global sectarian conflict by comparing him to the Joker, Heath Ledger's character in the 2008 movie, "The Dark Knight," whose central desire was "to watch the world burn."[10] The spike in sectarian attacks in Baghdad during the period surrounding Ja'afari's swearing-in was stunning. During a 13-day period from the end of April until May 11, 2005, AQI carried out 79 car-bombings against Shia targets. On the last day, the capital endured nine such attacks that killed 112 (Rayburn et al. 2019). An astounding 142 attacks were carried out by the end of May, the highest monthly total for 2005. Bombings and sectarian violence were unrelenting the next month as well, resulting in the deaths of 1,347 Iraqi civilians, the most since April 2003 when the country was in the throes of the coalition invasion.[11] While AQI and other Sunni groups launched car bomb and kidnapping raids into Shia neighborhoods, Jaysh al-Mahdi and other Shia militias carried out campaigns of intimidation, violence, and sectarian cleansing against Sunnis. In parallel, many Iraq police units had abandoned the sense of false neutrality and began a long campaign of extrajudicial arrests, torture, and execution of Sunnis. By midsummer, sectarian brutality had skyrocketed, with the Baghdad morgue receiving 1,100 bodies in July. Nearly all the victims showed evidence of torture or execution, such as cigarette burns, hands tied and bullet in the head, or wounds from power tools (Buncombe & Cockburn 2006).[12]

The Light at the End of the Tunnel? Or a Freight Train?

As the coalition approached the fall 2005 election period, which included the October constitutional referendum and the December parliamentary election, many senior American leaders hoped that they were finally on the cusp of reaping the benefits of their work towards establishing a democratic state. General George W. Casey, Jr., and other military officers believed that the twin elections would tamp down the insurgency and put Iraq on a new, positive trajectory. Military and civilian leaders alike assumed that democracy would usher in a time of reconciliation and provide an alternative to violence. Successful elections, they hoped, might even put an end to the violent resistance that had materialized almost as soon as the regime of Saddam Hussein had fallen. In reality Iraq's situation was dangerously fragile. Even if the elections went smoothly, many serious challenges remained. Al-Qaeda in Iraq's ruthless campaign against the Shia was accelerating. Sectarian tensions festered across the country, ready to ignite from the smallest provocation. Death squads from all confessionals, some wearing the uniforms of the Iraqi state, stalked the streets in a quiet campaign of ethnic cleansing. Faced with all these perils, Iraq was on the brink of civil war, not reconciliation, and elections held in such an environment would serve as the spark, not the damper.

The Iraqi Constitutional Referendum

One of the most significant consequences of the Sunni boycott of the January 2005 election was that Sunni leaders were effectively frozen out of the drafting of the Iraqi constitution. In May 2005, the Iraqi National Assembly nominated a constitutional committee that included only two Sunni Arabs out of 55 total members. Fearful of the dangers inherent in a constitution written by Kurdish and Shia Islamist parties, nearly 1,000 Sunni Arab notables demanded they be given more representation (Allawi 2007). American officials, cognizant of risks of another Sunni rejection of the political process, pressed Shia and Kurdish leaders to include more Sunni Arabs. By early July, U.S. Ambassador to Iraq Zalmay Khalilzad had persuaded Iraqi leaders to increase Sunni representation by 15 voting members and another 13 as nonvoting experts, but the change made little practical difference.[13] Later that month, two of the new Sunni members were assassinated, underscoring the message that their participation was not wanted.

As the committees began their work, other Sunni members received similar signals. "When the Sunni walked in, the Shia said, 'you sit over there. You are only here because the Americans made us let you come'" (Wright & Reese 2008) General Casey recollected in 2008. American officials pushed for the inclusion of Sunni Arab views but had little success in incorporating them into the final document. Perhaps more importantly, the Kurdish parties and the Supreme Council for the Islamic Revolution in Iraq (SCIRI) included language making Iraq a federal state whose provinces could vote to form autonomous regions. Those regions were also permitted to form their own regional governments, create internal security forces, and manage revenues from new energy discoveries. Sunni Arabs bitterly opposed these articles but had little power to resist them. On August 28, the Iraqi Government approved the draft constitution without consensus from the drafting committee.

On October 15, the day of the constitutional referendum, insurgents carried out only 88 attacks nationwide, down considerably from the 299 attacks during the January 2005 election. Attacks against polling sites also dropped, from 89 in January to 19 in October, as did the total number of casualties, from 213 to 49 (Katzman 2006). Unlike the previous election, several insurgent groups actively encouraged voting, as did Sunni political leaders. Turnout increased dramatically, jumping to 66%, as nearly the entire Sunni community hoped to reject the draft constitution and its federal articles. The final vote included a near-universal rejection of the constitution in the Sunni-majority provinces: in Anbar, 97% of voters opposed the constitution; and in Salahadin and Ninawa, the "no" votes were 82% and 55%, respectively. In the ethnically mixed Diyala Province, where Sunnis were a plurality, 49% of the population voted against the constitution. Despite the strong opposition in these provinces, Iraqi voters approved the constitution by a nation-wide majority of 78.6% (Katzman 2006). Sunni opposition fell barely short of the requirement that two-thirds of the voters in three provinces had to reject the draft constitution to block its acceptance. Thus, the constitution drafted primarily by Shia and Kurdish political parties became Iraq's new governing document.

The increase in nationwide and regional participation hid a darker reality. While many Sunnis had decided to join the democratic process, they were doing so to vehemently reject the political changes advanced by that process. Nearly all Sunnis who cast ballots were voting against a constitution they believed would destroy Iraq as they knew it and permanently marginalize them in society. Their participation in the political process was not an indicator of future stability, since they generally stressed Sunni identity politics, opposed federalism, and demanded the reinstating of old Iraqi Army ranks and positions – positions that the major Shia and Kurdish parties violently opposed. Ultimately, the identity-driven election only served to increase the animosity between Iraq's ethno-sectarian groups. In retrospect, the senior American commander in Iraq, General Casey, concluded that the constitutional referendum

> was not a national compact ... 70 percent of the Sunni went out and voted against it. You had this document that was written by Iraqis, but it was not a national compact of the whole of the country together. In fact, it was probably more divisive.
>
> *(Wright & Reese 2008)*

At the time, however, coalition leaders misread the adoption of the constitution, heralding the increased participation as a turning point. One week after the voting concluded, the U.S. headquarters' campaign assessment proclaimed, "Bottom Line: The successful referendum period was a strategic victory for the political process in Iraq and dealt a considerable blow to the enemy providing us with a unique opportunity to exploit success."[14] With what they viewed as a successful referendum behind them, many American officials breathed a sigh of relief as they prepared for what they thought would be the biggest danger related to the December election-insurgent attacks on polling sites.

Electoral Spoils: Shia Sectarians Commandeering the "Monopoly on Violence"

As coalition leaders planned their defenses for December's parliamentary election, Al-Qaeda in Iraq continued its relentless car-bomb campaign against Shia targets. While the effectiveness of those attacks dropped after early summer 2005, they continued to produce a steady drip of casualties that provoked Shia calls for reprisals. On September 14, Zarqawi's militants struck Baghdad with 12 car bombs, killing 167 and wounding nearly 600. Two days later, they hit Shia worshippers at a shrine in Tuz Khormato, 209 kilometers north of Baghdad, killing a dozen and wounding 23. In one gruesome incident south of Baghdad on September 26,

Sunni extremists masquerading as Iraqi police entered a school and executed 5 Shia teachers and their driver while their students looked on. Near-simultaneous car bombs struck Balad on September 29, resulting in 95 casualties. Large-scale attacks against predominantly Shia neighborhoods on November 18–19 resulted in another 324 civilian casualties (Rayburn et al. 2019).[15]

As AQI did its murderous work, a group of government ministries dominated by Shia militants began to withhold basic services such as water, power, and medical care in many Sunni areas, forcing Sunnis to trek into more dangerous neighborhoods. Along the routes into these neighborhoods stood checkpoints, which had become treacherous places where Sunnis were often intimidated or abducted by militia-allied police or even from militants in government uniforms. Caught between opposing sectarian elements, many civilians found themselves facing a terrible choice between accepting protection from the militia representing their confessional or succumbing to sectarian cleansing, as Jaysh al-Mahdi (JAM), Badr Corps, and Al-Qaeda in Iraq each took control of various neighborhoods in Baghdad. In some areas, JAM imitated Lebanese Hizballah's model of increasing popular legitimacy by providing public services. The militia gave cash to civilians affected by the fighting in Baghdad and provided housing, usually in abandoned Sunni homes, to Shia refugees displaced by the communal violence (Kukis 2011).

The situation became so dire that in October, Iraq's Sunni deputy Prime Minister and 9 other Sunni ministers wrote Prime Minister Ibrahim al-Ja'afari demanding action against Shia militants. The six-page letter documented alleged abuses of Sunnis by security forces associated with the Ministry of the Interior, including systemic torture, underground detention facilities, executions, and abductions. The ministers asserted that the perpetrators often used Interior Ministry uniforms and vehicles, and some even boldly acknowledged they were from the Interior Ministry's public order and special commando units. Many victims were tortured, with eyes poked out, noses cut off, or hands drilled, and many bodies were found bound or handcuffed. "Our people are being executed under the official or semi-official cover of the law," the Sunni ministers wrote, noting that

> these acts have transferred Iraqis from living under the fear of terrorism to living under governmental terror. It is unsafe for an Iraqi to be detained. Most [Iraqis] have come to think it better to resist and die in his home rather than having his head pierced or body burned, or parts cut off and his body thrown on the road to be eaten by the hungry animals.[16]

The Ja'afari government made little effort to probe the ministers' accusations. But on November 13, 2005, irrefutable evidence surfaced that seemed to confirm the Sunni allegations when U.S. soldiers searched a central Baghdad facility known as the Jadriyah bunker, run by the Interior Ministry's Special Interrogations Unit. After hearing stories about the facility, American officials arrived unannounced and demanded access to an area that Iraqi guides purposely avoided. Behind a locked door, they discovered 169 malnourished prisoners, 166 of them Sunnis, all showing evidence of torture. The secret bunker and the organization that ran it were not officially sanctioned, likely because they were under the supervision of senior Badr Corps officer Bashir Nasser al-Wandi, known colloquially as Engineer Ahmed, whom Interior Minister Bayan Jabr had appointed as deputy director of the ministry's intelligence directorate. When U.S. Ambassador Zalmay Khalilzad quizzed Interior Minister Jabr about what had transpired, Jabr told him that the detainees were terrorists and downplayed the abuse, claiming that the prisoners "weren't beheaded; they weren't killed; there was no torture."[17] As infamous as the Jadriyah bunker became, it was a mere fraction of the sectarian infiltration of the Interior Ministry and other government security offices in 2005. The U.S. military headquarters in Iraq estimated that the Iraqi government security ministries ran at least eight to ten more unauthorized facilities that held between 2,000 and 10,000 prisoners.

Shia sectarian infiltration of the interior ministry had become so severe and overt that worried American officials delivered stark warnings to senior leaders in the Pentagon. On September 19, 2005, James Steele, who had served as a civilian adviser to the Interior Ministry police forces in 2004 and was a trusted confidant of Secretary of Defense Donald Rumsfeld, wrote the secretary to alert him about what he observed during his time in Iraq. "There is a systematic effort by SCIRI and its Badr militia to take control of the high-end units within MOI (Ministry of the Interior)," Steele reported, adding that

> this effort ranges from assigning Badr officers to command units to protecting thugs like the commander of the Wolf Brigade who had been involved in death squad activities, extortion of detainees and a general pattern of corruption. Nearly all of the new recruits within the commandos are Shia, many of them are Badr members… [This effort] also contributes to the possibility of a Lebanon-type scenario where a civil war ensues with the Sunnis being driven into the arms of the insurgents as their militia. This would put us in an untenable position.[18]

The Interior Ministry was not the only government entity which faced deep sectarian challenges. Iraq's Health Ministry had also become infiltrated with Shia militiamen who used ambulances to carry out attacks and routinely euthanized Sunni patients. Sectarian fissures also extended to the highest levels of government. In early December 2005, Prime Minister Ja'afari ordered the disbanding of the Iraqi Joint Headquarters and replacement of ten Sunni generals with Shia officers (Rayburn et al. 2019). Among the purged would be three division commanders and the universally respected secular Shia officer Lieutenant General Nasier Abadi, the deputy commander of the Iraqi Joint Forces. Lieutenant General Mohan al-Furayji, whom American General Martin Dempsey described as "a bad piece of work," was selected to replace Abadi.[19] Recognizing the sectarian danger in Ja'afari's changes, the British deputy commander of coalition forces, Lieutenant General John Nicholas Houghton, warned that the overpowering importance of the proposed changes is the political impact they would have in marginalizing the Sunnis at a critical time and in placing the Ministry of Defense at the mercy of an extremist Shia agenda. The political motivation behind the proposed moves is self-evident.[20]

Providing more evidence of motive, Prime Minister Ja'afari had made his decisions without notifying the Sunni Minister of Defense, who, when learning of the orders, begged the coalition to oppose the changes, which they quickly did. Coalition officials were able to block the purge, but Ja'afari's attempted military push added to Sunni leaders' aggrievement and their perceptions of Shia sectarian misconduct being conducted under the guise of government action.

The December Parliamentary Elections

On December 15, 2005, Iraqis went to the polls again to elect their first government under the newly ratified constitution. As with the October referendum, voting occurred with little disruption from insurgents who carried out just 80 attacks that caused only 14 casualties nationwide. The relatively peaceful election day mirrored a two-month drop in violence: from the October 15 referendum to the parliamentary elections, the U.S. headquarters in Iraq estimated that attacks had dropped by 26% and casualties by 29%.[21] Voter turnout had also increased, echoing a trend across the three elections. Participation had grown from 58% in January to 66% in October and to 75% in December. The parliamentary elections on December 15 also seemed to indicate that Sunni involvement matched the statistics of other confessionals. In Anbar, overall voter turnout increased from 2% in January, to 38% in October, to a massive 86% in December. In Ninawa, participation notched up from 16% to 53%, to 70%, and Salahadin's reported turnout grew from 29%, to 90%, to 98% (Katzman 2006; Mozaffar 2006). The increased turnout, however, reflected a darker truth as voters had overwhelmingly cast their votes along sectarian lines, leading one Iraqi analyst to assert that the country had held "not an election, but a census" (Pan 2005).

Conclusion: Elections to Civil War

The October and December elections of 2005 left American leaders with the misguided belief that Iraq was finally on the path towards stability and normalcy. The coalition had satisfied the mandate in UN Security Council Resolution 1546 and was about to witness the formation of Iraq's first democratically elected government, a step that U.S. doctrine going back as far as the 1940 *Marine Small Wars Manual* considered a sign of progress in counterinsurgency campaigns. Many U.S. military leaders believed that the election results proved that Iraqis, especially Sunnis, were choosing the democratic political process over the insurgency, and that a properly supervised representative government could tamp down sectarianism. That the Iraqi security forces were able to ensure voting occurred with a progressively downward cascade in violence each election seemed to indicate that Iraqi forces were ready to take the lead in providing the country's security. Unfortunately, coalition leaders were misled by deceptive and inadequate indicators. The U.S. military's belief that violence had decreased came from statistics that primarily tracked attacks against coalition forces, which was no longer the focus of Al-Qaeda in Iraq and other sectarian groups whose goals had shifted to killing and terrorizing fellow Iraqis. The increase in voter participation across the three elections in 2005 reflected not faith in the democratic process, but sectarian influences competing in what Iraqis viewed as a zero-sum game of survival revolving around the capture of state institutions.

While virtually the entire U.S. government had assumed that elections would solve Iraq's challenges, the country continued its slow march toward civil war, showing in hindsight that U.S. leaders had applied the wrong prescription. Believing that the greatest danger to Iraq's security came from insurgent attacks against the coalition and nascent Iraqi government, U.S. leaders assumed that elections and the democratic process would remove most of the underlying causes for insurgents to continue fighting. But the conflict had already devolved into an intercommunal political struggle that teetered on the edge of civil war. Al-Qaeda in Iraq's car bombs, marauding sectarian militias, and government sponsored extrajudicial violence, among a long list of traumas, had ground down the possibility of goodwill between confessionals. Despite the U.S. faith in elections and belief that voting had improved security and fostered reconciliation, the deep tensions between Iraq's Shia and Sunni communities actually made the elections even more partisan than those in January. In such a scenario, elections were inherently destabilizing events that served as accelerants to civil war.

The haste with which the U.S. led coalition carried out the transformation from authoritarian state to parliamentary democracy – holding two parliamentary elections, drafting a constitution, and carrying out a referendum on that constitution in a single year – greatly exacerbated tensions by increasing the stakes of each event and provided insufficient time for reconciliation. In perfect conditions, such a transition would have been perilous. But Iraq suffered the strains of occupation, insurgency, and sectarianism. Such a pathway was not foretold, as opportunities existed to slow down the electoral timeline and ensure more balanced participation. But because those alternatives were rejected, Iraq progressed from the violent removal of the Sunni led Ba'ath regime to an approved constitution and an elected Shia government in roughly 30 months. By comparison, the fledgling United States – a nation with a longer tradition of participatory government and a robust civil society – spent 12 years navigating the hazards of constitutional development.

In the world outside the hubris of the coalition headquarters, Iraqis considered the 2005 elections not as stabilizing events, but rather as a preamble to civil war. In polls carried out between October and December by the State Department's Office of Research, most Iraqis in the key cities of Mosul, Tikrit, Kirkuk, and Baghdad were concerned about the possibility of civil war. In Mosul, 76% of respondents believed that civil war was looming, and in Baghdad, those anxious about the prospect of civil war had doubled since the same question was asked in March, jumping to 53%.[22] As Iraqis began 2006, they understood that sectarian violence was primed to explode and only needed a spark to plunge them into the abyss. That spark came shortly after midnight on February 22, 2006, when seven members of Al-Qaeda in Iraq entered the important Shia religious shrine at Samarra dressed as Iraqi police officers and set explosives that extensively damaged the mosque and collapsed its famous golden dome. In the days following the bombing, media sources estimated that more than 1,300 Sunnis were killed and over 100 Sunni mosques attacked by Shia militants (Cole 2007). In short order, the bombing revealed the reality that the central government could not protect its citizens, and that the population's basic security needs would become increasingly met through extrajudicial sectarian militias. Iraq's civil war had begun.

Notes

1 This chapter has been adapted from and influenced by my contributions to *The U.S. Army in the Iraq War, Volumes I and II*. As the principal author for the period from December 2003 until January 2007, I documented Iraq's path to civil war and the elections' role in that journey extensively in that work.
2 John Negroponte and General George Casey to Prime Minister Ayad Allawi, November 29, 2004.
3 Frank Sobchak, Interview with General George Casey. *CSA OIF Study Group,* October 1, 2014.
4 "PowerPoint Briefing," MNF-I, NSC SVTC, *MNF-Iraq Update,* January 31, 2005.
5 "Multi-National Force-West," in *Sunni Insurgency Study* (June 13, 2007).
6 "The Shape of the New Iraq, Part I: An Overview of the Transitional National Assembly," PowerPoint Briefing, *Embassy of the United States, Baghdad,* April 15, 2005.
7 Pete Connors, Interview with Brigadier General Mark A. Milley, Commander, 2d Brigade, 10th Mountain Division, *Contemporary Operations Study Team,* March 18, 2008.
8 "Gangs of Iraq: Interview with Bayan Jabr," *Frontline: PBS,* November 21, 2006.
9 "Multi-National Force-West," in *Sunni Insurgency Study* (June 13, 2007).
10 Frank Sobchak, Interview with Daniel Darling, Marine Corps Intelligence Activity Intelligence Officer, *CSA OIF Study Group,* March 18, 2014.
11 "Monthly Civilian Deaths from Violence," *Iraq Body Count,* 2003–2014, https://www.iraqbodycount.org.
12 A full 900 of the 1,100 deaths showed some type of torture or execution.
13 "Year in Review: Fact Sheet," Paper, MNF-I, November 30, 2005.
14 "PowerPoint Briefing," MNF-I, *Effects Assessment Synchronization Board (EASB),* October 22, 2005.
15 "Iraqi Market Struck by Car-bomb," *BBC,* September 30, 2005.
16 Iraqi Ministers and Deputy Prime Minister to Iraqi Prime Minister, October 4, 2005, MNF-I translation, *General George W. Casey, Jr., Archives,* National Defense University. The signatories included the minister of health, the minister of state for national assembly affairs, the minister of women's affairs, the minister of government affairs, the minister of commerce, the minister of culture, the minister of higher education, the minister of industry and minerals, the minister of human rights, and the deputy Prime Minister, Abid Mutlaq Hamood al Jaboori.
17 "Gangs of Iraq," *Frontline: PBS,* April 17, 2007, Video: 54:40. www.pbs.org/wgbh/pages/frontline/gangsofiraq/view/; "Interview with Matthew Sherman," PBS, Frontline, October 4, 2006, https://www.pbs.org/wgbh/pages/frontline/gangsofiraq/interviews/sherman.html.
18 "Iraq," memo, Jim Steele for SECDEF, September 19, 2005; See also "Texture," memo, Rumsfeld for Bush and Vice President Richard B. Cheney, September 23, 2005.

19 "Prime Ministerial Decrees on MOD Changes," memo, Deputy Commanding General, MNF-I, for Commanding General, MNF-I, December 3, 2005.
20 Ibid.
21 "Updated Notes Following POTUS SVTC," *Casey Files*, December 16, 2005; Paper, "Campaign Progress Review: June 2005-December 2005," *MNF-I*, December 20, 2005.
22 "Opinion Analysis: Confidence in Iraqi Army Rising in South; In Central Areas Many Fear for Their Safety," PowerPoint Briefing, *Department of State Office of Research*, Washington, DC: U.S., December 22, 2005.

Bibliography

Allawi, Ali A. *The Occupation of Iraq: Winning the War, Losing the Peace*. New Haven, CT: Yale University Press, 2007.

Batiste, John and Paul Daniels. "The Fight for Samarra: Full Spectrum Operations in Modern Warfare." *Military Review* (May-June 2005): 13–21.

Buncombe, Andrew and Patrick Cockburn. "Iraq's Death Squads: On the Brink of Civil War." *Independent*, February 26, 2006.

Cole, Juan. "Shia Militias in Iraqi Politics," in *Iraq: Preventing a New Generation of Conflict*. Edited by David M. Malone, Markus E. Bouillon, and Ben Rowswell. Boulder, CO: Lynne Rienner Publishers, 2007.

Diamond, Larry. *Squandered Victory. The American Occupation and the Bungled Effort to Bring Democracy to Iraq*. New York: Times Books, 2005.

Estes, Kenneth W. *U.S. Marine Corps Operations in Iraq, 2003–2006*. Quantico, VA: History Division, U.S. Marine Corps, 2009.

Grose, Peter. "U.S. Encouraged by Vietnam Vote." *The New York Times*, September 4, 1967, in George W. Casey, Jr. Papers. Washington, DC, National Defense University (NDU).

Katzman, Kenneth. "Iraq: Elections, Government, and Constitution." Report for Congress. Washington, DC: CRS, November 20, 2006.

Katzman, Kenneth. "Congressional Research Service (CRS) Report for Congress." Iraq: Elections and New Government. Washington, DC: Congressional Research Service, January 31, 2005.

Kukis, Mark. *Voices from Iraq: A People's History, 2003–2009*. New York: Columbia University Press, 2011.

McCarthy, Rory. "Pressure Mounts for Iraqi Election Delay." *The Guardian*, January 4, 2005.

Mizbana, Hadi. "Security Forces Find No Hostages in Iraqi Town Despite Reports of Captives." *Billings Gazette*, April 17, 2005.

Moss, Michael. "How Iraq Police Reform Became Casualty of War." *The New York Times*, May 22, 2006.

Mozaffar, Shaheen. "Elections, Violence, and Democracy in Iraq." *Bridgewater Review* 25, no. June 1, (2006): 5–9.

Pan, Esther. "Q & A: Iraq: Sunnis, the Elections, and the Insurgency." *The New York Times*, December 23, 2005 (part of a question and answer session at the Council on Foreign Relations).

Perito, Robert M. "U.S. Institute of Peace (USIP) Special Report. The Iraq Federal Police: U.S. Police Building under Fire." Washington, DC: U.S. Institute of Peace, October 2011.

Rayburn, Joel D., Frank K. Sobchak, Jeanne F. Godfroy, Matthew D. Morton, James S. Powell, and Matthew M. Zais, eds. "Strategy in Crisis, October–December 2006." *The U.S. Army in the Iraq War: Volume 2 Surge And Withdrawal 2007–2011*. Strategic Studies Institute, US Army War College, 2019.

Salman, Raheem and Patrick J. McDonnell. "Many Corpses, but Few Details." *Los Angeles Times*, April 22, 2005.

Worth, Robert. "Iraq Kidnapping Tale Combines Perilous Mix of Fact and Rumor." *The New York Times*, April 18, 2005.

Worth, Robert. "Iraqi Official Is Assassinated by Gunmen in Baghdad." *The New York Times*, April 19, 2005.

Wright, Donald and Timothy Reese. Interview with General (Ret.) George W. Casey, Jr. Contemporary Operations Study Team, February 5, 2008.

8

CONTEXTUALIZATION OF SECTARIAN CONFLICT AND VIOLENCE IN IRAQ

The Intersection of Identity, Power, and Conflict

Satgin Hamrah

Introduction

In the almost two decades since the invasion of Iraq by U.S. and coalition forces to oust Saddam Hussein in 2003, the country has been entrenched in a perpetual cycle of tension, conflict, and violence. In essence the invasion created a cascade phenomenon in which this cycle spread over time and space amplifying pre-existing societal fissures. This endless cycle has ebbed and flowed since 2003, but has nonetheless remained constant and has consistently been framed along the lines of identity. There have been continuing debates regarding the reasons why Iraqi society erupted into a state of conflict in the manner that it has in the post-invasion landscape. In order to understand the Iraq of today, and the challenges it has faced for nearly 20 years, it is important to dive deep into the policies, politics, and nuances that have influenced the country on both top-down and bottom-up levels. One of the starting points should be to ask candid questions and to pursue answers in an objective manner. This includes asking what the modern historical root causes are that have facilitated the major surge in the instrumentalization of sectarianism and communitarian identities that have been used to the detriment of Iraqi people and used by non-state actors to cause havoc across the country at an immense and unprecedented high human cost?[1] The 2003 invasion of Iraq and the subsequent death of Saddam Hussein were both deeply important watershed events not only for Iraq, but for the region as well. This undoubtedly had an influence on the rise of identity-based conflict. Were these the only influential reasons why conflict and violence have permeated Iraqi society on both micro and macro levels? In the post-invasion period, what followed was an unprecedented power vacuum on top-down and granular levels of society leading to unstable security and political landscapes across the country (MacAskill & Burkeman 2003). But were these and current challenges only associated with the invasion and subsequent events? The challenges facing Iraq during the post-Saddam period are highly complex,

DOI: 10.4324/9781003329510-9

layered, and interconnected. The enormity of identity-based conflict and violence, particularly sectarian based issues have contributed to ongoing challenges that the country continues to face. According to The Iraq Study Group Report (Baker et al 2006), these challenges can be attributed to an array of factors, including the Sunni Arab insurgency, Al-Qaeda, Shia militias, and death squads.[2] They are also attributable to external influences, as well as the policies and practices of Saddam Hussein.

Many of these challenges are associated with the cycle of violence that was unleashed on an unprecedented scale after the 2003 invasion. These stem from the significant changes that occurred in Iraq's socio-political, religio-political, and security landscapes during this period. It is often argued that the rise of sectarianism or identity-based conflict and violence in Iraq only arose after the invasion and the toppling of Saddam Hussein. It is true that the invasion and its subsequent chain of events did indeed facilitate massive instability across the country and by extension created an environment conducive to the rise of non-state actors. However, attributing the rise of these challenges solely to the invasion provides a skewed viewpoint, as well as an incorrect analytical starting point from which to engage in a comprehensive multi-pronged assessment of the challenges facing Iraq and the complexity associated with each layer of these challenges. This is particularly important, as the realities in post-2003 Iraq did not emerge from a socio-political, religio-political, or cultural vacuum. They emerged from a legacy of exclusion and an environment in which identity, both religious and ethnic, was utilized by the governing regime and its leader Saddam Hussein for strategic purposes. More specifically, these challenges are a reflection of his policies and practices, including his instrumentalization of sectarianism and communitarian identity for strategic purposes creating "us versus them" and "in-group and out-group" paradigms.

These divisions later came to full fruition after the invasion resulting in major fissures in Iraq along both sectarian and ethnic lines. As such, while it was initially believed that Iraqi society would emerge as a relatively peaceful democratic state after the invasion, the reality was quite different. On March 19, 2003, President George W. Bush in a nationwide televised address announced the launch of Operation Iraqi Freedom (Glass 2017).[3] During his speech he stated that key goals included helping Iraqis achieve a united, stable, and free country, as well as the restoration of control of the country to its people.[4] However, what actually occurred was quite different from what was stated during this speech. Against the backdrop of a complex web of emerging state and non-state actors, the post-Saddam period saw a brutal evolution of the strategies, policies, and tactics employed by the Ba'athist regime. These political entrepreneurs exacerbated existing fissures and markers of identity and in the process sharpened divisions across Iraqi society based on religious sect and ethnicity. The result was heightening levels of suspicion, tension, conflict, and violence. This, coupled with the power vacuum that was created, cascaded into a state of lawlessness providing an opportunity for non-state actors to take advantage of the rapidly declining state of the country. Moreover, similar to the period of Saddam Hussein's rule, sectarianism and communitarianism were both utilized to advance the agenda of these actors and to increase their sphere of influence and power. However, what was substantially different from the earlier period was the scale and the way in which sectarianism and communitarianism were used on both top-down and granular societal levels, as well as the sheer scale of conflict and violence that stemmed from the use of identity as a strategic instrument by political entrepreneurs (state and non-state). This was explicitly evident with the rise of non-state actors vying for power and influence in the country.

In the post-invasion environment, an insurgency consisting of Iraqis included dislocated Ba'athists and Sunnis that were unhappy with the shift in their political position in the country, as well as the the influx of Al-Qaeda inspired fighters that poured into the country. This combination facilitated the rise of sectarian conflict and violence and subsequently ignited a sectarian war and guerilla warfare tactics against U.S. troops.[5] This was evident as tension, conflict and violence between Shias, Sunnis, and Kurds escalated and resulted in widescale socio-political destabilization and the emergence of unprecedented security and socio-political landscapes that have mired the country in a cycle of sectarian conflict and violence that continues to plague the country. This stems not only from the invasion but also from the legacy of exclusion during Saddam Hussein's rule (Al-Qarawee 2014) as has been evident in the cycle of violence that emerged between the Sunni minority and the Shia majority. This became the center of conflict in the post-invasion environment, as well as Arab-Kurdish tensions (Al-Qarawee 2014). While the political entrepreneurs in the country had mostly changed, what continued in the new period were identity-based strategies and tactics and the process of instrumentalizing societal fissures for strategic purposes. This was clearly evident with the rise of non-state groups such as Al-Qaeda in Iraq (AQI) who not only utilized existing identity-based fissures (including sectarian) in Iraqi society, but also exacerbated sectarian cleavages to heighten chaos across the country. They capitalized on identity-based divisions in the country and thrived as a result of a vortex of fear and violence that was created. Similar to the Ba'athist regime, these groups operated in relative freedom and instrumentalized identity-particularly sectarian identity to expand the scope and scale of their power and influence. The result has been a country that has been ravaged by war and transformed into an almost contiguous conflict zone since the start of the Iran-Iraq War in 1980 at the expense of the Iraqi people.

While the shape and significance of sectarianism varies across the region and differs among sects (Valbjorn 2020), in Iraq it has played a strategic role for state and non-state political entrepreneurs, such as Saddam Hussein and AQI. In both periods ethnic (communitarian) and religious identity were mobilized, manipulated, and strategically utilized to advance the interests of political actors who formulated these plans. This chapter argues that the identity-based conflict and violence that emerged in the post-2003 landscape was not singularly due to the resulting power vacuum and socio-political instability that emerged after the invasion. Rather, it argues that the strategic utilization of identity, particularly religious identity, by Saddam Hussein as a key component of his rule fostered significant divisions within Iraqi society. This was evident[6] during the Iran-Iraq War (1980–1988) period and afterwards during the country's conflict with the West. More specifically, this chapter argues that identity, with a focus on religious identity, was strategically utilized by Saddam Hussein within the framework of his domestic and war-time strategies; thereby, establishing the foundation from which non-state actors such as AQI developed and implemented their brutal sect-based war and fomented a cycle of conflict and violence from which Iraq has not yet been able to free itself from.

The Rise of Political Islam

In the 1980s the greater Middle East and South Asia experienced a significant shift in the bridging of Islam and politics from both top-down and grass roots levels. This shift occurred on a transnational scale, including in Afghanistan during the Soviet-Afghan War,[7] Pakistan,[8] Iran,[9] as well as in Iraq. By extension the transnational shift that occurred had far reaching ripple effects which included a surge in sectarianism. Sectarian identity in the modern context has served as a pretext to inflict injury and death upon countless individuals who have been "othered" for strategic purposes. This has been and continues to be the underlying factor that has resulted in the death and injury of countless innocent people across the wider region since the 1980s. Before 1979 sectarian conflict and violence were not a common occurrence throughout the region (Warde 2016) despite an increasing shift towards bridging politics and Islam for strategic purposes in the 1970s by state and non-state actors. More specifically, despite the increased use of Islam for the advancement of political interests during the 1970s, sectarian narratives and conflict were minimal across the region compared to the 1980s, as were sentiments associated with sectarian discrimination. This was evident across both the greater Middle East and South Asia. For example, Fuchs argues that in 1979 Shias in Pakistan did not feel discriminated against nor was there a cycle of sectarian conflict despite occasional riots during the month of Muharram or the changes being implemented at the time by General Zia-Ul-Haq (Fuchs 2019). Some of the underlying factors that contributed to this change on regional and local levels are being examined as part of a larger project. However, overall, across the region Sunni-Shia cleavages were not extensive and sectarian conflict did not come to full fruition until the 1980s, including in Iraq and elsewhere.

This shift in the religio-political landscape contributed to the surging use of identity construction by political entrepreneurs for strategic purposes and consequently in sectarian conflict and violence across the Middle East and South Asia, which directly and indirectly impacted socio-political and security arenas. This pivot and the highly sectarian focused landscape that emerged were connected with the larger economic, security and political challenges that the wider region experienced in the 1980s (Nasr 2006). Thus, making the use of sectarianism as a strategy by political entrepreneurs highly provocative, as it not only advanced false narratives of "us versus them," it also promoted conflict under the guise of religion during challenging periods. As a result, the changes that occurred during the 1980s were profound and established deep roots of sectarian tension and conflict in the wider region including in Iraq.

The impact and consequences stemming from the strategic utilization of identity, particularly religious identity, which is the primary focus of this chapter, are highly complex, nuanced, and often interconnected requiring a comprehensive analytical framework to untangle. This not only provides an opportunity to delve into the strategies utilized by political entrepreneurs in this context and their "imagined communities" (Anderson 1983), it also helps in deconstructing overt and covert nuances and challenges associated with sectarianism, as well as its short and long-term consequences. Within the Iraqi context this is beneficial based on the need to examine the strategic utilization of religious identity on both state and non-state levels from the rule of Saddam Hussein onwards. This chapter primarily focuses on this time period and how Saddam Hussein influenced the post-invasion landscape, as a result of his identity driven policies and practices.

Analysis and discussion of sectarian conflict and violence in the Islamic world have tended to focus on ancient animosities between Sunnis and Shias often framing conflict and violence as one in which ideological incompatibility is at the heart of the challenges and one that dates back to ancient competition between these two sects (Haddad 2020). Consequently, the topic of sectarianism as it pertains to the Middle East and South Asia is often examined through a myopic lens. While sectarianism in its modern context does borrow some narratives of a much earlier period as tools of persuasion and coercion, critical analysis of the instrumentalization of identity, particularly sectarianism, requires an examination of this topic beyond the monochromatic way that is often utilized. As such, within the Iraqi context to understand the surge of sectarianism and related conflict that substantially increased in Iraq after the invasion in 2003, it is essential to understand the modern historical root causes that facilitated its rise and their subsequent impact their impact on religio-political, socio-political and geopolitical landscapes across the region.

In the pursuit of answering the question regarding why Iraq has been dealing with sectarian conflict and violence since 2003 at the level that it has, it is important to examine the background from which the post-invasion landscape emerged. Similar to other religions, Islam does not have a singular expression or a singular framework in which it is manifested by those that proclaim to be Muslim, including those that instrumentalize it. As such, in order to understand how and why the country's domestic landscape has evolved in the way that it has and its wider ramifications, this chapter briefly examines the instrumentalization of religious identity by political entrepreneurs and the process of identity construction and the development of in-group and out-group paradigms that were undertaken by these entrepreneurs, such as Saddam Hussein.

The Intersection of Identity, Religion, and Violence

Whether in Iraq, Iran, or in another country the strategic use of identity as well as the shift to political Islam, including the strategic use of sectarianism, was due to a power-based strategy utilized by state and non-state political entrepreneurs who sought to configure the socio-political and security landscapes to ones that were aligned with their interests. The process of materialization[10] of sectarian-based ideology within this context and subsequent conflict and violence between Sunnis and Shias made it possible to better control and manipulate individuals and communities (DeMarrasi, Castillo & Earle 1996). This was evident in the rhetoric, conflict, and violence that stemmed from Saddam Hussein's exploitation of identity and the process of othering, which were done within a broader framework of power, legitimacy, contestation, mobilization, and an outbidding process (Khatib 2015) that he engaged in on state and non-state levels. An outbidding process is one in which a dominant party tries to silence its perceived or real rivals. More specifically, it is a process in which political elites or other groups compete for the support of a particular religious or ethnic group at the expense of others. By focusing on ethnic and sect-based identities, Saddam Hussein strategically manipulated emotions and attachments to communities to create cohesive socio-political identities and religio-political identities that would further embed him in the in-group (i.e.:the Sunni Arab population) to enhance his power and position. Leaders often build on a foundation of shared social identity to incite fear and outrage towards out-groups among followers. This was highlighted in his overarching treatment of both Shia and Kurdish communities in the country. Within the Iraqi context this allowed Saddam to create an imagined community (Anderson 1983) of what according to him were true loyal Iraqis—Sunni Arabs. Thus, illustrating the similarity and overlap regarding the strategic use of ethnic and religious identities for the advancement of his political and security interests. While history and theology may have established the identities of perceived rival groups, the actual bones of contention were based on power and wealth, both important factors in shaping his strategies (Nasr 2006). This was illustrated by his framing of Iraqi nationalism within a Sunni Arab framework. As such, sectarian and ethnic identities, as well as emotions, served as proximate mechanisms by which he manipulated and strategically utilized identity to sustain cohesive cooperation among with the Sunni Arab Iraqi population and effectively othered Shia Iraqis and Kurdish Iraqis from the 1980s until the invasion of 2003.[11]

Shias, despite being a majority in Iraq, had been politically marginalized since the country's birth. While they were relatively marginalized since Iraq's independence, their level of marginalization continued during the rule of Saddam Hussein at a new heightened level resulting in further dividing Iraqi society along sect-based differences of discrimination (Pirsoul 2019). Their Shia identity was perceived as a threat to the Ba'athists nationalist project as their religious identity was portrayed as a distinctly Persian ethnic identity. Within this framework both sectarian and communitarian identities were used to increase in-group/out-group paradigms and by extension distrust, fear, and at times outrage. As a result, Saddam was able to exploit religion and Arab-Persian paradigms to further strengthen his position within the Ba'athist regime. Thus, exacerbating and solidifying societal divisions based on sect-based identities. Taking this into consideration, there is little doubt that the socio-political instability and the unstable security landscape of Iraq after the 2003 invasion have their roots in the Ba'ath Party's governance methodologies (Blayedes 2018). This was highlighted by the fact that sectarianism increased in Iraq stemming from an interaction between favorable underlying conditions and damaging government policies of the Ba'athist regime (Yousif 2010).

Many argue that 2003 marks the dividing line separating a sectarian Iraq from a non-sectarian Iraq (Haddad 2016). However, a distinct line does not exist, neither for the strategic utilization of religion as a whole nor with the instrumentalization of sectarianism.[12] This becomes especially relevant in this case, where Saddam Hussein himself and his institutional policies have been identified as being directly and indirectly responsible for heightening divisions among religious sects and ethnic groups. The manipulation and strategic use of identity was a key factor of Saddam's state building, ideology, domestic, regional and wartime strategies. The manipulation of sect-based identity was deemed useful for the state to react and outbid their perceived opponents, which in this context the other were the Shia and the Kurds.[13] Thus, resulting in a dangerous outbidding process that put in motion the construction of a vicious cycle of conflict and violence that deepened divisions in Iraq (Khatib 2015). This was highlighted, in a conversation between Saddam Hussein and Izzat al-Duri on March 1, 1987, in which they discussed the importance of morale, mobilizing popular support, and targeting Iranian cities. During this conversation Saddam stated that faith-based strategies should be utilized and aimed at Iraqi fighters and civilians to further motivate them to engage in the war effort.[14] Thus, illustrating the utilization of religion and religious identity for the advancement of state interests. Moreover, it highlights the coupling of religious identity with Arab nationalism in order to establish a strict "us versus them" framework from which to propagate effective rhetoric through carefully crafting embedding mechanisms for both the country's civilian and military populations. Within this same conversation Izzat an-Duri and Saddam Hussein also framed the war as an Arab war against the Persians (Nasr 2006). This was highlighted in the following statement,

> A sword, a shield, and an arrow. Sayidna-Umar (Caliph Umar ibn al-Khattab) during the conquest of Persia said when he embarked on his expedition of Persia:-God, I will beat the Kings of Persia with the Kings of Arabia, meaning, I will strike the Persians by the best Arabs-the best Arabs in combat, glory and courage. Therefore, we have to prepare our citizen fighters so that they can become fighters, believers and have principles.[15]

These comments were closely aligned with both his domestic policies during the 1980s and with his war policies.

124 Sectarian Conflict and Violence in Iraq

The strategic instrumentalization of identity, sectarian and communitarian, was at the forefront of his strategies during this period. The worlds overlapped within the larger context of short and long-term ramifications. During the Iran-Iraq War (1980–1988) the Shia population was suppressed based on their religious identity within Iraq (Nasr 2006). Rhetoric and propaganda espoused by the government involved a mix of nationalistic and religious elements in the discourse (Pirsoul 2019) surrounding the war and the country's Shia population. Saddam Hussein expelled about 200,000 Iraqi Shia of Iranian heritage stating that they were an Iranian fifth column threatening the stability of Iraq (Sciolino 1991: 4), jailed thousands, and executed hundreds. Shia festivals such as Ashoura were banned and some religious leaders were executed such as Mohammad Baqer al-Sadr in 1980 (Nasr 2006). Moreover, Shias did not have the same academic or employment opportunities as their Sunni counterparts and were always under a shadow of suspicion. Shia majority cities and towns were generally neglected as were religious centers unless Saddam chose to grant funding as part of his "carrot and stick" strategy (Nasr 206). On the other hand, if it was deemed strategically beneficial funding would be granted, as it was for the shrines at Najaf and Karbala in the early 1980s, as an attempt to garner support from the Shia population during the war and counter Ayatollah Khomeini's attempt to influence the Iraqi Shia community. There were clear lines of division between Sunnis and Shias with Shias being framed and suspected of being more loyal to Iran than to the ideals of Arab nationalism (Pirsoul 2019) despite the high numbers of Shia men serving and dying for Iraq during the Iran-Iraq War (Drozdiak 1984). This example illustrates the reluctance of the Iraqi Shia majority to follow the politics of the nascent Iranian government at the time. On balance, it is important to note that there were elements in the Shia community in Iraq during the Iran-Iraq War that were directly or indirectly affiliated with the Iranian government. For example, according to an unclassified British telegraph, the Iraqi Islamic Dawa party claimed in a communique that two of its members below up the Rafadin Bank in Baghdad and they set the ammunition depot of Al-Rashid Garrison on fire in 1981.[16]

The rhetoric, policies, and approaches the regime utilized both during and after the Iran-Iraq War not only highlighted the strategic significance of identity. It also quite clearly illustrated their highly influential impact within the framework of outbidding processes, enhancing legitimacy, and solidifying power. One interesting example was noted in an unclassified tele-letter regarding the strategic use of giving pep talks in Iraq during Friday sermons in mosques on the war against Iran and the need to keep fighting. This was part of a broader top-down state strategy intersecting ethnic and religious identity with the country's political and security interests.[17] Furthermore, this relatively simple example highlights the overarching approach by Saddam Hussein in instrumentalizing sectarian identity and Islam not out of ideological conviction, rather identity and religion were key tools in his domestic and international strategies (Helfont 2014). In addition to Saddam Hussein strategically utilizing sectarianism and communitarianism to his advantage, he also simultaneously increasingly bridged Islam and politics on another level, harnessing feelings of solidarity among Muslims to his advantage. This was evident in the increasing Islamification of the country. From the first months of the Iran-Iraq War, key members of the Ba'athist regime made a public showing of attending religious observances, and posters were displayed across the country depicting Saddam Hussein engaging in religious practices (Bush 2003).

In terms of the Islamification of the country arguably the pivot began in 1987 when the Ba'athist regime began to refer to the Popular Islamic Conference as the Popular Islamic Conference Organization (PICO) and allocated a building in Baghdad to be used as its permanent headquarters (Nasr 2006). At this point, this organization began publishing books on Islam and much of the scholarship was sectarian in nature framing Shias as heretical and Iraqi identity in Sunni-Arab terms. The establishment of the Saddam University for Islamic Studies established in 1988 in Baghdad, which played a significant role in international affairs, is another example of this increased pivot by the Ba'athist regime. This alone does not make it applicable to the examination of the instrumentalization of sectarianism in Iraq. What does make it applicable, though, is that this organization was used by Saddam's regime to publish books that explicitly argued that heterodox Shia movements and Iran during the 1980s were heretical.[18] There were a considerable number of examples in the 1990s as well. During the last decade of Saddam's rule, he increasingly referenced Islam and integrated Sunni Islam into his authoritarian system (Helfont 2014). According to Samuel Helfont, Saddam's Faith Campaign of the 1990s[19] was a culmination of his plan to use religion as a strategic tool for political purposes upon his assumption of the Iraqi presidency in 1979, during which time he began constructing the institutional capacity to control and monitor Iraqi religious institutions and different identity groups. The resulting authoritarian structures allowed him to employ Islamic symbols and rhetoric in public policy and practices (Helfont 2014).

It is important to note that Islam did not guide Iraqi polity. Rather it was a tool to achieve policy goals by the government. Yet the regime's use of religion was also more than a mere rhetorical shift. It was a long, detailed process of building institutions and networks to carry out policy and realize Iraq's strategic aims.[20] In doing so, Saddam worked toward shaping the country's religio-political landscape to meet his needs (Helfont 2014). For example, in 1991 with the war between Iraq and a Western led coalition looming, Saddam Hussein continued to weaponize Islam and wrote "Allah Akbar" or "God is Great" on the Iraqi flag. This introduced religion into the public sphere in a new way. Furthermore, the existence of newly co-opted religious leaders had very clear sectarian dimensions and provided the regime with the means to spread a particular interpretation of religion that reinforced Ba'athist rule in Iraq. This was also part of a broader strategy and included a call for Jihad against his enemies. His call for Jihad or holy war against "unbelievers" was rather odd as it delineated from Ba'athist norms. However, taking his long-term patterns into consideration regarding the strategic utilization of identity to advance his interests, such a pivot arguably fits within the larger framework of his domestic and regional policies and practices. After the war and throughout the last decade of his rule, the Ba'athist regime declared a "faith campaign" in which it built mosques, required increased religious education in Iraq and consistently allied with Islamists abroad. The result was not only an increased Sunnification of the country and further division of Iraqis based on their religious identification, but it also had long-term ramifications that were detrimental to Iraqi society (Coughlin 2002). Moreover, the Islamic Faith Campaign coupled with his strategic instrumentalization of religious identity dating back to the start of the Iran-Iraq War prepared the ground for Islamist insurgencies and a surge in sectarian conflict and violence after the 2003 invasion.

The merging of national and sectarian identities that took shape under Saddam Hussein in the previous decades continued in the 2000s. More specifically, the strategic utilization of Sunni Islam and the process of othering continued in the 2000s to strengthen his grip on power. He continued drawing on his exclusionary and xenophobic forms of identity politics-particularly those focused on Sunni-Shia sectarianism. In a more pronounced manner, Saddam continued to develop and implement policies involving the inclusion or exclusion of social groups based on identity and implemented these policies with varying degrees of repression (Valbjorn 2019). This was further illustrated by the opening of Iraq's borders by Saddam in 2003 to foreign fighters from Afghanistan, Syria, Saudi Arabia, Lebanon, and Tunisia and once again calling for Jihad. Moreover, the Iraqi National Intelligence Service allocated schools and mosques for their accommodation, especially in Al-Anbar, Kirkuk, and Tikrit. However, relations between the Iraqi National Intelligence Service and foreign fighters predated 2003. In 2001, Saddam's regime helped Al-Qaeda fighters who escaped from Afghanistan through Iran to establish their camps in the difficult terrain of the Kurdistan region in the border city of Biyara in the province of Sulaimanyah. These camps were the core of the "Ansar Al-Islam Group," the first branch of Al-Qaeda in Iraq (Schanzer 2004).

Based on contacts going back to the mid-1990s, Saddam Hussein also provided specialized training to Al-Qaeda in explosives and assistance to the group's biological and chemical programs (CIA 2002). Another aspect of the final years of Saddam's reign that contributed to post-2003 divisions are arguably the Islamization of some groups within the Iraqi Army, the Ba'athists, and the paramilitary forces of Fedayeen Saddam and Al-Quds Army which were part of "Saddam's Faith campaign." He inserted faith-sessions into the training manuals of some groups of his Republican Guard forces. Moreover, extensive religious, and faith sessions were integral parts of Fedayeen Saddam's trainings. Unquestionable obedience by its followers was required, as was staunch anti-Shia sentiments.[21] The evolving pattern of utilizing Islamic identity for strategic purposes highlights the contextualization of why and how sectarianism was used. It is also important to delineate competing national truths and contestation of claims that the government utilized within the framework of sectarian competition as a function of exclusivist claims to overarching religious categories. (Haddad 2016) for the advancement of strategic interests. Saddam Hussein's framing of sectarian identity and national identity not only bridged Islam and politics in Iraq on an unprecedented level, it also facilitated the creation of complex and conflicting forces that together paved the way for the cycle of conflict and violence that emerged in the post-invasion landscape.

Rather than succeeding in homogenizing Iraq within a specific Sunni framework, the actions of the Ba'athist regime deepened forms of ethnic, religious, and cultural cleavages to the detriment of Iraqi nationalist sentiment. According to Hashemi, the political context in which sectarianism often exists is the persistence of authoritarianism (Hashemi 2016). In the context of Iraq under Saddam Hussein the political mobilization and manipulation of sectarian identities was a key strategy for the advancement of his interests and regime survival. This by extension had both a direct and an indirect impact on the behavior of the Iraqi state, state-society relations, and on a more granular non-state level. A key tool for the Ba'athist state was the role that propaganda played in polarizing the Iraqi people. Saddam tried to harness sentiments of solidarity among the Sunni population to his advantage by portraying himself as a devout believer and invoking God in his struggles with the West. He used Sunnism in his policies against the Shia of Iraq, and an Arab identity in his policies against the Kurds. While the shape and significance of sectarianism varies across the region and among sects (Valbjorn 2020), its adverse impact on the societies it exists in, such as Iraq, is immense and often has unforeseen long-term ramifications. This has been vividly evident in Iraq since 2003 as sectarian polarization and antagonisms in Iraq have existed within a new paradigm since the invasion.

Post-2003 Iraq and the Rise of AQI

The weakness of the Iraqi state after the 2003 invasion has its roots in the construction of political identity and religio-social cleavage structures during and directly after Saddam Hussein's death (Blayedes 2018). This was evident in socio-political and threat landscapes that emerged both after the invasion and after Saddam's death. What resulted was a major transition in power relations from the minority Sunni sect to the majority Shia sect, as well as changes in power relations with and among the Kurds (Moaddel, Tessler & Inglehart 2008). For Shia politicians, the Ba'ath Party was the key political instrument that enabled the Sunnis to seize power and confine Shias within certain political, social, and security spaces. Based on their experience with the Ba'athist regime, especially Saddam Hussein, Shias were adamant in their call for the expulsion of the Ba'athist elements from state bureaucracy (Moaddel, Tessler & Inglehart 2008). Thus, resulting in a major shift within the country's domestic landscape. The once dislocated were in a newfound position of power and those that were in a position of power were at this point dislocated. As a result, this made many in the Sunni community feel deprived of power and influence, leading some to support the Sunni insurgency. Consequently, as Shias consolidated their power Sunnis became increasingly and overtly critical, building on the sectarian rhetoric espoused by Saddam Hussein and his regime, and further enhanced existing societal fissures (Moaddel, Tessler & Inglehart 2008).

On a non-state level, the strategic instrumentalization of sectarianism significantly increased after the invasion of Iraq in 2003, as did related tension, conflict, and violence. A perpetual cycle of conflict and violence was unleashed in the country on a level that the nation and its people had never grappled with before.

This was related to the rise of Al-Qaeda in Iraq (AQI) – a militant Sunni extremist organization that became active in Iraq after the U.S. led invasion of 2003. It was comprised of Iraqi and foreign fighters fighting against the U.S. occupation and the Shia dominated Iraqi government. Similar to the previous regime, AQI used religious identity to mobilize people of the Sunni sect of Islam in order to embed itself into the Sunni segment of society with the goal of targeting the previous out-group-Shias. As a political entrepreneur, Zarqawi instrumentalized sectarianism in the organization's mobilization and recruitment efforts, as well as its messaging strategies and acts of violence. This included the unleashing of propaganda campaigns against not only Americans, but also the Shia-led government and Shias as a whole. This was evident on Islamist forums and websites. Another core component of his strategy was attacking Shias with the goal of provoking a sectarian war in Iraq. Zarqawi strongly believed that given Iraq's sectarian context and chaotic political landscape, he could establish himself as the leader/defender of Sunnis in Iraq. More specifically, his strategy was to wage a sectarian war, work closely with Ansar El Islam and Iraqi insurgency groups, then take advantage of the ensuing chaos to control the Sunni areas of Iraq and their people.

AQI first appeared in 2004 when Abu Musab al-Zarqawi, a Jordanian born militant already leading insurgent attacks in Iraq, formed an alliance with al-Qaeda, pledging his group's allegiance to Osama bin Laden in return for bin Laden's endorsement as the leader of al-Qaeda's franchise in Iraq.[22] Zarqawi ,one of the most destructive militants in Iraq at the time, organized a wave of attacks, often suicide bombings targeting security forces, government institutions, and Iraqi civilians with a focus on Iraqi Shias. A primary tool in AQI's strategy of chaos, instability, and division was to target Shias to inspire militant Sunni Islamists and to significantly enhance existing sectarian conflict and use it to its advantage. This was particularly evident in 2005 when AQI declared an "all-out war" on the Shia in Iraq[23] unleashing a series of atrocities against Shia civilians and shrines eventually provoking the war Zarqawi was seeking to create a cycle of bloody chaos throughout the country (Laub & Masters 2014). By targeting Shias and espousing very explicit sectarian narratives against this population, AQI intended to deepen existing sectarian tensions. This was evident in AQI's construction of narratives in *Inspire* magazine in which the in-group was framed as honorable and real Muslims and the out-group were portrayed as oppressive and effectively othered. The diagnostic frames of oppression and grievance were attributed to the "other" while simultaneously projected a collective identity from the in-group based on shared values, beliefs, and grievances, thereby, providing justification for violent actions against members of the out-group.

This included targeting Iraqi Shias, including during religious processions or at Shia mosques and shrines. One example is the 2006 attack destroying the golden dome of the Al-Askariyyah Mosque in Samarra, which is one of Shi'ism's holiest mosques (Worth 2006). The result of all these activities was the amplification of an existing cycle of conflict and violence that the country has yet to recover from which increased the level of sectarian violence, eventually contributing to a full-scale sectarian civil war. In essence, AQI was successful in further dividing the country and facilitating sectarian and ethnic violence across Iraq (Cordesman 2007) by building upon the societal fissures and in-group/out-group paradigms created during the previous period. This pattern was exacerbated when the United States withdrew its forces from Iraq in 2011 as AQI substantially increased attacks mainly on Shia targets. Achieving high levels of success and seeking to enhance its position among jihadist groups, in April 2013 AQI changed its name to ISIL (Islamic State of Iraq and the Levant).[24] The name change was an expression of its broadened ambitions as its fighters had crossed into Syria to challenge the Assad regime, secularists, and Islamist opposition groups there, in addition to its continued challenge of the Iraqi government.[25] As such, the strategic utilization of sectarianism and communitarianism by Saddam Hussein to secure and enhance his power and position was activated and motivated on an even more profound scale and scope, unleashing an unprecedented surge of sectarian conflict and violence, the likes of which the country had never seen before (Cheterian 2021). While the exact context of each period is different in terms of geopolitics, as well as socio-political and security realities, the framework in which these tools have been used remain the same. In the current context, it has contributed, and continues to directly contribute to, tension, conflict, and violence throughout the country resulting in the injury, death, and migration of countless people.

Conclusion

Whether you are examining the Iraqi region after the British seized it from Ottoman Turkey during World War I or after Iraq attained its independence, particularly in the 1970s and later in the 1980s, 1990s, early 2000s or directly after the fall of Saddam Hussein until today, a common theme has been, and continues to be, the strategic utilization of identity, particularly sectarianism by political entrepreneurs with the goal of advancing their interesting, including enhancing their legitimacy, power, and influence. While the exact context of each period may have been different in terms of its geopolitical, socio-political, and security realities, the framework in which these tools have been used remain the same. This includes the time period after the 2003 invasion of the country in which the political, security, and socio-cultural realities starkly changed with the fall of Saddam Hussein, the end of the Ba'athist regime and the onset of a new power dynamic in the country on both state and non-state levels. However, a theme that continued in Iraq from the previous regime was the strategic utilization of identity, particularly sectarian identity, contributing to a surge in tension, conflict, and violence throughout the country resulting in the injury, death, and migration of countless people. As a result, Iraq has faced enormous challenges in the last 20 years, which continue to shape the lives of the women, men, and children of the country. I do not think that the country's immense identity-based challenges are impossible to overcome. However, it is important to recognize that Iraq is a highly complex landscape. As such, it is essential to pragmatically approach who has and is strategically using sectarian identity and religious ideology to his or her advantage, the reasons behind their instrumentalization of identity, and the short and long-term ramifications associated with this strategy.

This chapter aimed to provide a glimpse into the complex reality of some modern historical factors that have contributed to the rise of sectarian tension, conflict, and violence in the post-2003 landscape. It predominantly focuses on the influences of Saddam Hussein's policies and practices on the conflict and violence that arose after his fall. Saddam Hussein's Islamic Faith Campaign coupled with his strategic instrumentalization of religious identity dating back to the start of the Iran-Iraq War in essence established the foundation from which Islamist insurgencies were able engage in sectarian conflict and violence after the 2003 invasion and create chaos and bloodshed across the country (Helfont 2018). Conflict and violence within a Sunni-Shia context or the use of Islamic based rhetoric is not necessarily related to, or stem from, a specific feature of the Islamic religion itself or the diverse cultures and people that identify with the faith as has been evident by the strategic instrumentalization of religious identity by Saddam Hussein and its ripple effects.[26] Rather, during his rule such rhetoric, conflict, and violence were based on the exploitation of identity, particularly religion for power, legitimacy, mobilization, and outbidding processes on state and non-state levels, highlighting Nasr's argument that history and theology may have established the identities of rival groups within the Islamic faith (Khatib 2015). However, what drives tension, conflict, and violence is not based on religious ideology or deep-seated spirituality. Rather it is generally based on issues pertaining to power, influence, and wealth which can be more easily garnered by political entrepreneurs who can be legitimated with the manipulation of identity (Nasr 2006).

Notes

1 The Iraq War coupled with the actions of non-state actors resulted in millions of children being orphaned, at least 100,00 people were killed just in the first ten years alone and over five million Iraqis were displaced. This had enormous immediate consequences on an inter-generational level as well.
2 The insurgency in Iraq is attributed to former members of Saddam Hussein's regime, Sunni Arab Iraqis, criminals, and external elements. According to a speech given by President George W. Bush at Fort Bragg, North Carolina foreign fighters were pouring into the country from Saudi Arabia, Syria, Sudan, Egypt, Yemen, and other nations and made common cause with Iraqi insurgents and remnants of Saddam Hussein's regime who were seeking to restore the Ba'athist regime. In essence they were fighting against the possibility of freedom and democracy in Iraq.
3 On 15 December 2011, "The Chairman of the Joint Chiefs of Staff and other top U.S. military leaders observed the official end of U.S. Forces Iraq's mission after nearly nine years of conflict that claimed the lives of nearly 4,500 troops (Torreon)."
4 According to Naval History and Heritage Command, "20 March 2003 marked the beginning of Operation Iraqi Freedom with preemptive airstrikes on Saddam Hussein's Presidential Palace and military targets followed by approximately 67,700 'boots on the ground' with 15,000 Navy personnel on ships in the region (Belasco)." "Iraqi forces were overwhelmed quickly, and Baghdad fell a mere five weeks after the invasion began;" "Operation Iraqi Freedom," Naval History and Heritage Command, August 6, 2020, https://www.history.navy.mil/browse-by-topic/wars-conflicts-and-operations/middle-east/operation-iraqi-freedom.html.

5 Ibid.
6 Saddam Hussein instrumentalized identity to assist him in maintaining, as well as expanding the scale and scope of his political power. In this context Saddam Hussein used Sunnism as part of the Ba'athist political process, manipulating and emphasizing in-group similarities and out-group differences to engage in identity mobilization and to add credibility to his rule. He utilized this approach to engage in the political construction of socio-political and religio-political relationships to create an imagined community.
7 Islam was mobilized by the United States during the Cold War as was evident in Afghanistan in which it was deemed a useful weapon against the spread of Soviet influence. Islamists were mobilized by the United States and its regional allies in the fight against the Soviets in Afghanistan. The Afghan jihad was predominantly comprised of Sunni Islamists and had very explicit sectarian dimensions that were influenced by regional actors and exacerbated as a result of ideological cross-fertilizations that occurred among the fighters.
8 The salience of sectarianism also arose in Pakistan starting in the 1980s. Sectarian conflict in Pakistan is not a monocausal phenomenon as it has deep roots in the changes and trends that began in the wider region since the late 1970s, including the increased interjection of Jama'at-i Islami in the domestic politics of Pakistan
9 In the Shia Revival, Nasr argues that Iran under Khomeini during the Iran-Iraq War created a cult of martyrdom in the country and a willingness to die for the Shia cause among many in the Iranian populace. Nasr argues that the Iranian Revolution imposed its own radicalizing logic. the Iranian Revolution and the resultant Shia religio-political activism by Iran under Khomeini. Ayatollah Khomeini also used Shi'ism within a religio-political framework with immense domestic and regional ramifications. After Shariati's death, he rose to political dominance and united the masses-religious and secular-by using Shi'ism and its symbols. In the post-revolution landscape, the role of Shi'ism in Khomeini's strategies changed. What was once used to unite and motivate the masses against the Pahlavi Dynasty, at this stage gave clerics political power, legitimacy, and allowed them to exert unprecedented political influence.
10 By materialization I am referring to the use of ideas, values, stories, myths, ceremonies, rituals, and symbols, etc. in order to influence sectarian-based ideology. Through this process it is possible to shape the beliefs of individuals into a collective framework of "us versus them" and by extension enhances the possibility of violent action against individuals that are deemed to be part of the out-group collective.
11 Consequently, he was able to leverage extant psychological mechanisms to cultivate a strong Sunni Arab identity for the Ba'athist regime as well as the country. The attachment of the in-group to their Sunni Arab identity was an effective strategy on both top-down and bottom-up levels, with its full impact coming to fruition during the post-invasion period.
12 Historically the Shia majority has been discriminated against by Sunni Muslims that have governed the country. The Shias express their dissatisfaction in a popular saying, "The roads and mail are for the Sunnis, the taxes for the Shias;" Sciolino (1991: 4).
13 While the primary focus of this chapter is not on Saddam's treatment of the Kurdish population, it is important to have clear understanding of the sheer brutality associated with this "us versus them" framework regarding the Kurds. In March of 1988 Saddam and his regime committed one of the worst atrocities of the modern era-the chemical attacks on Kurdish towns and villages including Halabja. In Halabja alone it resulted in the death of thousands of Kurds and countless were physically injured. It is believed that Napalm was used, as well as mustard gas and nerve agents including sarin, tabun, and VX. According to a report by Human Rights Watch in 1993, this was a campaign of extermination against the Kurds of northern Iraq.
14 During the Iran-Iraq War religious identity was not only strategically used within domestic and war time strategies by Saddam, but also in Iraq's regional policies as was evident in the country's partnership with Saudi Arabia to create a Sunni wall around Iran and his attempt to influence Sunnis in Pakistan. This included those in the country's Baluchistan region. It is important to note that the nascent Iranian government and its

leader Ayatollah Khomeini also strategically utilized religious identity in the country's domestic, war time, and regional policies.
15 Ibid.
16 *Iran-Iraq War,* Telegram from Brit Int. Sect. Tehran 090900z Jul to Priority FCO-Telegram Number 290 of 9 July 1981, Info Priority Moduk (For D14), Baghdad, Washington, July 12, 1981.
17 *Iraq/Iran: The View from Baghdad,* Unclassified Teleletter, Baghdad TL 338, GRS 1400, from S. L. Egerton 020/324/1, June 1, 1981.
18 According to White House archives from the presidency of George W. Bush, Saddam Hussein's regime engaged in the oppression of the country's Shia Muslims. Restrictions on Shia Muslims included: placing conditions and outright bans on communal Friday prayer, prohibited Shia Mosque libraries to lend books, denied permission for Shia programs on government-controlled radio and television, banned Shia centric books – including prayer books and guides, banned many funeral processions and other funeral observances other than those organized by the government and prohibited certain processions and public meetings commemorating Shia holy days; Bush (2003).
19 Saddam defined his faith campaign of the 1990s on an Islamic revival which was evident in the state structures, policies and strategies that emerged during this period. Ordinary Iraqi citizens understood the underlying message given by him and behaviors on the street began to change including the number of women wearing hijab.
20 According to White House archives from the period of George W. Bush's presidency, during the Persian Gulf War, Saddam exploited the fact that non-Muslim troops were fighting Muslims Iraq and portrayed the war as a war against Islam. He appealed to Muslim suspicion of Western morality and Western attitudes toward Islam and asserted that coalition forces had desecrated holy sites.
21 *The New York Times* reported early in 2003 that "United States military commanders say foreign fighters are being actively recruited by loyalists of Saddam Hussein to join the resistance against American forces in Iraq, ...military officials say that American troops in Iraq have had to contend with Syrians, Saudis, Yemenis, Algerians, Lebanese and even Chechens" Gordon & Jehl (2003).
22 Zarqawi became known to Osama Bin Laden in 1998. In 2004 he pledged allegiance to Osama Bin Laden. Moreover, he saw a benefit to the chaos that was ensuing after the 2003 invasion. AQI embraced a Salafist-jihadist ideology which was staunchly anti-Shia and stressed the need to expel the United States and its western allies from Iraq. Additionally, he worked to undermine the country's rising Shia government and community at any cost including igniting a brutal sectarian war between the Sunnis and Shia.
23 "Al-Zarqawi declares war on Iraqi Shia," *Al Jazeera,* September 14, 2005.
24 "Profile: Islamic State in Iraq and the Levant (ISIS)," *BBC News,* August 2, 2014.
25 Ibid.
26 During his rule Saddam utilized different definitions of Iraqi identity. His strategy included emphasizing one identity over the other depending on the circumstances at hand – including political and security considerations. This occurred at the expense of other facets of Iraqi identity. During the Iran-Iraq war he elevated Iraq's Arab identity, and often framed Iraqi identity within Sunni terms. More specifically, an Arab identity, Sunnism and the country's Islamic identity when it was strategically beneficial. The latter was evident during the later period of his regime.

Bibliography

Al-Qarawee, Harith Hassan. "Iraq's Sectarian Crisis A Legacy of Exclusion." Carnegie Endowment for International Peace. April 23, 2014.

Anderson, Benedict. *Imagined Communities: Reflections on the Origins and Spread of Nationalism.* New York: Verso, 1983.

Baker, James A.III, Lee H.Hamilton, Lawrence S.Eagleburger, Vernon E.Jordan, Jr., EdwinMeese III, Sandra Day O'Connor, Leon E. Panetta, William J. Perry, Charles S. Robb, and Alan K. Simpson. *The Iraq Study Group Report: The Way Forward-A New Approach*. New York: Vintage Books, 2006.

Blayedes, Lisa. *State of Iraq Under Saddam Hussein Repression*. Princeton: Princeton University Press, 2018.

Bush, George W. *Apparatus of Lies: Saddam's Disinformation and Propaganda, 1990–2003*. Washington, D.C.: The White House, 2003.

Cheterian, Vicken. "Framing Sectarianism in the Middle East." *Journal of Historical Sociology* 34 , no. 1 (March 8, 2021): 186–201.

CIA. "Iraq and al-Qaida: Interpreting a Murky Relationship." June 21, 2002. https://irp.fas.org/congress/2005_cr/CIAreport.062102.pdf.

Cordesman, Anthony H. "Iraq's Sectarian and Ethnic Violence and Its Evolving Insurgency Developments through Spring 2007."Center for Strategic and International Studies, January 29, 2007.

Coughlin, Con. "Con Coughlin Discusses His New Book, 'Saddam: King of Terror.'" Interview by Robert Siegel. All Things Considered, NPR, November 8, 2002.

Drozdiak, William. "Iraq's Shiites Enlist Under Saddam Hussein's Flag." *The Washington Post*, March 20, 1984.

DeMarrais, Elizabeth, Luis Jaime Castillo and Timothy Earle. "Ideology, Materialization and Power Strategies." *Current Anthropology* 27, no. 1 (February 1996): 15–31.

Fuchs, Simon Wolfgang. *In a Pure Muslim Land: Shi'ism between Pakistan and the Middle East*. Chapel Hill: University of North Carolina Press, 2019.

Glass, Andrew. "Bush Announces Launch of Operation Iraqi Freedom, March 19, 2003." *Politico*, March 18, 2017.

Gordon, Michael R. and Douglas Jehl. "After the War: Militants: Foreign Fighters Add to Resistance in Iraq, U.S. Says." *The New York Times*, June 22, 2003.

Haddad, Fanar. "Shia Centric State Building and Sunni Rejection in Post-2003 Iraq." Carnegie Endowment for International Peace, January 7, 2016.

Haddad, Fanar. *Understanding Sectarianism Sunni-Shia Relations in the Modern Arab World*. Oxford: Oxford University Press, 2020.

Hashemi, Nader. "Toward a Political Theory of Sectarianism in the Middle East: The Salience of Authoritarianism over Theology." *Journal of Islamic and Muslim Studies* 1, no. 1 (2016): 65.

Helfont, Samuel. *Compulsion in Religion: Saddam Hussein, Islam, and the Roots of Insurgencies in Iraq*. New York, NY: Oxford University Press, 2018.

Helfont, Samuel. "Saddam and the Islamists: The Ba'athists Regime's Instrumentalization of Religion in Foreign Affairs." *Middle East Journal* 68, no. 3 (2014): 352–366.

Khatib, Hakin. "Political Instrumentalization of Islam in a Violent State Crisis: The Case of Syria." *Journal of Applied Security Research*, 10 no. 3 (July 2015): 341–361.

Laub, Zachary and Jonathan Masters. "Islamic State in Iraq and Greater Syria." Council on Foreign Relations, June 12, 2014.

MacAskill, Ewen and Oliver Burkeman. "Power Vacuum That Has Taken U.S. by Surprise." *The Guardian*, April 10, 2003.

Moaddel, Mansoor, Mark Tessler and Ronald Inglehart. "Saddam Hussein and the Sunni Insurgency: Findings from Values Surveys." *Political Science Quarterly* 123, no 4 (2008): 623–644.

Nasr, Vali. *The Shia Revival: How Conflicts Within Islam Will Shape the Future*. New York: W.W. Norton & Company, 2006.

Pirsoul, Nicolas. "Sectarianism and Recognition in Iraq." *Democratic Theory* 6, no.1 (2019): 49-72.

Schanzer, Jonathan. "Ansar al-Islam Back in Iraq." *Insight Turkey* 6 no. 1 (January–March 2004): 94–104.

Sciolino, Elaine. "After the War; Iraq's Shiite Majority: A Painful History of Revolt and Schism." *The New York Times*, March 30, 1991.

Valbjorn, Morten. "What so Sectarian about Sectarian Politics? Identity Politics and Authoritarianism in New Middle East." *Studies in Ethnicity and Nationalism* 19, no. 1 (2019): 127–149.

Valbjorn, Morten. "Beyond the beyond(s): On the (many) third way(s) beyond primordialism and instrumentalism in the study of sectarianism." *Nations and Nationalism* 26, no. 1 (January 2020): 91–107.

Warde, Ibrahim. "Wagering on Sectarianism: The Political Economy of Extremism." *The Muslim World* 106, no. 1 (January 2016): 205–216.

Worth, Robert F. "Blast Destroys Shrine in Iraq, Setting Off Sectarian Fury." *New York Times*, February 22, 2006.

Yousif, Bassam. "The Political Economy of Sectarianism in Iraq." *International Journal of Contemporary Iraqi Studies* 4, no. 3 (December 2010): 357–367.

9
SECTARIANISM AND COUNTERTERRORISM

Explaining the "Silent Space" between Policy and Practice[1]

Heidi E. Lane

Introduction

Over the span of only two decades, Middle East and North African states have transformed in ways that most veteran observers would never have predicted. Since 2001, the traditional autocratic regimes that made up the MENA region have all but disappeared. Long-standing autocratic governments in Egypt and Tunisia have been overturned while others, such as Libya, Syria, and Yemen have disintegrated into proxy conflicts. Across the region there has been a dramatic realignment of bi-lateral and multi-lateral relationships and regional organizations. Despite these momentous changes, some familiar attributes of the "old" MENA remain. First, there is still a tendency among states, regardless of ideological and religious identity, to view aspects of their security, internal and external, through a sectarian lens. Sectarian politics, it would seem, are on the rise (Abdo 2016). Second, the region has seen an increase in securitization that grew after 9/11 and accelerated especially following the Arab Spring.

This chapter focuses on sectarianism and counterterrorism in the MENA region and examines where these two trends have intersected to shape state behavior. It looks at where sectarian attitudes have been preserved, newly created, or modified within this period of expanded securitization and how, if at all, sectarianism is expressed in counterterrorism policies and frameworks. Despite the enduring salience of sectarian practices within state institutions, a key question that arises is why do counterterrorism policies and related security architecture tend to omit direct references to sectarian fears? Is it purely the result of instrumentalist behavior on the part of less than democratic states who rely on what Bellin coined the "coercive apparatus" (Belin 2004). I argue that the reasons for this disconnect between policy and practice are more complex and can be viewed within the larger scope of international relations where domestic and international interests intersect and compete for dominance. Within the international system, less powerful states, such as those within the MENA region, have found ways to maximize key interests while at the same time, navigating areas of disagreement with US foreign policy. Sectarian strategies have been useful tools for state and non-state actors and organizations. With the War on Terror and international emphasis on counterterrorism that followed after 9/11, MENA states have also learned to deemphasize sectarian strategies and language within the context of counterterrorism even as it remains a central component of state security narratives.

This chapter first briefly revisits some of the academic debates surrounding the scholarship on sectarianism and places it within the larger context of securitization. Second, it discusses the potential impact of past and present international policies on sectarian behavior by considering the possible role that such policies have played in shaping the way in which states view sectarian issues. The third part of the chapter examines a range of counterterrorism measures that MENA states have used, particularly in response to the Arab Spring, where sectarian strategies have been institutionalized. The final section addresses the gap or "silent space" between policy and practice in some states and considers some preliminary explanations as to why states with traditionally deep sectarian cleavages and a long pattern of suppression against specific groups have pursued counterterrorism programs that make almost no mention of sectarian actors.

Establishing a lexicon: Securitization and Sectarianization

There is little consensus among scholars regarding the definitional scope of sectarianism, even as interest in this subject has grown in recent years. Early treatments of sectarianism were largely *ascriptive* and elevated primordial explanations, while more recent scholarship has incorporated both agency and dynamism. Some also expand the parameters of what constitutes "sect" beyond Sunni-Shia and include other communities such as Druze, Yazidi, and Kurdish populations that straddle ethnic and religious definitions while the broadest treatments also include intra-religious ideological divisions such as those embraced among *salafis*. Sectarianism, whether practiced by states or non-states, "sharply emphasizes boundaries with the 'Other', particularly when politicized or when claiming a monopoly over religious truth" (Hinnebusch 2019). Syria, Iraq, Bahrain, Saudi Arabia, and Lebanon have histories of employing sectarian practices, but a broadening of the definition also invites inclusion of Algeria in their treatment of the *pieds noir* during the Algerian Revolution, as well as Israel's sectarian policies towards Druze and Palestinian citizens of Israel.[2] In Jordan and Egypt, sectarian strategies have been used to diminish the appeal of *salafist* narratives, opening the aperature to intra-religious forms of sectarianism. Sectarian strategies, broadly defined, can be employed by states or by other actors, and become important tools of statecraft.

Two additional areas in the literature on sectarianism are relevant here. First is the question of *where* sectarianism takes hold or defines the way politics unfolds? This chapter is primarily focused on the state as actor and when states choose to use sectarian strategies in response to external or internal pressures or in response to perceived security threats that stem from ethnic or religious groups. However, there is much work to be done within this wider definition of sectarianism to place state behaviors in a more precise geopolitical context. In many scholarly treatments, sectarianism is associated with states that are weak or suffer internal ethnic and religious divisions. However, a closer look at the ways in which sectarianism is consciously utilized would suggest that *all* states, at some point or another, engage in some type of sectarian politics. Hashemi and Postel favor the term *sectarianization* to describe a set of self-conscious strategies, often used by states "to manage matters of sect, religion, and ethnicity that the state finds threatening or potentially damaging to its security or legitimacy."[3]

The second question has to do with temporality. That is, *when* rather than *where* does sectarianism become an important driver of politics? One familiar argument is that sectarianism rises during periods of intense state rivalry, such as the decades-long contest between Saudi Arabia and Iran and spreads to ignite other regional conflicts (Fisher 2016).[4] But do certain periods really experience more sectarianism than others? Again, Hashemi and Postel argue that the periods following 1979, 2003, and 2011 were notable turning points (Hashemi & Postel 2017). Sectarianization, therefore, unlike sectarianism, is dynamic and responsive to internal and external political conditions, particularly when linked to questions of security or legitimacy. Moreover, sectarian strategies have often been attributed to weak states or states with histories of internal divisions and civil war, but a closer look reveals that almost all states, at some point or another, utilize sectarianization in order to preserve core interests. For Hashemi and Postel, "authoritarianism, not theology, is the critical factor that shapes the sectarianization process" (Hashemi & Postel 2017).

Democracy Promotion and the Sectarian Variable

If Hashemi and Postel are correct and authoritarianism does indeed shape the sectarianization process, what role then do periods of relative reform and democratization have on this process? From the end of the Cold War until 2001, US and international policies were largely devoted to "security and stability" within the MENA region. The end of the Gulf War in 1991 gave new impetus to the "stability" paradigm and the promotion of democracy through political and economic liberalization. Democracy promotion and its associated programs were funded by various US agencies to include the State Department and USAID, but many were actually administered through NGOs and civil society organizations and were intended to boost efforts to liberalize political and economic systems through electoral and institutional reform. In practice, US foreign military and economic assistance to MENA states was linked, explicitly or implicitly, to states' willingness to commit to internal political and economic reforms, particularly in the area of civil society. Consistent with the theoretical underpinnings of neo-liberal globalization, democracy promotion programs emphasized liberalization, privatization, and deregulation of state institutions (Guazzone & Pioppi 2012: 4–6). However, democracy promotion did not directly address sectarian issues except as a subset of minority rights.

For US policymakers, the paradigm of "security and stability" was thus, both an optimal outcome and a dominant means intended to foster a peaceful post-Cold War regional balance and assure the free flow of natural resources as well as advance international idealism and democratic ideals. The idealistic proponents of democratization, including many in the scholarly community, saw the MENA as ripe for the fourth wave of democratization.[5] In the field of Middle East politics, liberalization tended to be viewed as a collective good that would be beneficial, rather than harmful, to the respective political systems where it was adopted.[6] Though the "fourth wave" never came, regional governments in the Middle East and North Africa seem to have learned important lessons about how to manage the demands of international donor organizations and NGOs who carried out the work on the ground. In some rare cases, liberalization and reform was tolerated, but far more commonly, MENA governments protected the interests of long-standing autocrats by finding ways to appear as though they were implementing recommended reforms without substantively changing existing power-structures or state behaviors.

While US foreign military and economic assistance to regional states was linked, explicitly and implicitly, to states' willingness to entertain reform of their political and economic institutions, these prerequisites were rarely enforced. In fact, rather than incentivize, the very premise of much of the liberalization and reform efforts directly threatened regional governments in significant ways. Democracy promotion raised concern in many states since it necessarily included pressing for better treatment of marginalized groups who often had ethnic, religious, and sectarian affiliations. Many of these same groups were exactly those that regional governments had long sought to control through sectarian based strategies. In Bahrain, for example, political liberalization necessarily included empowering the Shia majority which the Bahraini monarchy had long resisted. Kuwait, for its part, had a long record of what might be called positive sectarianization. Wells has demonstrated that the Kuwaiti government has utilized sectarian strategies for several decades in different ways, but always with the objective of weakening any formidable opposition to the Al-Sabah rulers (Wells 2017). When Kuwaiti rulers were threatened by vocal tribal and Sunni Islamist groups, the monarchy gave additional leverage to Kuwait's Shia minorities as a means to galvanize support for the government. In Lebanon, sectarian strategies were baked into formal power sharing arrangements of the Taif Accord which that many believed had been the glue that held the country together since the end of the Lebanese Civil War. In post-invasion Iraq, the Lebanese example, though hardly ideal and one which effectively codified sectarianism, served as a model for the constitutional arrangements after the fall of Saddam Hussein in 2003 (Wells 2017).

In key instances, the era of democracy promotion and the pushback that it created did little to mitigate sectarian practices. To the contrary, in some cases, democracy promotion may have inadvertently furthered sectarian practices.[7] During the George W. Bush years, the War on Terror significantly increased the profile of democracy as a matter of policy. In Iraq and elsewhere, the promotion of a liberal model of democracy did not deliver what was originally noted and fell short of expectations (Bridoux & Russell 2013). The US also invested in numerous interagency initiatives that were intended to direct resources and attention to address the underlying causes of terrorism. As part of COIN (counterinsurgency) and CT (counterterrorism) frameworks, US agencies such as USAID had a potentially important role to play in creating broad cross-sectarian practices within the context of counterterrorism. In large part, the participation of development agencies and organizations was based on the premise that terrorism could only be stopped through long-term strategies that addressed marginalized and underrepresented populations. Many of these programs were designed for implementation in African countries. However, the normative values and prescriptions nonetheless were part of the overall approach to counterterrorism and were advanced by USAID and DOS in particular(Baltazar and Kvitashvili 2007).

In some states, limited liberalization and reform programs were tolerated and even promoted. In Jordan and Egypt, for example, modest electoral reforms took place during the 1990s. In the Gulf, the Bahraini monarchy debated how it might placate demands by its citizens for more political voice by increasing power-sharing arrangements within its nascent legislative assembly. Far more commonly, however, regional ruling elites continued to guard the interests of long-standing autocrats by delaying international pressures for reform and did not resist altering existing power structures or state behaviors. For many regional governments, democracy promotion itself directly threatened the existing political balance, in part because such programs tended to focus on marginalized groups who often had ethnic, sectarian, and religious affiliations.

After the failures that accompanied the 2003 US-led invasion of Iraq, democracy promotion faded. As early as 2006, it began to recede from the US foreign-policy agenda as the War on Terror consumed more and more human and financial resources. The most muscular permutation of the concepts and objectives behind democracy promotion had been the Bush Administration's "Freedom Agenda," which was integral to the logic behind the US invasion of Iraq in 2003.[8] Even before the invasion, the Freedom Agenda began to erode the political will of long-time US allies. Former Saudi foreign minister, Prince Saud al-Faisal, for example, was quoted in the New York Times stating "if there is stability, if there is peace in the Middle East, that is the way that it will bring about a democratization and an opening of society, not through war."[9] By the time President Obama took office in 2008, democracy promotion began to rapidly disappear from official rhetoric and policy debates. Most importantly, democracy promotion encountered significant pushback by many MENA states who believed that their own security was at risk and blamed what they considered "terrorist elements" for internal dissent and unrest. Security, rather than democracy promotion, they argued, should be the focus of US and international efforts. Regional leaders pointed to political instability and insurgency in Iraq as evidence that democracy promotion had failed and blamed the sectarian divides squarely on the ill-advised policies of the United States.

Ample evidence of the gradual shift in US policy away from democracy promotion is also found in official documents. The 2006 US Strategy for Combating Terrorism mentions al-Qaeda 17 times and invokes "democracy" 17 times, making the assertion that "in effective democracies, freedom is indivisible… [democracies] are the long-term antidote to the ideology of terrorism today."[10] By contrast, in the 2018 US Strategy for Counterterrorism, there were only three mentions of democracy.[11] While the wording of these documents provides only one window into complex and dynamic foreign policy initiatives, the move away from an era that prioritized liberal reform became clear as the decade progressed. Indeed, the 2020 US National Strategy for Combatting Terrorist and Other Illicit Financing mentions "terrorist" 93 times but the word democracy did not appear even once.[12] As former US President Donald Trump boldly proclaimed in 2017, "we are not nation building again, we are killing terrorists" (Miller 2017). There was one critical problem that had plagued the policymaking community long before 2001; there remained almost no consensus on the definition of terrorism nor how to best prevent it.[13] Some observers viewed the eclipse of democracy initiatives as counterproductive. One widely-circulated RAND study concluded that abandoning the pursuit of democracy promotion was premature and that in order to effectively engage in successful counterterrorism, democracy promotion "if carried out carefully, should remain in the toolbox" (Kaye at al. 2008). However, private and public pressure that prevailed after the invasion of Iraq led many US officials to conclude that the war on terrorism could not be waged with soft power initiatives such as those that had been so prevalent in the 1990s. While the shift away from democracy promotion in US policymaking circles can be traced directly to US failures at statebuilding in both Iraq and Afghanistan, regional allies, for their part, continued to argue that democracy promotion had fueled increased radicalization and sectarianism across the region. Saudi Arabia and Egypt, for example, repeatedly voiced their opinion in public and private venues that US liberalization policies were to blame for the growth of movements like the Muslim Brotherhood who they argued, shared the extremist views like that of Al-Qaeda. Many pointed to the sectarian fragmentation of Iraq and the growing strength of Iranian influence across the region.

At the same time, MENA states invested heavily in improved security architecture that centered on counterterrorism and anti-terrorism. As democracy promotion policies receded, the War on Terror and the international emphasis on mitigating and preventing further attacks by al-Qaeda offered regional states lucrative political and economic incentives to invest in their own robust counterterrorism architecture. After 2001, the MENA region became one of the world's fastest-growing markets for global military sales.[14] Between 2000 and 2009, military expenditures in the MENA rose a total of 83% going from US$51.4 billion to US$91.4 billion.[15] While these figures do not specifically single out how much was spent on counterterrorism and internal security, the top priority of most MENA states remained that of domestic security. In the years following 9/11, every MENA state, from Egypt to Algeria, adopted new counterterrorism laws, established special security courts, and otherwise re-tooled their existing security establishments as part of their participation in the fight against terrorism. As broad securitization grew exponentially in the years following 9/11, there was also a marked increase in debates about state-sponsored terrorism and the sectarian motives of specific actors in the region. Iran, some states argued, fueled sectarian violence between Sunnis and Shia in Iraq. As early as 2007, the late Saudi monarch, King Abdullah remarked, "in beloved Iraq, blood flows between brothers in the shadow of illegitimate foreign occupation and hateful sectarianism, threatening a civil war" (Holland 2007). In post-invasion Iraq, but especially following the final withdrawal of US troops in December 2011, a number of MENA states had still refused to restore diplomatic posts in Iraq because of what they considered sectarian favoritism. Saudi Arabia refrained from opening its own embassy in Iraq until 2015, only after the death of Abdullah. Many regional leaders, publicly and privately agreed with the Saudi view that the vacuum left by the US departure had led directly to Iran's growing influence in Iraq and strengthened Iran's influence with Shia organizations in Lebanon, Syria, and Yemen. The "Shia Crescent" which grew in the vacuum left by the United States, they argued, furthered sectarian tensions across the whole region.[16]

The Relationship Between Terrorism and Sectarianism

Discussions of sectarianism as it related to terrorism were at first bound up in a larger discussion of the "root causes" thesis, which dominated in both academic and policymaking communities especially after 2001. "Root causes" of terrorism, it was argued, stemmed from social and political conditions found in many MENA states that left citizens without avenues for non-violent political participation. Indeed, the idea that terrorism was related to "root causes" drew directly from the key concepts that had shaped liberalization and reform policies during the 1990s and early 2000s. Countering Samuel Huntington's "clash of civilizations" thesis, policymakers along with civil society and human rights organizations argued that "root causes" were tangible and measurable variables, and tended to be found in societies that lacked freedoms, had poor or corrupt governing institutions, and where citizens were routinely subjected to arbitrary and repressive security apparatuses. However, as the War on Terror progressed and MENA states suffered their own attacks, terrorism became easily associated with sectarian actors and motives. Although empirical evidence between terrorism and sectarianism remains weak, discussions of sectarianism and terrorism often overlapped. Moreover, the persistence of violent conflicts across the region before and after 2001, have aided sectarian narratives and at times, entered into the official rhetoric of state actors.

Accompanying these contentious debates about the causes of terrorism was a steady decline in public support for pluralism, nationalism, and cross-sectarian organizations among citizens in the MENA region. Guazzone and Pioppi claim that, starting in the 1980s, top-down liberalization was accompanied by a marked decline in nationalist ideology (Guazzone & Pioppi 2012: 10).[17] The exuberance that many Arab citizens felt when local NGOs briefly found openings to advance reformist agendas during the heady period of the 1990s grew dimmer. By 2005, advocates of reform reported very little progress, a general fatigue caused by persistent and stronger autocratic rule and an increase in divisive forms of ethno-religious nationalism and sectarianism. Therefore, the sectarian variable became a probable accelerant for terrorism in the minds of many policymakers. In general, across the region, segmented ethnic and religious identity-based politics seemed to overtake inclusive national narratives. Not surprisingly, these conditions also created greater insecurity for regional governments that were being swept into the fight against terrorism. For many, the failures associated with the US-led invasion of Iraq revived fears of sectarian violence even as the rest of the world focused more on the threat of extremism carried out by Islamist organizations like Al-Qaeda.

Within this regional context, the US, as well as other key Western nations, and international organizations, encouraged MENA governments to move swiftly to address internal problems that could lead to further terrorist incidents. On the one hand, governments were incentivized to examine "root causes" of terrorism. On the other hand, new international frameworks were also adopted that placed responsibility as well as outright demands on MENA states to create and then report on what measures they were taking to prevent and counter terrorism at home. MENA nations found themselves being criticized for not doing enough, but also for approaching the problem with weak tools. From approximately 2004 onwards, more than a few MENA governments quickly adopted counterterrorism frameworks in response to the international frenzy. Many of these frameworks have included sectarian strategies that limit citizens' rights rather than mitigate the formation of violent extremist organizations. Whether these outcomes were intended or not, the ways in which counterterrorism has been practiced by most MENA governments has given fuel to critics who see securitization and sectarianization as conscious processes that are mutually reinforcing (Matthiesen 2017).

The Impact of International and Regional Counterterrorism Frameworks

Adding to the association of sectarianism with terrorism was the expansion and growth of international organizations and global initiatives aimed at countering terrorism. For MENA states, the international focus on a generic terrorism provided both limits and opportunities. The European Union, United Nations, and NATO all established new or renewed frameworks to address global terrorism. The United Nations reinvigorated the UN Counterterrorism Committee (UNCTC), already in existence prior to 2001, as part of the UN Security Council. Terrorism, though recognized as a UN area of interest, had previously been only a minor item on the UN agenda. After 2001 however, the UN took a leading role in raising the profile of global terrorism under the mandate of UNSCR 1373. The

UNCTC, for its part, set forth a global agenda with a common set of standards for states that were intended to assist them in fighting terrorism at home. These standards also required states to submit periodic reports[18] that detailed the measures that were being taken to fight terrorism on their own home fronts. At the beginning, most MENA states furnished periodic reports, but over time, the reports declined in frequency. For some MENA members, the UN actions provided an international stage on which government spokespersons could showcase their *bona fides* in the area of preventing and countering global terrorism in their own backyards. The UNCTC also offered individual states greater access to a global audience when it came to showcasing efforts to fight terrorism abroad. Despite these global efforts, terrorism and by extension, counterterrorism continued to lack a concrete definition or specific parameters. This opened the door to a variety of interpretations as some member states began to question UNCTC efforts. Some MENA states viewed these measures as encroaching on state sovereignty.[19]

Another entity that grew out of this period was the UN Office of Counterterrorism. Separate from the UNCTC, the UNOCT is donor-based which also provided wealthy states with access and agency surrounding the debates about terrorism and counterterrorism. In recent years, more than three quarters of UNOCT funding has come from Qatar and Saudi Arabia (Kessels & Lafas 2021). The top five donors, according to the UN, are Qatar, Saudi Arabia, the European Union, China, and the United States.[20] NATO also established its own framework to address global terrorism. NATO's swift response to 9/11 by invoking Article 5 of its charter drew the postwar defensive organization into the business of counterterrorism. Beyond the NATO mission in support of Operation Enduring Freedom (OEF) in Afghanistan, it also revived counterterrorism as one of its core missions. Though some European members argued against this addition, NATO ultimately drafted "Counterterrorism Policy Guidelines" as well as a "Military Concept for Defence Against Terrorism" (North Atlantic Treaty Organization 2022). In recent years, NATO members and its "partners"[21] contributed to the 85-member Global Coalition to Defeat ISIS/ISIL which itself included several MENA states whose own counterterrorism policies had grown in scope and scale during the two decades since 2001. Other cooperative international forums that grew out of this period include the Global Counterterrorism Committee (GCTC) which also courted the participation of MENA states and served as an important venue for shaping their counterterrorism approaches.

None of these international organizations or committees, however, included guidelines on how partner states would handle their own internal matters when it came to terrorism nor did they establish guidelines for addressing sectarian concerns. While there is some evidence that these international forums have played a role in dissuading MENA states from overt expression of sectarian strategies when it comes to counterterrorism, once MENA states became partners, the means they used to counter terrorism at home have rarely been criticized by these same bodies. At a regional level and in response to the rise of ISIL, The Islamic Military Counterterrorism Coalition (ICMTC), (also known as the Islamic Military Alliance or IMA), was formed by Saudi Arabia in December 2015. Based in Riyadh, the establishment of this intergovernmental counterterrorism alliance was viewed in some circles as an overtly sectarian response to Iranian involvement in the Yemeni conflict. Its membership grew and now currently boasts membership of thirty-four countries. A fairly sizeable number of these nations have conducted numerous military operations in Yemen.[22] Though its primary stated objective is to protect Muslim states from terrorism regardless of sect, it functions more as a loosely coordinated group of nations with the similar interest of appearing to support a collective counterterrorism framework at a regional level. The ICTMC, however, does not include Iraq and Syria in its membership on the grounds that these two nations are under Iranian or Iranian proxy influence. While the success of such regional counterterrorism frameworks has been unclear, it is increasingly evident that regional and international counterterrorism policies have provided a formula for some MENA states to pursue sectarian strategies under the guise of counterterrorism.

Counterterrorism Policies and Practices: Explaining the Silent Space

In the initial years following 9/11, the counterterrorism policies adopted by MENA states were sometimes drafted in consultation with the UNCTC. However, as the years passed, this coordination diminished as other areas of counterterrorism cooperation increased. For example, between 2003 and 2006, Morocco, Jordan, Tunisia, Bahrain, Turkey, and Qatar passed their own versions of counterterrorism legislation (Whitaker 2007). In some cases, the impetus for doing so came not from international pressure, but rather from deadly attacks that took place within these states. For example, in 2003, Morocco was rocked by suicide bombings in Casablanca while Jordan suffered suicide bombings in Amman in November 2005. Whitaker has found that there was an additional correlation between how quickly a country sought to pass counterterrorism legislation and its Freedom House scores measuring political rights. Those states that were eager to pass counterterrorism laws were also among the most authoritarian (Whitaker 2007).[23]

Another practice in the first years of the War on Terror was to use soft power as a tool of anti-terrorism. In later years, these approaches became better known as "counter-extremism initiatives" and spawned an entire industry of private companies who delivered full programming to interested parties. One notable example of a soft power approach was Jordan's "Amman Message" which provided the public, both at home and abroad, with an authoritative and mainstream interpretation of Islam.[24] The document, though intended for domestic consumption, ultimately gained little traction except in receptive international audiences where it was viewed as an example of how some Muslims were speaking up against extremist voices such as those of al-Qaeda and its associated counterparts. Such soft power initiatives coupled with the adoption of robust security measures, showcased to the international community the extent to which some MENA states were willing to go to support the larger objectives of the War on Terror. Many MENA governments still engaged in sectarian strategies, but under the auspices of the War on

Terror, learned that international support tended to be more forthcoming when direct sectarian references were absent from official documents. Counterterrorism frameworks, therefore, appear to provide a "silent space" for sectarianization in the absence of an agreed upon definition of terrorism and the global emphasis on countering terrorism. Thus, willing governments were able to "counter the global threat" in ways that both validated these international frameworks and protected the individual prerogatives of states. This delicate balance between policy and practice shifted after the onset of the Arab Spring. The onset of the Arab Spring dramatically transformed regional security interests and presented many MENA governments with existential threats. Events in Egypt, Libya, Tunisia, and Syria threatened the stability of other MENA governments in ways that were much more profound than anything that had occurred during the War on Terror. Unlike the occasional terrorist attacks that most states had experienced, the mass protests and rage that broke out in Tunisia, Egypt, Saudi Arabia, Bahrain and elsewhere were, in fact, mainly cross-sectarian.

In the aftermath of the Arab Spring sectarianism underwent a transformation in the MENA region. Some regional leaders stoked theories that the Arab Spring was the work of outside powers such as the US and Iran (Mikail 2014).[25] Arab citizens themselves, though they expressed cross-sectarian objectives at the outset, soon became fearful that the removal of even repressive governments could lead to the violent conditions that prevailed in Iraq after the removal of Saddam Hussein. In some cases, Sunnis supported protesters in one state, but not another based on largely sectarian affiliation. For example, one study showed that in Kuwait, Kuwaiti Shia were in favor of the protest movements in Bahrain, but against those led by Syrians while among Sunni Kuwaitis, the inverse was true (Albloshi 2016: 109–126). In response to protests, however, in almost all cases, MENA governments fell back on security measures that were strengthened after 2001 in order to counter terrorism. Counterterrorism frameworks, therefore, offered states a new set of tools to address sectarian fears and objectives but also allowed governments to make claims that these measures were not targeting one or another community, but rather aimed at "terrorists" and extremists. Jordan, UAE, Bahrain, Saudi Arabia, and Oman introduced new laws that were somewhat generic in their intent which were directed at mitigating the spread of "extremist ideologies."[26] While many of these laws were originally promulgated for use against violent Islamist and salafist organizations, evidence from the Arab Spring suggests that these laws have and will likely again be utilized during times of crisis or unrest against citizens who pose "national security risks."

Other state institutions that were securitized during the War on Terror and became tools to suppress the Arab Spring are security courts and special legal bodies that were promulgated to deal with counterterrorism or security violations. The majority of these courts or special counsels are overlaid on already weak and largely ineffective legal structures and tend to be heavily staffed by military or security personnel. In some instances, institutional securitization also accompanied changes in constitutional documents where amendments to existing constitutions have been made to accommodate a state's turn towards greater securitization with emphasis on counterterrorism. Even though some of these institutions underwent modest liberalization and reform in recent decades that resulted in some rollback of emergency laws, the post-Arab Spring security environment has prompted MENA governments to offer new justification for counterterrorism and counter-extremist measures. The UAE, for example, which has been historically unresponsive to calls for reform, has invested very heavily in the area of counterterrorism in internal security services at the domestic level and in counterterrorism forces that have the ability to be deployed outside the UAE. Given the high monetary investment in this sector in recent years, it would seem likely that UAE counterterrorism policy reflects a reframing of foreign and domestic security policies that includes sectarian strategies to protect security interests within the UAE. While Emirati official rhetoric typically identifies Iran as the main threat, there has been relatively less emphasis on discourse that reveals overt sectarian strategies even when it appears that sectarian preferences are clearly at play.

Bahrain[27] has also fallen back on counterterrorism and anti-terrorism to mitigate sectarian fears (Möller 2018). It is worth noting that sectarianism is not codified in either the Bahraini constitution or in other official documents, but sectarianization strategies are routinely used by security forces.[28] For example, the constitution of Bahrain does not refer directly to sectarian affiliation, nor does it make reference to different religious affiliations except to note that the official religion of the state is Islam (*din wa dawla*).[29] Official documents to include passports also do not refer to religion or sect (Möller 2018). Regardless of the implicit right to practice one's own religion, religious processions, gatherings and associations are illegal until granted a permit. Official data on how often gatherings are prohibited or impeded by the state because of their religious or sectarian intent is not available, but prohibitions are routinely reported by international watchdog groups (Bassiouni et al. 2011). In some cases, Bahrain has utilized arguments about terrorism proactively. In the case of Bahraini cleric and spiritual leader of the Bahraini opposition movement al-Wefaq, Ayatollah Isa al-Qasim, Bahraini officials revoked the cleric's citizenship on the grounds that he was "spreading extremism."[30] While Bahrain has allowed some to reapply for citizenship, this tactic has been used with more frequency since 2011.

Counterterrorism measures in Kuwait have also increased since the onset of the Arab Spring and many have revolved around the Lebanese Hezbollah. In 2017, a plot by Kuwaitis who sympathized with the organization was uncovered and the plotters were convicted of belonging to a "terrorist cell"[31] but the case of Kuwait is instructive. Some of the most vociferous sectarian politics has come not from the security establishment, but from the Kuwaiti National Assembly. Former Kuwaiti MP, for example, Waleed Tabatabai called for legislation that would criminalize Kuwaitis who were members of the Lebanese Hezbollah. Although the proposed legislation was never adopted, Tabatabai was subsequently charged with several crimes in Kuwait. Kuwait, while still employing sectarian strategies, has often used them to suppress overt sectarian initiatives that have emerged from the various political blocs within the National Assembly.[32]

Sectarianization and the Armed Forces

Given that counterterrorism frameworks have mainly been implemented by the institutions that govern the security of the state such as the armed forces and interior ministries, what role, if any, have the armed forces played with regard to sectarianization? Do liberal international policies such as democracy promotion reach these audiences in non-democratic states? How do the armed forces of MENA approach the question of sectarianism, if at all? While this question merits much further inquiry, it is integral to the discussion of securitization in a region where sectarian strategies shape state politics and institutions.

Until recently, scholarship about the MENA region has been weak on the role of armed forces and how they interact and shape state decisionmaking, particularly in times of crisis. For more than a generation, scholars viewed militaries as irrelevant to the political landscape except as guardians of authoritarian structures. More recently, there has been a rediscovery of the nuanced roles that armies and other armed forces have had, particularly during the Arab Spring, in the making (or breaking) of politics (Albrecht et al 2016). Albrecht et al. have examined a variety of different responses among MENA militaries during the Arab Spring and the conclusions vary greatly depending on context and circumstance (Albrecht et al 2016). Indeed, they found that the outcome of several of the Arab Spring uprisings were either partly or fully dependent on how the armed forces behaved at the moment of crisis for the government. In the case of Egypt, for example, the military sided with the protestors. In the case of Syria, it did not. What do we know about the use of sectarian strategies within the armed forces and how might counterterrorism frameworks be used to manage sectarian behaviors? If past is an indicator of the future, sectarian strategies have often been carried out by the armed forces and their composition, in some instances, is itself based on sectarian belonging. In the Syrian example, unofficial sectarianization through conscription was precisely what led to an eventual dominance of Alawi within the military and security sectors. More recently, since the onset of the Syrian civil war, many have argued that the complete sectarianization of the Syrian state has unfolded during the past decade to the extent that it has despite Assad's continued control of some parts of state. Syria as one nation no longer exists and is instead comprised of small proxy states governed by sectarian militias. While the Syrian case may be extreme, similar patterns are evident in Libya.

In other MENA states, the situation is different. Although the defense budgets of almost every MENA country have been on a steady incline (particularly in the case of Saudi Arabia and UAE in recent years) many militaries do not have a citizen base that will support a sectarian turn. For instance, in the cases of Qatar and UAE, the percentage of non-citizens and non-Arabs who serve in the military exceeds 30% and in Qatar, whose military is by far the smallest, non-Qataris make up more than two-thirds of those in uniform. No reliable figures are published for how many non-citizens work in the supportive structures of the defense establishment. At present, the inability for several Gulf nations to fully provide for their own defense without hiring non-citizens may mute the immediate potential for overt sectarianization of the armed forces at this time. More study is needed to draw any firm conclusions, but it is clear that both the security sector in MENA nations, and militaries in particular, have undergone significant change in the past three decades. It is not clear how much of this change has been structural and how much has been doctrinal and related to new norms such as jointness or combined operations. Some of this change is driven by international engagement through agencies such as the Defense Security Cooperation Agency (DSCA) whose mission is to encourage, foster, and fund cooperation between US and other militaries across the world.[33] Many countries provide some type of foreign military training which ranges from tactical to strategic. The US, as the largest provider of foreign military training, offers courses to a variety of nations on a wide range of different areas and subjects. In a recent study of foreign military training, Miles-Joyce found that despite the extensive amount of training to impart liberal norms, "norm conflict" led military respondents to fall back on organizational cohesion and group interests (Miles-Joyce 2022). Though Miles-Joyce draws from data on Liberia, her findings have salience for MENA militaries given the high degree of corporate belonging and institutional cohesion that exists in most of the region. If such results are translated to MENA militaries, it is likely that sectarian strategies have been practiced without the explicit reference to such practices in counterterrorism documents and frameworks, thus allowing for further "silent space" between policies and practices.

Conclusion

If there is "silent space" between actual state practices and the *official* articulation of counterterrorism policies, what are the most salient explanations? Do states consciously omit sectarian references from official counterterrorism documents and frameworks when presenting their counterterrorism strategies to the domestic or in international forums in order to preserve their strategic options? Does "omission" of such references represent the opportunity for "commission" or more flexibility within individual national security? And is it possible that this "silent space" between policy and practice actually constrains the state in certain instances? Full exploration of this topic will require further empirical data, however, the relationship between securitization and sectarian strategies, particularly within the context of counterterrorism seems undeniable given present evidence. In the previous sections, I have argued that a decade of democracy promotion in the 1990s, followed by a hard turn after 2001 towards securitization, likely pressured MENA states to accommodate international norms that many did not share. Policies associated with democracy promotion and liberalization threatened the traditional ways in which many MENA states had previously managed sectarian issues. In response, these states resisted such pressures, but often found themselves in conflict with expected international norms associated with liberalization and reform. By contrast, the War on Terror, although it also came with international pressures, gave states new tools that allowed them to develop new strategies to deal with security threats and enjoy international approbation rather than punishment. In fact, if anything, in some cases, states that failed to adopt counterterrorism platforms were instead criticized for being weak on terrorism.[34] Sectarian strategies therefore remained prevalent and though never openly encouraged, were rarely questioned by international proponents of the War on Terror. Thus, they occupied a "silent space" that often was either unnoticed or ignored. Perhaps as a consequence, most MENA states have also refrained from codifying their own national counterterrorism policies and instead, fall back on the frameworks and reports that they furnish for international forums such as the UNCTC. The vague and noncommittal content of these reports offers little in the way of substance on who can be and will be considered as a terrorist in the future and the practice of sectarianization across a range of institutions of state are likely to remain prevalent.

Notes

1 Disclaimer: The views in this chapter are those of the author and do not represent or reflect, officially or unofficially, the views of the US Naval War College, the US Navy, or the US Department of Defense.
2 Notable examples of states that fuel the process of sectarianization even in the absence of active internal wars include Israel, Saudi Arabia, and even Bahrain at the local level of policing. In the Israeli case, participation by some minorities in the security of the state has institutionalized this type of sectarianization (this would include the Druze, the Bedouin in border security).
3 The term "sectarianism", they argue, is static, Orientalist in origin and typically associated with primordial narratives (Hashemi and Postel 2017).
4 On the Cold War origins of the Saudi-Iranian rivalry, see Hiro (2018).
5 Much of the research of this period was ground breaking, but also adopted a normative approach that assumed that such liberalization programs would do more good than harm to the respective political systems that underwent some degree of transformation. For two overviews of this period, see Baaklini et al. (1999); Teitelbaum (2009).
6 For two excellent examples of this scholarship, see Baaklini et al. (1999) and Teitelbaum (2009.)
7 The 2003 invasion of Iraq and the subsequent ousting of Saddam Hussein served as catalysts for the surge of sectarian conflict of violence throughout the country. Chaos and insecurity from both top-down and bottom-up levels of society, provided an opportunity for sectarian identity to be instrumentalized by state and non-state actors. This often translated to high levels of violence as evidenced by the actions of Al-Qaeda in Iraq and later ISIL.
8 George W. Bush, "President Discusses the Future of Iraq." Remarks by the president at the American Enterprise Institute. The White House, Office of the Press Secretary, Washington DC, February 26, 2003. President Bush Addresses the American Enterprise Institute (archives.gov).
9 "A Nation at War; Arab Criticism: Saudi Arabian Foreign Minister urges US to pause from invasion," New York Times, March 23, 2003.
10 "US National Strategy for Combating Terrorism," 2006, p. 9. https://2001-2009.state.gov/s/ct/rls/wh/71803.htm.
11 "National Strategy for Counterterrorism," Office of the Director of National Intelligence, October 2018. https://www.dni.gov/index.php/features/national-strategy-for-counterterrorism.

12 "National Strategy for Combating Terrorist and Other Illicit Financing," United States Department of the Treasury, 2020. https://home.treasury.gov/system/files/136/national-strategy-to-counter-illicit-financev2.pdf.
13 For an excellent and comprehensive treatment of how terrorism was viewed prior to 2001, see Zoller (2021).
14 "The Arab Thermidor: The Resurgence of the Security State." Project on Middle East Political Science (POMEPS). For a general view of counterterrorism activities in the region, see US Department of State Reports on Terrorism – The Middle East and North Africa, 2017. https://www.state.gov/reports/country-reports-on-terrorism-2017/.
15 "The Global Militarization Index (GMI)," Bonn International Center for Conversion, February 2011, p.11.
16 "The Arab Thermidor: The Resurgence of the Security State Memos," project on Middle East Political Science, https://pomeps.org/the-arab-thermidor-memos; for a more general overview of counterterrorism activities across the region, see US Department of State, "Country Reports on Terrorism – The Middle East and North Africa," 2017. https://www.state.gov/j/ct/rls/crt/2017/282844.htm. See also "A Shia Crescent? What Fallout for the US?" Edited transcript of the proceedings of the 41st Capitol Hill Conference, Middle East Policy Council, October 14, 2005 in *Middle East Policy*, vol. 12, no. 4 (Winter 2005).
17 The Guazzone-Pioppi volume is particularly useful because of its organizational framework. The authors included in the volume analyze the changes in four Arab countries that have taken place since the 1980s in three sectors: politics, economics, and security. See methodology, pp. 8–15.
18 Reports were supposed to be submitted by member states between the years of 2001–2006. Many states complied in all six years, but the quality and content of the reports varies greatly from country to country.
19 The exact wording of Item 7 in the UN document 56/88 (24 January 2002) titled "Measures to Eliminate International Terrorism" reads: "The General Assembly urges all States that have not yet done so to consider, as a matter of priority, and in accordance with Security Council resolution 1373 (2001), becoming parties to relevant conventions and protocols as referred to in paragraph 6 of General Assembly resolution 51/210, as well as the International Convention for the Suppression of Terrorist Bombings and the International Convention for the Suppression of the Financing of Terrorism and calls upon all States to enact, as appropriate, domestic legislation necessary to implement the provisions of those conventions and protocols, to ensure that the jurisdiction of their courts enables them to bring to trial the perpetrators of terrorist acts, and to cooperate with and provide support and assistance to other States and relevant international and regional organizations to that end."
20 United Nations, "Funding and Donors," 2020, https://www.un.org/counterterrorism/funding-and-donors.
21 The term "partner" has a number of usages and depending on context, denotes a formal or informal relationship with an organization or state. In the case of NATO, for example, partners are named states who have agreed to a certain set of standards under a NATO umbrella. In the case of the US, partnerships tends to be a more flexible term applied, sometimes in lieu of ally.
22 The actual number of members may be closer to 45 as of June 2022. See the official website at: The Islamic Military Counter Terrorism Coalition (imctc.org).
23 Whitaker looks at all countries rather than those just in the MENA region.
24 Amman Message – The Official Site: https://ammanmessage.com/.
25 See also Farha (2016: 8–60).
26 Some of these were also modeled on the language found within international frameworks such as that of the UN Counterterrorism Committee.
27 The current population of Bahrain, by way of comparison, is approximately 1.25 million, 46% of which are Bahraini citizens. There is no official data that expresses population

breakdown by sect within Islam and the census does not reflect the differences between non-Muslim citizens (Möller 2018).
28 The most meticulous inquiry into the Bahraini case is found in Bassiouni et al. (2011).
29 The reference to official religion appears in Article 2 (2002).
30 Revocation of Bahraini Cleric's Citizenship Marks Sectarian Tension in Gulf Region – Center for Security Policy. Article 17 of the Bahraini Constitution states that "Bahraini nationality shall be determined by law." Furthermore, "A person enjoying Bahraini nationality shall not be stripped of his/her nationality except in cases of treason and other types of cases prescribed by law" (English translation from Constitute.org). See also articles in Bahrain Mirror (English and Arabic) online. Note: *treason* (الخيانه) It is worth noting that earlier constitutions (including that of 1973) included dual-citizenship among the reasons for revocation of Bahraini nationality.
31 "Kuwait MP Proposes Jail Terms for Hizballah Supporters," *The New Arab*, July 24, 2017.
32 "Kuwait: Counter Terrorism Legislation Proposed by MP," Library of Congress, August 3, 2017; "Kuwait Sentences MPs to Jail Terms for storming into Parliament," Reuters World News, November 27, 2017; In November 2020, the Court of Cassation suspended the seven-year jail sentence against Tabatabai.
33 DSCA was established in 1971 and is based in Arlington, VA. See www.dsca.mil.
34 In 2004, the Indonesian constitutional courts ruled a number of terrorist prosecutions were unconstitutional. The court was subsequently criticized by the US and Australia (Whitaker (2007).

Bibliography

Abdo, Geneive. *The New Sectarianism: The Arab Uprisings and the Rebirth of the Shi'a-Sunni Divide*. Oxford: Oxford University Press, 2016.

Albloshi, Hamad H. "Sectarianism and the Arab Spring: the Case of the Kuwaiti Shia." *The Muslim World* 106, no. 1 (2016): 109–126.

Albrecht, Holger, Aurel Croissant and Fred H. Lawson. *Armies and Insurgencies in the Arab Spring*. Philadelphia: University of Pennsylvania Press, 2016.

Baaklini, Abdo et al. *Legislative Politics in the Arab World: The Resurgence of Democratic Institutions*. Boulder: Lynne Rienner Publishers, 1999.

Baltazar, Thomas, and Elisabeth Kvitashvili. "The Role of USAID and Development Assistance in Combating Terrorism." *Military Review* 87, no. 2 (March 2007): 38–40.

Bassiouni, Mahmoud Cherif, Nigel Rodley, Badria Al-Awadhi, Philippe Kirsch and Mahnoush H. Arsanjani. "Report of the Bahrain Independent Commission of Inquiry." The Bahraini Independent Commission of Inquiry (November 23, 2011). https://www.bici.org.bh/BICIreportEN.pdf.

Bellin, Eva. "The Robustness of Authoritarianism in the Middle East: Exceptionalism in Comparative Perspective." *Comparative Politics* 36, no. 2 (2004): 139–157.

Bridoux, Jeff and Malcolm Russell. "Liberal Democracy Promotion in Iraq: A Model for the Middle East and North Africa?" *Foreign Policy Analysis* 9, no. 3 (2013): 327–346.

Farha, Mark. "Searching for Sectarianism in the Arab Spring: Colonial Conspiracy or Indigenous Instinct." *The Muslim World* 106, no. 1 (2016): 8–60.

Fisher, Max. "How the Iranian-Saudi Proxy Conflict Tore the Mideast Apart: Foreign Desk." *The New York Times*, November 19, 2016.

Guazzone, Laura and Daniela Pioppi, eds. *The Arab State and Neo-liberal Globalization: The Restructuring of State Power in the Middle East*. Ithaca: Ithaca Press, 2012.

Hashemi, Nader and Danny Postel, eds. *Sectarianization: Mapping the New Politics of theMiddle East*. Oxford: Oxford University Press, 2017.

Hinnebusch, Raymond. "Sectarianism and Governance in Syria." *Studies in Ethnicity and Nationalism* 19, no. 1 (2019): 41–66.

Hiro, Dilip. *Cold War in the Islamic World: Saudi Arabia, Iran, and the Struggle for Supremacy.* Oxford: Oxford University Press, 2018.

Holland, Steve. "US Rejects Saudi View of Iraq as Occupied." Reuters, March 29, 2007.

Karlsrud, John. "From Liberal Peacebuilding to Stabilization and Counterterrorism." *International Peacekeeping* 26, no. 1 (2019): 1–21.

Kaye, Dalia Dasse et al. *More Freedom, Less Terror? Liberalization and Violence in the Arab World.* Santa Monica, California: RAND Corporation, 2008

Kessels, Eelco and Melissa Lefas. "What the Review of UN Global Counterterrorism Strategy Tells Us." *Just Security*, July 27, 2021.

Matthiesen, Toby. "Sectarianization as Securitization: Identity Politics and Counter-Revolution in Bahrain," in *Sectarianization: Mapping the New Politics of the Middle East.* Edited by Nader Hashemi and Danny Postel. Oxford: Oxford University Press, 2017.

Mikail, Barah. "Sectarianism after the Arab Spring: An Exaggerated Spectre." *ASPJ Africa & Francophonie*, 1st Quarter, 2014.

Miles-Joyce, Rennanah. "Soldiers' Dilemma: Foreign Military Training and Liberal Norm Conflict." *International Security* 46, no. 4 (Spring 2022).

Miller, Paul. "Trump's Presidential Afghanistan Speech." *Foreign Policy*, August 22, 2017.

Möller, Lena-Maria. "Bahrain." In *Encyclopedia of Law and Religion.* Edited by Gerhard Robbers, October 1, 2018.

North Atlantic Treaty Organization. "*Counter Terrorism*," last updated August 3, 2022, https://www.nato.int/cps/en/natohq/topics_77646.htm#:~:text=NATO's%20counter-terrorism%20work%20spans%20across%20NATO's%20three%20core,Intelligence%20Cell%20has%20been%20established%20at%20NATO%20Headquarters.

Teitelbaum, Joshua ed. *Political Liberalization in the Gulf.* New York: Columbia University Press, 2009.

Telhami, Shibley. "Arab Public Opinion: A Survey in Six Countries." University of Maryland, March 16, 2003. https://sadat.umd.edu/publications-media/arab-public-opinion-survey-six-countries.

United Nations. "Funding and Donors," 2020, https://www.un.org/counterterrorism/funding-and-donors.

Vincent, Droz. "The Security Sector in Egypt: Management, Coercion and External Alliance under the Dynamics of Change," in *The Arab State and Neo-liberal Globalization: The Restructuring of State Power in the Middle East.* Edited by Laura Guazzone and Daniela Pioppi. Ithaca: Ithaca Press, 2012.

Wells, Madeleine. "Sectarianism, Authoritarianism, and Opposition in Kuwait," in *Sectarianization: Mapping the New Politics of the Middle East.* Edited by Nader Hashemi and Danny Postel. Oxford: Oxford University Press, 2017.

Whitaker, Beth Elise. "Exporting the Patriot Act? Democracy and the 'war on terror' in the Third World." *Third World Quarterly* 28, no. 5 (2007): 1017–1032.

The White House. "National Strategy for Combatting Terrorism," 2006. https://georgewbush whitehouse.archives.gov/nsc/nsct/2006/.

Zoller, Silke. *To Deter and Punish: Global Collaboration Against Terrorism in the 1970s.* New York, NY: Columbia University Press, 2021.

10

OLD STATELY FRIENDS, NEW SECTARIAN FOES

The Modern Saudi-Iranian Roots in Shia-Sunni Sectarianism

Pouya Alimagham

Introduction

There is a tendency to look at history backwards as it pertains to Shia-Sunni sectarian conflict. The assumption is often that since they are fighting across the Middle East today then they must have always been fighting. This is premised on the belief that Shia and Sunnis have been locked in a conflict since the early Islamic period when there was a dispute over Prophet Mohammad's succession eventually evolving into two distinct sects. This divide, according to prevailing logic, is still unfolding as a blood feud in the Islamic world today. In 1987, for example, when Iranian pilgrims were killed during the *Hajj* pilgrimage in Saudi Arabia, *Time* magazine concluded that this violence was a modern manifestation of conflict between the two sects dating back centuries:

> As the world's only Shia-ruled Muslim country, Iran seeks to export its brand of Islamic revolution throughout the region and to overthrow the Sunni-ruled Muslim regimes in countries like Kuwait and Saudi Arabia. The two religious factions have been fierce rivals for centuries.
>
> (Greenwald 1987)

Time's narrow lens has endured in the eyes of other publications. In 2015, for instance, *The Wall Street Journal* likewise surmised that "in today's Middle East, deep political and religious divisions are fueling insurgencies and proxy wars. One key driver of this instability is the 1,400-year-old sectarian split between Sunni and Shia Muslims that goes back to the origins of Islam."[1]

Unsurprisingly, Western political leaders with little background in the region anchor their opinions in these mainstream media sources by echoing such a view of the Middle East. American senator, Rand Paul, for example, argued against the

DOI: 10.4324/9781003329510-11

continued American military presence in the Middle East as according to him "Sunnis have been killing Shia since the massacre at Karbala in 680 AD. If we wait until they stop killing each other, we will stay for a thousand years or more. I agree with @realDonaldTrump. Bring the troops home."[2] To be clear, Senator Paul's intentions or demand to withdraw U.S. troops from the Middle East are not at issue. Rather, the point of contention in focusing on Paul's words is the backward reading of history prevalent across the media and political landscape of the U.S. The increasingly Orientalist explanation assumes that Shias and Sunnis are monoliths locked in a bitter, timeless dispute that unleashes a doctrinal, unyielding need to kill each other indefinitely.

In contradistinction, this chapter argues against this view by positing that the Shia-Sunni sectarian conflict is *not* rooted in time immemorial conflict, but rather in modern geostrategic rivalries between Iran and Saudi Arabia. That the two happen to be Shia and Sunni powerhouses has lent their struggle for political supremacy a sectarian tinge – not the inverse in which they are competing *because* of a dispute over religion. To support the thesis, this chapter outlines pre-revolutionary Iran's friendship and tactical alliance with Saudi Arabia by way of their coordination over the Dhofar Rebellion. Before the Iranian Revolution of 1978–1979, the two conservative monarchies were stalwart allies of the United States in the Cold War – with mutual enemies in the Soviet Union, Nasserist Republicanism, and Arab socialism. Their strategic relationship was so deep seeded that they coordinated with the Omanis to suppress a Marxist rebellion in Oman's Dhofar region. The intricacy and fraternity in this undertaking dispels such superficial explanations of today's Shia-Sunni divide. Indeed, the two quintessential Shia and Sunni countries worked together closely over Dhofar.

After chronicling the Saudi and Iranian coordination in suppressing the rebellion in Dhofar, the chapter proceeds to demonstrate how the Iranian Revolution radically changed the political calculus of the region. Iran went from being an ardent defender of the American-led regional order to calling for revolution across the Islamic world in general – and the Middle East and Persian Gulf in particular. Revolutionary Iran not only empowered Shias, but also Sunnis – even becoming the flagbearer of Palestinian liberation. As such, the chapter will show that today's Shia-Sunni war is not rooted in a 7th century dispute, but in the Saudi counter-revolutionary sectarianism that aimed to blunt Iran's ability to export its Islamic Revolution. I argue that it is this very reaction that forms the basis of today's sectarian war in the Middle East.

Background: Iran and Saudi Arabia in the Cold War

In January 1968, the British declared that their policy of withdrawing their naval presence East of the Suez Canal Zone extended to the Persian Gulf – the world's most important oil transit corridor. The United States feared that a pro-Soviet state would fill the British void and jeopardize Western and Japanese access to oil. With Mohammad Reza Shah Pahlavi at the helm, Iran and the U.S. had been close allies since the Central Intelligence Agency ousted Iran's democratically elected government in his favor in 1953 (Rāhnamā 2015). Their relationship would take on greater strategic importance after the British announcement. The U.S. military was bogged down in the Vietnam War and looked to pro-American, right-wing governments to help in its global struggle against Communism. Iran and Saudi Arabia, two conservative pro-American monarchies that straddled the Persian Gulf were obvious candidates for safeguarding the vital oil passageway. The Nixon Administration believed that the latter, according to one Cold War historian of the Middle East, was "both unwilling and unable" to take on the role (Alvandi 2014). The former, however, was eager to harness American political and military support to become the preeminent power in the region.

As early as 1966, the Shah believed that radical Arab governments in Egypt and Iraq, both of which were supported by Moscow, constituted a threat to the Persian Gulf and Iran. The Shah was concerned about Nasserist Egypt's military intervention in North Yemen as well as the joint Soviet-Chinese backing of the Dhofar Rebellion in Oman. He viewed Gamal Abdel Nasser – the head of state of a predominantly Sunni Muslim country until his death in 1970 – not through the prism of religion, but as a Middle Eastern ally of Soviet Communism. That Nasser came to power through a military coup that deposed the country's monarch served as a frightening precedent in the eyes of the Shah. Iraq and Yemen, followed suit in 1958 and 1962, respectively, to further affirm that such fears were not born of paranoia. The spread of pan-Arabist republicanism and Arab socialism indeed threatened the Shah. He worried that the popularity of Leftism would spread to Iran, and he feared that the Iranian military may one day overthrow him and likewise proclaim a republic. In the 1970s, the Shah also grew increasingly worried that Soviet power was encircling Iran. From the east in Afghanistan, the north, which at the time bordered the Soviet Union, the west through Iraq's military build-up and the construction of a Soviet naval base at Umm al-Qasr – near Iran's oilfields – and the south through its support for Marxist rebels in Dhofar. The Shah felt the Soviet noose tightening around Iran's neck.

The Saudis were even more worried about Nasserism, especially since Nasser's revolutionary message of pan-Arabism, anti-imperialism, and republicanism was a direct challenge to Saudi Arabia for being aligned with the United States. The foremost imperial power of the 1960s and 1970s in much of the Third World. Furthermore, that the Saudi state was a monarchy in a land that lacked a long tradition of the institution only augmented the threat it felt in the face of Arab republicanism spreading throughout the Arab world. These real concerns prompted the two pro-American monarchies to band together against Nasserism and Marxist insurrection in the region. The tactical alliance took place despite the Saudi state's anti-Shia, Salafist ideology.

Since the establishment of modern Saudi Arabia in 1932, the ruling Saudi royal family discriminated against its Shia subjects as a matter of state policy, considering them heretics worse than non-Muslims. No quote better exemplifies this sentiment than the words of the founder of the Saudi state, Ibn Saud, to his British confidant, John Philby:

> I should have no objection in taking as a wife a Christian or a Jewish woman… The Jews and Christians are both people of the book; but I would not marry a Shia…who have been guilty of backsliding and shirk [polytheism]…
>
> *(Nakash 2006: 44)*

Such prejudice was not confined to the state's early years, but was echoed in the 1990s by the Grand Mufti of Saudi Arabia, Abdul Aziz ibn Baz, who issued a "ruling against the Shia, reaffirming that they were infidels…" (Nakash 2006). Thereby, "prohibiting [Sunni] Muslims from dealings with them" (Nakash 2006). This is significant as the ultra-conservative clerics in Saudi Arabia are partners in the country's power structure and such an edict is legally binding (Nakash 2006). Doubtless, this anti-Shia worldview has had real-life consequences for Saudi Shia. However, it did not affect the state's foreign policy vis-à-vis the quintessential Shia majority country, Iran. In other words, there was no Shia-Sunni divide, nor was there an existing sectarian split between them dating back to the 7th century. In fact, Iran and Saudi Arabia had friendly relations before the Iranian Revolution. As with any relationship, they had their disagreements. The Saudis, for instance, disagreed with the Shah's claim that Bahrain was historically a part of Iran – a claim the Shah abandoned in 1970 on the eve of Bahrain's independence from Britain in 1971 in favor of militarily claiming the three islands situated close to the Strait of Hormuz – Abu Musa and Greater and Lesser Tunbs.

The announced British withdrawal from the Persian Gulf served as an opportunity for the Shah, who – with American backing – aspired to make Iran the primary power in the region. Initially, the Nixon Administration worried that supplanting the Twin Pillar policy of support for Saudi Arabia and Iran in favor of a tilt towards the latter might garner the ire of the former. Eventually, however, the administration decided that the Shah's regime was more stable than the Saudi state and that supporting the Shah militarily would enable it to one day come to the aid of the Saudi royal family if necessary (Alvandi 2014). In September 1969, the Shah indeed reassured King Faisal at the Islamic Summit Conference in Morocco that should an emergency situation arise then the Saudis could rely on Iran for whatever support was needed (Alvandi 2014). The Saudis were not alone in thinking that Iran's ascendancy would benefit them. The American ambassador to Iran, Douglas MacArthur II, observed that the Arab states of the Persian Gulf increasingly believed that Iran was the only "moderate neighbor with both the will and the capacity to come to their aid" (Alvandi 2014). When Yemenis attacked Saudi Arabia soon after the summit, Iran "quickly airlifted anti-aircraft guns and anti-tank recoilless rifles to Saudi Arabia to repel the Yemenis" (Alvandi 2014). In sum, despite the Saudi government's anti-Shiism, Iran was immensely close to the Saudis that it interpreted an attack on such an ally as a threat to the regional order, and sent advanced weaponry to safeguard Saudi security. In fact, years later when the Shah was in exile, he had positive words for his Saudi ally:

Twice I had the great joy of making the supreme pilgrimage. As a faithful Muslim and Defender of the Faith, I hope that Saudi Arabia will always remain the guardian of these holy places, Mecca and Medina, where millions of pilgrims travel every year on the path to God. History has recorded the stature of Ibn Saud, founder of Saudi Arabia. He was wise and brave and an excellent administrator. When one considers the fatal events for which Iran is now the theater in 1980, one cannot but rejoice at seeing Saudi Arabia still free and independent. One can only pray to God that it remains so.

(Pahlavi 1980)

The feelings between pre-revolutionary Iran and the Saudis were hardly one-sided.

In one of the Shah's *Hajj* pilgrimages, the Saudis organized displays of support for the Shah in which "...little girls and boys draped in the green of the Saudi flag and the green, white and red of the Iranian flag recited poetry and songs for [the Shah] about the love of the two Moslem brothers peoples for each other" (Adams Schmidt 1968). According to *The New York Times*' coverage of the Shah's visit to Saudi Arabia, the two leaders were "keenly aware of their mutual interest in seeing to it that the newly independent sheikdoms of the Gulf do not follow the revolutionary political example of Aden when Britain withdraws from the Gulf some time before the end of 1971" (Schmidt 1968). To be sure, there was no sectarian conflict, and Sunnis were not "killing Shia since the massacre at Karbala in 680 AD." Instead, these Shia and Sunni powerhouses worked together on a number of regional issues (Ghattas 2020).

Iranian Intervention in the Arabian Peninsula

Resistance to the British-backed Omani Sultan, Said ibn Taymur, had been gaining ground throughout the 1960s against his increasingly repressive rule. The most sustained armed challenge to ibn Taymur was centered in the province of Dhofar. A coastal plain with a backdrop of mountains, the 150,000 inhabitants had more contact with neighboring Yemen than the relatively far-off Omani capital, Muscat (Goode 2014). By the end of the decade, however, the multi-faceted rebellion gave way to the flagbearers of the Popular Front for the Liberation of Oman and the Arab Gulf (PFLOAG), which was backed by the People's Democratic Republic of Yemen, the Soviet Union, and initially China. To the indignation of the conservative neighboring states, PFLOAG's ideological zeal coupled with their guerrilla training to make headway in their revolutionary struggle against the central government. In 1970, the British supported a bloodless coup in which Prince Qabus toppled his ineffectual and "arch-conservative" father who had resisted social change and was reluctant to use the country's growing oil sales to improve the underdeveloped country (Pace 1975). Before the coup, Oman was a largely agricultural-based economy, with only six elementary schools; the population of less than a million was without a single secondary school or a single newspaper (Pace 1975).

The Shah believed that Qabus, however, was better suited to not only govern, but to also ensure through reforms that the country did not fall into the hands of the Marxists. They gradually improved relations, and the Shah believed that investing in safeguarding Qabus was a worthwhile endeavor. Thus, he resolved to support the new Sultan to stamp out the insurrection in order to prevent Arab radicalism from spreading to the Trucial States, which were even less prepared to deal with a guerrilla uprising. That the rebels openly declared that "freeing Dhufar is only the first step in our campaign to free all of the Persian Gulf from imperialism" meant that the Shah saw them as a direct threat to Iran should they succeed in toppling Sultan Qabus (Goode 2014). Several years later when Iran had dispatched troops to Oman, the Shah gave an interview with *Kuwait Daily*, and affirmed as much when he said that Iran was in Oman to ensure "that the entrance in front of Iranian port city of Bandar Abbas will not fall in the hands of the wrong people."[3]

In 1972, the Shah began Iran's involvement in Oman by fulfilling the Sultan's request for a shipment of arms and supplies (Goode 2014). The arms, however, were not enough to turn the tide of the war in favor of the government. The Dhofari rebels were well-funded, trained in guerrilla warfare, and empowered with *espirit de corps*. By the end of the year, small numbers of Iranian special forces began to arrive as the Shah was determined to help Sultan Qabus suppress the rebellion not only with Iranian treasure, but also with blood. At its peak, Iran had 4,000 troops under the command of Iranian officers fighting in Oman (Goode 2014). While the rebel's numbers were not high, as a guerrilla army their strength was not in their quantity, but in their tactics. The fluidity of a small band of guerrillas can harness difficult terrain to outmaneuver an enemy larger in size with more advanced weaponry. As such, half of Oman's 12,000-manned military was unable to put down an undermanned revolt, and Iran's special forces proved highly consequential in turning the tide of war against the rebels and in favor of the young Sultan. Iran's intervention extended beyond boots on the ground, encompassing Oman's airspace. With one of the most advanced air forces in the world, the Shah pledged his American made fighter jets to "guarantee the inviolability of Oman's airspace against any foreign intruders..." This was an indirect threat against the People's Democratic Republic of Yemen (South Yemen), which was accused of violating its neighbor's airspace in support of the rebels (Pace 1975).

The Saudis were not thrilled about the presence of Iranian troops on the Arabian Peninsula. They worried about Iran's growing assertiveness and the Shah's potential for Iranian hegemony, especially after he ordered the occupation of Abu Musa and Greater and Lesser Tunbs Islands near the Strait of Hormuz. At the same time, Saudi attention was diverted to the far more pressing Arab-Israeli theatre of conflict, particularly after the Yom Kippur War of 1973. As such, they did not have the means to come to the aid of the Sultan. Moreover, the Saudis did not want to be seen as too close to the Shah since Arabs across the region in general knew that the Shah's government was close to the Israelis (Alvandi 2014).

Simultaneously, the Iranian intervention was not entirely difficult for the Saudis to accept. The Shah was fighting communism to buttress a monarch and a form of government that aligned with the Saudis. Moreover, the struggle against the guerrillas in this relatively small theatre of war was in accordance with the interest of the Saudi and Iranian patron, the U.S., which was engaged in a global struggle against Communism. That is, the Saudis deduced that defeating the radicals would strengthen the U.S. position against the Soviets, a state they suspected of having subversive designs in the Middle East. Consequently, they backed the Iranian intervention. Beyond lending the Shah support for the undertaking, they also provided aid to Oman's central government so that it may help ameliorate some of the economic and development problems that, in part, gave rise to the rebellion in the first place. The Saudis gave as much as $200 million, half of which was allocated to help the Omani government with development projects.[4] In sum, Iranian and Saudi support for Sultan Qabus complemented one another. One deployed troops and military hardware, while the other deployed its checkbook.

The Shia-Sunni divide was nowhere at issue. The Saudis never once objected to Iran's involvement because it was a predominantly Shia country. Put differently, they did not see it as a Shia intervention in a Sunni country. While some Arab leaders balked at the Omanis for accepting help from a non-Arab country, Oman's foreign minister, Qais Zawawi, retorted that it was an internal Omani manner, and that no military support was forthcoming from anywhere but Iran (Goode 2014). In other words, the only issue – a minor one at that – was more about ethnic politics than a sectarian one. Nor did Iranian soldiers see their presence in sectarian terms. They did not ask why Shia Muslims like themselves were tasked to fight and die for a distant Sunni Muslim country. For them, the only issue was that many were confused as to why they were being sent to fight far from home in the first place. They were trained and indoctrinated to defend Iran's territorial integrity but were now sent abroad to safeguard a foreign government in its war with its own people. In fact, one soldier, Gholamreza Khalili Shahanqi, returned to Iran dismayed with the Shah because he had dispatched him, a Muslim, to kill other Muslims. For him, the Dhofaris were downtrodden brothers in Islam regardless of their sect, and he was upset that an avowed Muslim king had sent him to shed the blood of other Muslims.[5]

In sum, despite some minor reservations, the Saudis supported the Iranian mission in Oman, and used their checkbook in the service of the same end goal of defeating the rebellion. The kingdoms of Iran and Saudi Arabia saw eye-to-eye in Oman – irrespective of their religious convictions – and Iranian troops were stationed in the Arabian Peninsula from 1972 until the completion of the mission in the mid 1970s. This ultimately ended the rebellion on terms favorable to Iran, Saudi Arabia, and Oman. Iran and Saudi Arabia grew so close that they formed the Safari Club, a pact of intelligence agencies that also included Egypt, Morocco and France to conduct covert anti-Communist operations in Africa in 1976 after the U.S. Congress began to limit CIA interventions abroad (Scott 2007). However, the Iranian Revolution of 1978–1979 changed the entire calculus not just of Iran-Saudi relations, but also relations between Sunnis and Shias overall.

The Iranian Revolution

The Iranian Revolution was a watershed moment in the history of the Middle East (Keddie 1995). It marked the first time that a popular and protracted uprising brought down a government. That the Iranian state was backed by the world's preeminent superpower that had armed it with some of the most advanced weaponry, made the revolution's success all the more unprecedented. *The Observer* noted in 1979 that the revolution sent a "shock-wave" that was "felt around the world."[6]

Nowhere else was this shockwave better felt than the Middle East. The revolution inspired Iranians, Arabs, and Afghans alike – those with a state and those without one. Beirut, for example, where the stateless Palestine Liberation Organization was stationed at the time of Iran's revolution, "echoed with machinegun fire" as fighters "saluted" the revolution's triumph.[7] That the revolution's leader was an Islamist cleric, however, naturally carried more meaning for Islamists. Even Sunni fundamentalists, who disagreed with Shiism as a matter of theology, believed that there were lessons to be learned from the Iranian Revolution. For instance, Ahmed Yousef, one of the founders of Hamas – the militant Sunni Islamist group in the Palestinian Territories, would later note that "The Iranian revolution gave us a strong belief that the tyrants can be brought down" (Gambrell 2019).

Iran's revolution indeed became an exemplar for action for the disparate peoples of the Middle East and wider Islamic world. What gave the revolution's global application urgency was Ayatollah Khomeini's pan-Islamist declarations. The revolution's leader Ayatollah Khomeini did not recognize the ethnic and national divisions among Muslims as he argued that the Muslim community is not confined to the national boundaries of countries. For him, the suffering of Muslims in Afghanistan, Palestine or elsewhere was not confined to the national boundaries of the countries in question, but concerned Muslims all over the "Islamic world":…

> We do not regard Islam as being confined to Iran. Islam is Islam everywhere. It is the same Islam in Egypt, Sudan, Iraq, the Hijaz, Syria and other places. We cannot separate our fate from that of other Muslims… We cannot consider the Arabs or the destiny of the Arabs nor that of the other (Muslim) countries as being separate from ours. It is the same Islam everywhere, and all Muslims—us included—are duty bound to protect Islam wherever it is.
> *(Khomeini 1981)*

In his book *Kashf al-Asrar (The Revealing of Secrets)*, published nearly four decades before he would go on to lead a revolution, he argued forcefully that "the walls that they have erected throughout the world in the name of countries are the products of man's limited ideas" and that the world is "the homeland of all the masses of people… under the law of God…." (Khomeini 1943). Almost 30 years later in his seminal tract, *Islamic Government*, he argued against the continued existence of such nation-states, blaming the imperial powers for dismembering the Ottoman Empire when they "separated various segments of the Islamic nation from each other and artificially created separate nations... about 10 to 15 petty states" (Khomeini 1970). Consequently, he called upon the Muslim faithful – Sunni and Shia – to heed Iran's example by rising up and overthrowing their "godless" governments, especially the ones beholden to the United States. To be sure, the heads of state across the region predictably trembled at the thought of their own people rising up.

There has been much focus on the revolution's appeal among the region's Shias. That Khomeini was a Shia clerical leader explains part of that focus. It is true that factions within Lebanese, Iraqi, Kuwaiti, Bahraini, and Saudi Shias were most receptive to Khomeini's brand of Islamism given that they all had long experienced state persecution that had resulted in a history of anti-state activism. In other words, the region's Shias were not the only ones receptive to Khomeini's revolutionary appeal, but they were especially primed for militancy, because of their disenfranchisement, poverty, and subjugation. Yet, it would be wrong to suggest that the revolution only appealed to Shias, thereby giving birth to today's sectarianism. It would equally be wrong to assume that Iran supported the predominantly Sunni Palestinians to pre-empt any allegation of sectarianism.[8]

"Islamic Palestine"

For Iran's Muslims before and after the revolution, Palestine had a distinct importance beyond the scope of any theological dispute. Ayatollah Morteza Mottahari, one of the leaders of the Iranian Revolution and an architect of Iran's Islamic system, warrants mention, because he effectively underscored Palestine's Islamic importance:

> What would the Prophet of Islam do if he was still alive today? What issue would occupy the Prophet's thoughts? By God we are responsible regarding this crisis. By God we have responsibility. By God we are being ignorant. By God this very issue would break the heart of the Prophet today. The problem that would fill Husayn ibn Ali's heart with sorrow today is this issue. If Husayn ibn Ali was here today, he would say "if you want to mourn for me today, if you want to lament over me, your slogan today must be 'Palestine'." The Shimr[9] of 1300 years ago is dead and gone. Get to know the Shimr of today. Today the walls of this city should tremble to the slogan of Palestine. And what efforts have we Muslims exerted for Palestine? By God it's a shame for us to call ourselves Muslims. It's a shame to call ourselves Shiites of Ali ibn Abi Talib. The enemy has ravaged our fellow Muslim's land, murdered and imprisoned their men, violated their women and took their jewelry from their ears and hands... Are they not Muslims?[10]

For the likes of Mottahari, Shias were the flagbearers not of Shias liberation, but of Islamic emancipation, and Palestine, which had virtually no Shias, was the quintessential Islamic issue.

For the militant clergy, however, Palestine was not simply a Muslim issue because Palestinians were predominantly Muslim, but also because Palestine is home to Islam's third holiest site – Jerusalem (*al Quds* in Arabic). Muslims believe Jerusalem to be the site that the Prophet Mohammad visited in his Night Journey and from which he ascended to heaven, met and prayed with the great prophets of the Abrahamic tradition, and returned. What's more, following the Jewish tradition, it is also Islam's original *qiblah* – the direction in which the first Muslims prayed. So important was Palestine to the generation that made the revolution that the issue transcended the clergy. Radical activists received guerrilla training in Palestinian camps[11] in Lebanon in the 1970s with explosive consequences. Some stayed and fought side-by-side with Palestinian groups against Israel.[12] Others returned home, several with Palestinian wives at their side,[13] in order to wage guerrilla war. Upon their return to Iran, they staged bold attacks against the regime, American installations and personnel. For example, official American cables noted "twenty-eight confirmed explosions (11 of which [were] directed against US presence)" in the four months spanning the spring and summer of 1972.[14] Targeting the U.S. presence in Iran was also connected to international conflicts whereby the U.S. fought or supported the fight against popular forces in such places as Vietnam, Oman, and, more to the point, Palestine (Ervand 1989). Furthermore, in 1972, guerrillas bombed the Jordanian embassy to protest King Hussein's state visit and avenge Black September – the month in 1970 when King Hussein's army routed the PLO in Jordan (Ervand 1989).

In the post-revolutionary period, the Iranian government did not render Sunnis as the self-affirming "Other" – as evidenced by the state's uncompromising support for the Palestinians to this very day – but juxtaposed itself against the United States and Israel. In other words, its ideology was not defined by its opposition to Sunni co-religionists, but rather U.S. imperialism and what it considered its regional outpost. Khomeini supported Shias and Sunnis alike, and spoke of Iran's revolution not in Shia specific terms, but in Islamic terms not confined to Iran: "Just as the Prophet was from Arabia, but his Islamic message was not only for his land, Iran's Islamic Revolution belongs to all lands" (Khomeini 1979). This is what made Iran's message so dangerous for the region's governments and served as one of the catalysts for conflict, alongside the Saudi state's response.

The Saudi Roots in Today's Shia-Sunni War

Before the Iranian Revolution, anti-Shiism was a matter of Saudi domestic policy, and did not guide its foreign policy. The Dhofar example is a case in point. Sunni Saudis and pre-revolution Shia Iranians worked together to roll back common threats. After the revolution, however, the calculus of the entire region had dramatically changed, and Saudi foreign policy changed with it. The first priority of any unelected government is to ensure its survival, and Saudi anti-Shiism became a foreign policy as a matter of regime survival. For the Saudi state, ensuring that Iran's revolution did not spread to the region was indeed about domestic state security. If another Muslim country followed the Iranian example and rose up and toppled its respective government, then it would add to the momentum of the Iranian Revolution to potentially inspire restive Saudi citizens. On the other hand, if the Saudi government could convince the region's Muslims that Iran's revolution was an abomination, then Khomeini's calls for uprisings throughout the Muslim world would go unheeded. As such, the Saudi state preyed on Iran's Achille's heel – that it hailed from the minority branch of the Islamic tradition.

To that end, the Saudi state began to export its anti-Shia creed in order to convince Sunni Muslims – who adhered to the majority sect in Islam – that Iran's Islamic Revolution was born of a heretical subversion of Islam and not to be emulated. To be clear, exporting hardline Salafi Islam was not merely a matter of conflicting religious truths. According to one specialist, the real objective was not only to turn away Muslims from Iran's example and leadership, but to steer them in the direction of the Saudis through the consolidation of "their political and ideological influence by establishing a network of supporters capable of defending the Kingdom's strategic and economic interests" (Daou 2012). However, the Saudis would not condemn their counterparts as heretics when facing them directly.

In a meeting between the Iranian foreign minister and the Saudi king in 2009, for example, the monarch protested Iranian support for Hamas – the Sunni Islamist movement – which prompted Foreign Minister Manouchehr Mottaki to respond that the issue involved Iran because "these are Muslims." King Abdullah retorted not in sectarian but in ethnic terms: "You as Persians have no business meddling in Arab affairs."[15] Whereas before the Iranian Revolution, the Saudis backed the Iranian military mission in the Arab country of Oman in the Arabian Peninsula of all places, afterward they objected on ethnic terms when it came to face-to-face encounters and religious terms everywhere else. A case in point is a Saudi state-published book, titled: *Dispelling Darkness and Alerting the Unsuspecting to the Danger of Shiism to Muslims and Islam*, which was first printed in 1988. It is still in circulation today, has been digitized and is available for free online (Al-Jabhan 1988). Accordingly, Shias exist outside of the realm of "Muslims and Islam," dehumanized as "apes," "pigs," "apostates," "asses," "defectors," "deceivers," "agitators," "dogs of fire," "human dogs," "cows," and "agitators" (Abukhalil 2015). They are also referred to as "Jews" and "Manicheans," which in Salafi parlance is without question meant to be derogatory (Abukhalil 2015). Furthermore, the Saudi state deploys its petrodollars across the world by funding anti-Shia mosques and preachers, religious schools (Daou 2012), Sunni extremist jihadi groups, and transnational Arabic-language media, much of which is owned by the Saudis, with the express goal of fostering anti-Shia sectarianism in order to prevent the spread of Iran's Islamic Revolution. The Saudi government provides scholarships so Muslim students can come from afar to receive training in what one critic of Saudi extremism referred to as the "bigotry of Salafism" (Husain 2014).

In their crusade against Iran, the Saudis have left no proverbial "stone unturned," even taking advantage of the opportunity of the presence of thousands of migrant workers that come from Pakistan and elsewhere to indoctrinate them in anti-Shiism. When their work is completed, many of these workers return home harboring these newfound prejudices that they spread to friends and family (Matthiesen 2013: 34). Another strategic benefit of a policy of anti-Shiism is to prevent Sunnis from making common cause with Shias against the ruling Al Saud family in Saudi Arabia or Al Khalifa Dynasty in neighboring Bahrain. When unrest occurs, the state fosters anti-Shiism among its Sunni majority, members of which are then unleashed to physically attack Shias, whom the state presents as seditious agents of Iran. The government then intervenes to facilitate order thereby presenting itself to those very Shias as the guarantor of their security – that the only alternative to the government is the state-manufactured extremism of their countrymen (Al-Rasheed 2017). Moreover, across the region, especially in Saudi Arabia and Bahrain, Shia dissidents are cast as fifth columnists loyal to Iran – underscoring both their *alleged* treachery and heresy. This dehumanization of Shia has had consequences far beyond the Iranian-Saudi rivalry.

Conclusion

The Iranian Revolution and the subsequent policies of Iran instigated a Saudi reaction that continues to this very day to the great detriment to the world's Shias. Not only did Saudi Arabia finance Saddam's invasion of Iran, but it also sought to ensure that Iran's revolutionary message fell on proverbial deaf ears. To that end, the Saudis deployed billions in petrodollars in a soft war against Iran via sectarianism – an ideological cold war infused with a dangerous religious dimension. This strategy became increasingly hot after the United States invaded Iraq in 2003 and inadvertently paved the way for Iran's allies to come to power. From transnational Arabic media, much of which is controlled by Saudi Arabia, to Sunni mosques across the Muslim world, Saudi-funded analysts, commentators, and preachers preyed on Iran's Achilles' heel – that it hails from the minority branch in Islam. They presented Iran's leaders as heretics, the country's branch of Islam as a heresy, and the revolution as a perversion not to be emulated but to be destroyed, all to make certain that Iran's call for Islamic Revolution went unheeded both abroad and at home in the Arabian Peninsula. Integral to the strategy was the cultivation of Sunni extremism that rendered Shias as "the Other."

The Saudi attempts to bifurcate the Muslim world have had a wide-reaching impact. Moreover, before Iran supported oppressed Shia and Sunnis alike, from Shia in Lebanon and Iraq to Sunnis in Bosnia and Palestine, it resisted for decades the *self-defeating* urge to talk about regional conflicts in sectarian terms. Today, however, Iran is increasingly expressing its world view in sectarian terms. This was evident in a televised commemoration of Hussein's 7th-century death – a martyrdom that constitutes a key moment in Shiism's origin story. While the event has long been replete with Shia leitmotifs, the *Ashura* ritual in 2018 was different. It included highly charged words that attest to the divide in which Iran unwittingly finds itself:

> Takfiris [Excommunicators], Wahhabis, and Daesh [ISIS] have united against us at the behest of the US, yet we feel the divine spirit of Allah among us...

Soon everyone will hear the name of Husayn, the spirit of resistance and legacy of Khomeini will triumph the world over… The flag of Shiism will be hoisted—and whoever loves Ali is our countrymen.

Before 1979, Saudi Arabia and Iran were two pro-American kingdoms that worked in tandem with each other to combat shared threats of Marxism and Republicanism. The Saudis even acquiesced to the presence of Iranian troops on the Arabian Peninsula in Oman. The doctrinal differences between Shiism and Sunni Islam were not at issue whatsoever in terms of a political divide. Only after its revolution when Iran called for the overthrow of the Saudi royal family did the Saudis respond with vitriolic anti-Shiism, giving birth to the region's current bloody sectarianism. Thus, today's Shia-Sunni divide is not necessarily rooted in a timeless theological dispute, as the likes of Senator Rand Paul have argued, but a nation-state rivalry between two influential neighbors going back 40 plus years. Therefore, the conflict is more a modern political dispute than an age-old religious one. As such, ending this senseless violence must begin by bridging the gap between the Kingdom of Saudi Arabia and the Islamic Republic of Iran.

Notes

1 "Saudi Arabia vs. Iran: The Sunni-Shiite Proxy Wars," produced by Reem Makhoul, Mark Scheffler and Airelle Ray. *Wall Street Journal*, 7 April 2015, Video: 4:26. https://www.youtube.com/watch?v=I7cdBjYd2Bo.
2 Rand Paul (@RandPaul), "Sunnis have been killing Shia since the massacre at Karbala in 680 AD. If we wait until they stop killing each other, we will stay for a thousand years or more. I agree with @realDonaldTrump. Bring the troops home," Twitter, 16 Jan 2019, 10:10 AM, https://twitter.com/RandPaul/status/1085600177682071552.
3 "Kuwaiti Editor Interviews Shah," telegram, from Kuwait City, Kuwait to Bahrain Manama, Department of State, et. al., December 28, 1974.
4 "Saudi Aid to Oman," telegram from Jeddah, Saudi Arabia, to U.S. Department of State, May 13, 1975.
5 "Khāṭerāt-i man az ma'mūrīat-i jangī dar ẓofār." *Fars News*, November 10, 2010.
6 "Shock-wave felt round the world," *The Observer*, January 7, 1979.
7 "PLO jubilant over Khomeini victory," The *Jerusalem Post*, February 13, 1979; For a more detailed discussion regarding the global impact of the Iranian Revolution, see Esposito (1990).
8 Asʿad AbuKhalil wrote in 2014 that tensions between Hamas and Iran over the war in Syria "hurt Iran (and Hezbollah) as that relationship helped dispel the sectarian cast of Iranian policies in the Arab East." "Some determinants of Iranian policy in the Arab East". *al-Akhbar English*, November 3, 2014. Such a statement seemed to suggest that Iran supported Hamas, a militant Sunni Islamist organization, in order to refute allegations of sectarianism in which Iran only supported Shia groups such as Hizbullah in Lebanon, and SCIRI and others in Iraq.
9 Shimr, the commander of Yazid's army, massacred Husayn and his band of followers in the Battle of Karbala in 680 AD.
10 The text of his famous speech is posted in full online, and the actual audio clip can be found see Ruh, "Shahīd morteżā mottaharī va felestīn," *Doshmantarin*. November 15, 2010. http://doshmantarin.blogsky.com/1389/08/24/post-10/; Alireza Bahmanpour, "Ayatullah's Historical Speech about Palestine," *YouTube*, June 18, 2010. http://youtu.be/-SxOUMLfX7c.

11 In his memoirs, Massoud Rajavi, the Mujahedin leader, confirms that the MKO received military assistance from Arafat's al-Fatah organization. See Rajavi (1984). Also, see Saxon (1979: A9).
12 "Facing the New Realities: After the changes in Iran, it's now or never at Camp David," *Time*, March 4, 1979, 40.
13 According to Taleqani's chief aide, Taleqani's son, Mojtaba, a Mujahedin who sided with the Marxist faction during the schism that produced two groups—one that stayed true to its original Islamic worldview and the other, the Marxist Mujahedin, which eventually became Paykar. Mojtaba, imprisoned in pre-revolutionary Iran for such memberships, fled the country upon his release and went to Lebanon to collaborate with Palestinian factions. While in Lebanon, he wed a Palestinian woman who returned with him to Iran and occasionally served as a translator between Ayatollah Taleqani's office and the Palestinian diplomatic corps that established an official presence in Iran after the revolution. See Shanehchi (1983).
14 Farland, Tehran, to Secretary of State, telegram, August 10, 1972.
15 Riyadh Fraker to Dubai American Consulate, et al., telegram, March 22, 2009.

Bibliography

Abukhalil, Asad. "Origins of Sectarian Warfare in the Middle East: Saudi Wahhabi Hate Rhetoric Against Shias." The Angry Arab News Service, October 26, 2015.
Adaki, Oren and David. A. Weinberg. "Preaching Hate and Sectarianism in the Gulf." *Foreign Policy*, May 5, 2012.
Adams Schmidt, Dana. "Shah of Iran and Saudis' King Seek Persian Gulf Cooperation." *The New York Times*, November 14, 1968.
Al-Jabhan, Ibrahim Suleiman. *Dispelling darkness and alerting the sleeper to the danger of Shiism to Muslims and Islam*. 1988. https://www.noor-book.com/en/ebooks-Ibrahim-Suleiman-Aljabhan-pdf.
Al-Rasheed, Madawi. "Sectarianism as Counter-revolution: Saudi Responses to the Arab Spring," in *Sectarianization: Mapping the New Politics of the Middle East*. Edited by Nader Hashemi and Danny Postel. Oxford: Oxford University Press, 2017.
Alvandi, Roham. *Nixon, Kissinger, and the Shah: The United States and Iran in the Cold War*. Oxford: Oxford University Press, 2014.
Daou, Marc. "How Saudi petrodollars fuel rise of Salafism." *France24*, September 29, 2012.
Ervand, Abrahamian. *The Iranian Mojahedin*. New Haven: Yale University Press, 1989.
Esposito, John. *The Iranian Revolution: Its Global Impact*. Miami: Florida International University Press, 1990.
Freeman, Colin. "Islamic State executioner who devised deadly 'Quranic quiz' killed by US airstrike." *The Telegraph*, May 9, 2016.
Gambrell, Jon. "Iran's revolution bridged sectarian rift before deepening it." *Associated Press*, Feburary 10, 2019.
Ghattas, Kim. *Black Wave: Saudi Arabia, Iran, and the Forty-Year Rivalry That Unraveled Culture, Religion, and Collective Memory in the Middle East*. New York: Henry Holt and Company, 2020.
Goode, James F. "Assisting Our Brothers, Defending Ourselves: The Iranian Intervention in Oman, 1972–75." *Iranian Studies* 47, no. 30 (May 2014): 441–462.
Greenwald, John. "At War on All Fronts." *Time*, August 17, 1987.
Husain, Ed. "Saudis Must Stop Exporting Extremism." *The New York Times*, August 22, 2014.
Keddie, Nikki R. *Iran and the Muslim World: Resistance and Revolution*. New York: New York University Press, 1995.
Khomeini, Ruhollah. "Ahamīat-i ḥefẓ-i jomhūrī-ye islāmī – naqsh-i rohānīat dar ṭūl-i tārī kh –ṭarḥ-i khīānatbār-i sāzesh bāisrā'īl" (The Importance of Preserving the Islamic

Republic – The Role of the Clergy throughout History – The Treacherous Designs of Normalization with Israel) *Tehran* 15 (November 16, 1981): 369–370.

Khomeini, Ruhollah. *Ḥokūmat-i islāmī: vilāyat-i faqīh. mu'aseseh-ye āmūzeshī-ye pazhoheshī ye emām khomeinī* (The Islamic Republic, The Guardianship or Governance, Imam Khomeini Education and Research Institute). Qom, Iran: Imam Khomeini Education and Research Institute, 1970.

Khomeini, Ruhollah. *Kashf alasrār* (Unveiling of Secrets). Qom, Iran: Imam Khomeini Education and Research Institute, 1943.

Khomeini, Ruhollah. "Sokhrānī dar jam'-i dāneshjūyan-i 'arabestanī-ye moqīm-i īrān" (Speech to a Group of Arab Students Living in Iran). *Qom* 10 (November 2, 1979): 446–449.

Ladjevardi, Habib. Interview. Paris, France. Iranian Oral History Collection, Harvard University, Transcript 4 (seq. 66–67), March 4, 1983.

Matthiesen, Toby. *Sectarian Gulf: Bahrain, Saudi Arabia, and the Arab Spring.* Stanford: Stanford University Press, 2013.

Nakash, Yitzak. *Reaching for Power: The Shi'a in the Modern Arab World.* Princeton and Oxford: Princeton University Press, 2006.

Pace, Eric. "Iranian Troops Helping Oman to Quell Rebels." *The New York Times*, February 7, 1975.

Pahlavi, Mohammad Reza. *Answer to History: By Mohammad Reza Pahlavi The Shah of Iran.* New York: Stein and Day Publishers, 1980.

Rāhnamā, 'Alī. *Behind the 1953 Coup in Iran: Thugs, Turncoats, Soldiers, and Spooks.* Cambridge: Cambridge University Press, 2015.

Rajavi, Massoud. Interview recorded by Zia Sedghi. Paris, France. Iranian Oral History Collection, Harvard University, Transcript 2 (seq. 21), May 29, 1984.

Ruh. "Shahīd morteżā mottaharī va felesṭīn" (The Martyr Morteza Mottahari and Palestine). *Doshmantarin*, November 15, 2010.

Saxon, Wolfgang. "Arab leaders Call Iran Shift Historic: Saudis Are Worried About Anarchy and Others are Cautious, but the P.L.O. Appears Joyful". *The New York Times*, February 14, 1979.

Scott, Peter Dale. *The Road to 9/11: Wealth, Empire and The Future America.* Berkeley: University of California Press, 2007.

Taylor, Joshua. "Boy, 6, beheading in front of screaming mum in Saudi Arabia 'for being wrong religion.'" *The Mirror*, February 1, 2019.

CONCLUSION: THE CONTEXTUALIZATION OF SECTARIANISM

The Role of Identity, Money, and Competition

Ibrahim Warde

Introduction

From 1979 onwards the greater Middle East and South Asia experienced major shifts in the realms of socio-politics, religion, and security as a result of the rise of political Islam and the spread of sectarianism. As Islam and sect-based identity were increasingly instrumentalized by political entrepreneurs, societal fissures expanded along sectarian lines and tensions and conflicts were exacerbated. To understand the complexities associated with sectarianism and the factors that have and continue to propel its use forward, it is essential to examine the factors that contributed to its rise both within historical and modern contexts. By utilizing this approach within an interdisciplinary analytical framework, one has an enhanced capacity to contextualize complexities associated with this phenomenon, as well as an ability to gain depth of insight on the overt and covert factors that have influenced it. This includes but is not limited to outbidding processes, the role of money, the manipulation of identity, as well as issues pertaining to identity construction. While recognizing the deep scars left by great power rivalries and the battles for independence and nationalism (most recently the 1951–53 developments in Iran which saw the nationalization of oil by the Mossadegh government and the coup organized by the CIA to bring back the Shah to the throne), we predominantly focus on the chain of events that began in the 1970s. Through the utilization of an interdisciplinary approach, the authors of this volume have sought to provide depth of insight into factors that have influenced landscapes marred by sectarianism and its impact, and to deconstruct popular misconceptions regarding this phenomenon across the greater Middle East and South Asia.

Within this framework one is better able to analyze the changes and continuities that contributed to the surge of sectarianism. This includes key policies and watershed events that directly and indirectly contributed to the rise of sectarian

DOI: 10.4324/9781003329510-12

tension, conflict, and violence, that have had devastating costs on state and societal levels. Moreover, in order to better contextualize sectarianism in the greater Middle East and South Asia within the framework of identity, competition and conflict, it is also essential to analyze the changes and continuities that led to a specific period in which these shifts are increasingly apparent. A key example is the Nixon Doctrine, which was a realist approach to U.S. foreign policy and national security strategy. This Doctrine and its supporting strategies were related to the country's relationship with the Soviet Union within a Cold War context and the relationship of the United States with other nations (Laird, Griffin, McGee & Schelling 1972). In essence it combined both U.S. foreign policy with its national security interests and emphasized negotiation, power, and partnership (Laird, Griffin, McGee & Schelling 1972), which was clear in the Twin Pillar policy (al Saud 2003). More specifically, the United States chose to rely on Iran and Saudi Arabia to advance U.S. interests in the Persian Gulf region during the Cold War. Iran was a military power and consequently had a major security role in the Persian Gulf region within the framework of the Twin Pillar policy, while Saudi Arabia was primarily a financial power (Ramazani 1979: 821–835). It is important to note that both Saudi Arabia and Iran were not just important allies to the United States, they also enjoyed, despite sectarian and ideological differences, cordial relations. Throughout the wider region sectarian tension and conflict were minimal compared to 1979 and later. However, with the success of the Iranian Revolution in 1979 and the birth of the Islamic Republic of Iran, the period of cooperation between the two countries ended and their relationship changed to one of competition for regional hegemony couched in stark sectarian rhetoric and proxy conflicts. Thus, the changes that the region underwent in 1979 and the 1980s, resulted in redefining the parameters regarding the strategic use of sectarian identity.

Watershed events in the greater Middle East and South Asia included the seizure of the Grand Mosque in Mecca, the Soviet-Afghan War, the Iran-Iraq War, and the religious radicalization of the government of Pakistan under General Zia ul-Haq (Warde 2016: 205–216). They each had immense immediate and long-term influence on local and regional levels. However, the fact that these events in essence intersected within the same time period exacerbated their impact significantly. As such, this intersection propelled modern sectarianism forward at a heavy human cost, and worsened state and regional security. Consequently, these watershed events and the political entrepreneurs behind them transformed South Asia and the greater Middle East on socio-political, cultural, religious, and security levels (Ghattas 2020). This was evident in the countless lives lost across the region due to wars, as well as sectarian conflict and violence, not to mention physical and psychological injuries that were sustained as a result. Given the level of complexity involved and the need to understand these changes and their impact, which continues to influence the wider region, it is essential to examine the nuances behind the strategic use of identity by state and non-state political entrepreneurs, as well as the role of money in keeping sectarian tensions alive and moving forward (Warde 2016).

Without funds, political entrepreneurs (state and non-state) would not be able to engage in such endeavors – at least not successfully. Nonetheless, the money factor is often overlooked as a tool in perpetuating sectarian tension and conflict throughout South Asia and the greater Middle East despite its foundational role in this regard. This has been vividly clear during the past four decades, including in the Soviet-Afghan War, the Iran-Iraq War, and in Pakistan which became a battleground for proxy conflicts between the United States and the Soviet Union, as well as between Iran and Saudi Arabia in the 1980s. These events have had profound ripple effects that are still reverberating across the region today, such as in Afghanistan, Pakistan, Iraq, Syria, Yemen, and Lebanon. None would have been possible without financial support and funding mechanisms by which sectarian identity and its strategic utilization were honed by political entrepreneurs.

The combined effect of these events had an enormous impact on local, regional, and international politics (Warde 2015). Moreover, they not only transformed South Asia and the greater Middle East, but the Muslim world from top-down and bottom-up levels. The examples noted above provide a glimpse into the complexities of sectarianism in different contexts. For example, the Soviet-Afghan War was a catalyst for empowering and training militant Islamists within the context of fighting the Soviets. In addition to the strategic utilization of religious identity to create a sense of unity among the Islamists and enhance their motivation to fight the Soviet Union in Afghanistan (Kepel 2003), they had the money (Gates 2007) and resources needed to fight and win (Bearden & Risen 2003). The Sunni fighters of the mujahideen were mainly financially supported by the United States and Saudi Arabia, with the latter matching dollar for dollar U.S. financial support of the mujahideen (Warde 2016). Shia fighters were supported by Iran and the two groups predominantly fought the Soviets separately based on sectarian divisions. These changes were also evident on a domestic level as religiosity reshaped politics and society. The distinction between sectarian identities in this context was a part of the exploitation of identity and the process of othering, which were done within a broader framework of power, legitimacy, contestation, mobilization, and an outbidding process (Khatib 2015).

The Iran-Iraq War was another war in which sectarian identity was instrumentalized by both nations involved on varying levels. Both Iran and Iraq utilized Islam strategically both within a war context and in their regional policies. However, when it came to finding the lines of division between "good" and "bad" lines were drawn in the proverbial sand (Mamdani 2004). This was evident as Saudi Arabia and other Arab states financially supported Iraq in its war against Iran (Warde 2016). This was happening both within the context of the Iran-Iraq War which was also often framed as one between Arab Iraq versus Persian Iran, but also against the backdrop of the Iranian government empowering Shias across the Muslim world and attempting to export the so-called revolution.

In Pakistan, the realities associated with sectarian tension and conflict were a bit different. It was directly and indirectly influenced by the Soviet-Afghan War, the proxy war between the United States and the Soviet Union, as well as the escalating competition for regional hegemony between Iran and Saudi Arabia – all with dire consequences for its people. These changes were occurring against the backdrop of General Zia-Ul-Haq's Islamization efforts in Pakistan accompanied by the strengthening of the Jamaat-i-Islami (Warde 2016). Moreover, bound by their socio-political contexts and influenced by the sectarian conflict that emerged between Iran and Saudi Arabia, Shia and Sunni transnationalism became tied to specific states. Within Pakistan cleavages were further exacerbated as a result of new Shia organizations founded by Iran in the 1980s during the Iran-Iraq War, and the Soviet-Afghan War. It was also increased by Saudi Arabia who significantly expanded its pre-existing ideological and financial efforts that it already had in the country (Jalal 2008) (e.g.: madrassas) According to Nasr, there is a clear link between Pakistan's madrassas, the rise in sectarianism, Sunni militancy in the country and Saudi funding (Nasr 2000: 139–180). On balance, whether in Iran, in Pakistan or elsewhere, the shift to political Islam, including the strategic used of sectarianism, was due to a power-based strategy utilized by state and non-state actors to configure the socio-political and security landscapes in line with their interests.

What these examples have in common, along with the topics analyzed by the authors in this volume is the manipulation of sectarian identity for strategic purposes at varying levels by political entrepreneurs and the fundamental role of money – without which fissures are less likely to be exacerbated, tension is less likely to escalate, and conflict is less likely to occur. Overall, given the complexity associated with this phenomenon, it is important to analyze sectarianism through an interdisciplinary approach and examine diverse themes, including the political economy of sectarianism, counterterrorism, identity, and the intersection of politics and identity, which this volume has done. Thus, building on existing scholarship through diverse voices, while simultaneously challenging popular narratives that use sectarian divisions between Sunnis and Shias as an unchanging feature and all-encompassing explanation for conflicts across the Muslim world.

Bibliography

al Saud, F.B.S. *Iran, Saudi Arabia and the Gulf: Power Politics in Transition 1968–1971.* London: I.B. Tauris, 2003.

Bearden, M. and J. Risen. *The Main Enemy: The Inside Story of the CIA's Final Showdown with the KGB.* New York: Random House, 2003.

Gates, Robert M. *From the Shadows: The Ultimate Insider's Story of Five Presidents and how they Won the Cold War.* New York, NY: Simon & Schuster, 2007.

Ghattas, Kim. *Black Wave: Saudi Arabia, Iran, and the Forty-Year Rivalry That Unraveled Culture, Religion, and Collective Memory in the Middle East.* New York, NY: Henry Holt & Co., 2020.

Jalal, Ayesha. *Partisans of Allah: Jihad in South Asia.* Cambridge: Harvard University Press, 2008.

Kepel, Gilles, *Jihad: The Trial of Political Islam.* Cambridge: Belknap Press, 2003.

Khatib, Hakin. "Political Instrumentalization of Islam in a Violent State Crisis: The Case of Syria." *Journal of Applied Security Research* 10 no. 3 (July 2015): 341–361.

Laird. Melvin R., Robert P. Griffin, Gale W. McGee and Thomas C. Schelling. "The Nixon Doctrine." AEI's Town Hall Meeting. A Town Hall Meeting on National Security Policy sponsored by the American Enterprise Institute, 1972.

Mamdani, Mahmood. *Good Muslim, Bad Muslim: American, The Cold War and the Roots of Terror.* New York: Pantheon, 2004.

Nasr, S.V.R. "The Rise of Sunni Militancy in Pakistan: The Changing Role of Islamism and the Ulama in Society and Politics." *Modern Asian Studies* 34, no. 1 (2000): 139–180.

Ramazani, R. K. "Security in the Persian Gulf." *Foreign Affairs* 57, no. 4 (1979): 821–835.

Warde, Ibrahim. "Wagering on Sectarianism: The Political Economy of Extremism: Wagering on Sectarianism." *The Muslim World (Hartford)* 106, no. 1 (2016): 205–216.

Warde, Ibrahim. "Avatars of Checkbook Diplomacy: From the Afghan Jihad to the Arab Spring." *Fletcher Security Review*, February 2015.

INDEX

Abdullah II, King of Jordan 20–21
Adams Schmidt, Dana 157
Aden 157
advice columnists, Egypt 52–62; advice columns 55–59; approaches to extremism 60–62; covert approach 62; good life 52, 59–60; humanist 52, 53–54, 55–58, 59–60, 60–61; letter-writers 58; religious 52, 54–55, 55, 58–59, 59–60, 61–62; sarcasm 55; writers 53–55
Afghanistan. *see* Soviet-Afghan War
Ahl-e-Sunnat wa Jamaat, the 10
Ahmadiyya Muslim Community 14–15, 20–34; contested Muslim identity 22–23; exclusion 21, 23–24, 29, 33, 34; fatwas against 24; finality of Prophet Mohammad 21, 28–29, 29–30; Ghulam Ahmad and 21, 26–34, 34n2; Islamic identity 28; and Islamic orthodoxy debates 21; jihad 25, 26–28, 33; and Mohammad 25, 26; piety through persecution 28–29; Promised Messiah 21, 27, 32–34; and prophecies 32–33; self-identity as the True Islam 21, 24–26, 28, 29, 31, 32, 33, 34
Ahmad, Nazir 12–14
Akarli, Engin 67
Akbar, Emperor 11
Al-Ahram 53–54, 58–59
al-'Arabi, Ibn 30
Al-Azhar University 54
Albrecht, Holger 147
Al-Farabi 10

Algerian Revolution 136
Al-Ghazali 8
Aligarh movement 12
Allawi, Ayad 103
Al-Qaeda 49, 126, 140, 142
Al-Qaeda in Iraq (AQI) 2, 101103, 105–107, 109–110, 112, 112–113, 114, 119, 126, 128–129
Amin, Hafizullah 40–41
Amman Message 20–21, 144–145
Anderson, B. 121
Anjuman-i-Sipah-i-Sahaba 15–16
annihilation, fear of 3
Arab-Israeli war, 1973 14
Arab nationalism 84–85, 91
Arab Spring 135, 136, 145, 147
Asad, Talal 23
assimilation, fear of 3
authoritarianism 137
Ayesh 12–13

Bad Muslims 25
Badr Corps militia 110
Bahrain 136, 138, 139, 145, 146, 149n2, 150–151n27, 164
Bangladesh 14, 17, 18
Barany, Zoltan 89
Barelvi-Deobandi debates 29–30
Batiste, John 104
Bellin, Eva 135
belonging 14
Beydoun, Ahmad 80
Bhutto, Zulfikar Ali 14

174 Index

bin-Laden, Osama 44, 128, 132n22
Black September 87
blasphemy law 15
Brahimi, Lakhdar 102
Brooks, Risa 83
Browne, Walter 68
Bush, George W. 100, 118, 139

Central Intelligence Agency 43, 154, 159, 168
Chehab, Fuad 86, 87–88
Chiha, Michel 73–74
Christians 59
citizenship rights 15
civilian-military relations 84, 87–88, 90–91, 94, 97
coercive apparatus 135
Cold War 39, 41, 131n7, 154–157, 169
Collier, Paul 81
colonialism 68–70
communal thinking 80
community, decontextualization and deconstruction 1
competition 169
Conference on the Limitation of Armaments, Washington D.C. 68
confessionalism 80
Confucius 59
consociationalism 81–82, 98
constructivism 4
counterterrorism 5; armed forces sectarianization 147–148; democracy promotion 137–141; international and regional frameworks 142–144, 150n19, 150n21; justification 146; policies and practices 144–146, 148–149; sectarianization 136–137, 145; sectarian lens 135; sectarian strategies 136; securitization 141; soft power 144–145; state behavior 135–149; U.S. initiatives 139

Danforth, Loring M. 79
Daniels, Paul 104
Daoud, Qasem 104
Daou, Marc 163
Da'wa Party 104
deconstruction 1
decontextualization 1
defense budgets 140–141, 147
Defense Security Cooperation Agency 148
democracy promotion 137–141
Deobandis 15
Dhofar Rebellion 154, 155, 157–159
difference 18

discrimination 18
divorce 58–59
domination, fear of 3
al-Duri, Izzat 123

Eddé, Emile 73
education 10
Egypt 136, 139, 140, 145, 155; advice columnists 52–62; advice columns 55–59; approaches to extremism 60–62; extremism 52; good life 59–60; number of mosques 52; reforms 52–53
El-Tayeb, Sheikh Ahmed 54–55
Enloe, Cynthia H. 81
ethnic cleavages 79–80
ethnic identity 3, 4
ethnicity 79–80
ethno-sectarian cleavages 91
European Union 142
exclusion 18
extremism 60–62

Farah, Caesar E. 65–66
fard al-ayn 46, 50n8
Fatemiyoun Brigade 47
Fatima 12–13
fatwas 12, 24, 27, 102
Fearon, James D. 81
female circumcision 59, 62n10
Firro, Kais 69, 70
Francis, St. 59
Frangieh, Suleiman 87
Freedom House 144
Fuchs, Simon Wolfgang 120

Gambrell, Jon 160
gender relations 58–59
al-Ghazali, Muhammad 62n14
Ghulam Ahmad, Mirza 21, 26–34, 34n2, 35n14, 35n15, 35n16
GIA 49
Global Coalition to Defeat ISIS/ISIL 143
Global Counterterrorism Committee 143
globalization 17, 137
God 27, 33
good life, the 52, 59–60
Greater Lebanon 69, 71, 76n1
group mobilization 79
Gulf War, 1991 92, 94

Haddad, Fanar 64, 80
al-Hakim, Abdul Aziz 102
Hamas 163, 165n8
al-Haq, Sheikh Gad 54–55

Hashemi, Nader 2, 3, 4, 65, 74–75, 127, 137
Helfont, Samuel 125
Helou, Charles 87–88
Hezbollah 146
Hinduism 16
Hindutva brigades 16
Hinnebusch, Raymond 136
Hizbollah 90
Hoeffler, Anke 81
Houghton, John Nicholas 111–112
Husain, Sohail 32–33
Hussein, Saman Dlawer 106

Ibn Sina 10
identity 5, 117, 169; boundaries of 99; decontextualization and deconstruction 1; ethnic 3, 4; framing 4; imagined 1; Iraqi case study 77; Iraqi Security Forces case study 91–97, 98; Lebanese Armed Forces case study 77, 84–91, 98; manipulation 3, 170–171; and the military 77–99; mobilization 3; out-group 80; politicization 98; religious 2, 4, 5, 121, 122–127, 128, 131–132n14; sect-based 2; socially constructed 77, 97; strategic utilization of 120–121, 122–127, 131–132n14, 132n26; territorialization of 65, 65–68
identity-based conflict, Iraq 117–130
identity cleavages 81–82
identity formation 121, 122–127: consociationalism 81–82; cultural characteristics 79–80; and ethnicity 79–80; military institutions 82–84; national 78–79; nationalism and 78–79; sectarian narratives 97–98; security elite considerations 80–81
identity politics 75, 122–127
imagined communities 78, 121, 122
imperial manipulation 66
India 18; 1857 Rebellion 26; Ahmadiyya Muslim Community 20–34, 21; British colonial rule 11–12, 21, 22, 26–34, 35n15; Citizenship Amendment Act 17; and Kashmir 16–17; Mughal period 10, 11; Muslim identity 27; National Register of Citizens 17; rise in anti-Muslim feelings 16–17; sectarianism in 10–14; state promoted religious bigotry 17
in-group/out-group paradigms 1, 3
institutional analysis 77
instrumentalism 3
integration 90

interdisciplinary approach 168–169
interdisciplinary transnational approach 5
inter-group dynamics 99
intermingling 89
Iqbal, Muhammad 2
Iran 2, 39, 49, 137, 141, 168; Achille's heel 163; Cold War background 154–157, 169; intervention in the Arabian Peninsula 157–159; Palestine and 161–162; pre-revolutionary relations with Saudi Arabia 154–159, 165; Soviet-Afghan War involvement 42–43, 46–48; world view 164–165
Iranian Revolution 131n9, 154, 159, 160–161, 162–163, 164
Iran-Iraq War 15–16, 39, 92, 95, 120, 124–125, 130, 131–132n14, 164, 169–170, 170, 171
Iraq 2, 4, 99, 136, 139, 140, 141, 145, 155; AQI car-bomb offensive 106–107, 109–110, 112–113; Ba'ath Rule 92; Badr Corps militia 105, 106; battle for Fallujah 103; challenges facing 117–118; Civil War 113–114, 128–129; Coalition Provisional Authority 95–96; Constitution, 2005 94–95, 102; Constitutional Referendum 107, 108–109; cycle of violence 117, 118, 119, 123, 127–128; de-Ba'athification 94–95, 95, 96, 127; December 2005 parliamentary election 107, 112; descent into sectarian conflict 101–114; distribution of political power 101; elections 101–114; ethno-sectarian cleavages 91; Faith Campaign 125–126, 132n19; fall 2005 election period 107–108; identity-based conflict 117–130; identity in 117; initial electoral decisions 100; instrumentalization of sectarianism 118; insurgency 119, 127, 130, 130n2, 140; Interim Government 102; invasion of, 2003 117, 118–119, 127, 139, 142, 149n7, 164; Islamification 125–126; Ja'afari Government 104–105, 110–112; the Jadriyah bunker 110–111; January 2005 election 100–104; January 2005 election aftermath 104–108; January 2005 election vote 103; Jaysh al-Mahdi 106, 107; Kurds 91, 94, 94–95, 95, 96, 97, 98, 108–109, 119, 123, 131n13; lack of U.S. planning 101–102; legacy of exclusion 119; Mada'in hostage crisis 104–105; modern historical factors 117–130; overthrow of the monarchy 92; police forces purged 105; Post-2003 127–129; rebellions 92; rise of

Index

sectarian violence 105–106, 119; role of sectarianism 117–130; Samarra shrine bombing 114, 128; sectarian cleansing 110; Shia marginalization 122–127, 131n12, 132n18; Shia militias 106, 107; Shia ministerial control 105; Shia sectarian misconduct 110–112; shift in religio-political landscape 120–121; strategic utilization of identity 122–127, 129–130; Sunni electoral boycott 103; Sunni representation 108–109; Transitional Government 104–105; Umar Brigades 105–106; U.S. military failure 112–113; U.S. Role 101–114; U.S. strategy 103

Iraqi Security Forces 91–97, 98; Ba'ath Rule 92; chain-of-command 96; civilian-military relations 94, 97; and Constitution, 2005 94–95; de-Ba'athification 95, 96; deployment 93, 97; ethno-sectarian cleavages 91; organization 93, 96; post-2005 95–97; promotion 93, 96; recruitment 92, 95–96; Republican Guard 92, 93, 94; sectarian quotas 96; Special Republican 92, 93, 94

Iraq Study Group Report 118

Islam: interpretative community 9; number of sects 8; penchant for sectarianism 10–14; sectarian competition 8; weaponization of 15

Islamic Military Counterterrorism Coalition 143–144

Islamic orthodoxy debates 21, 22–23, 34, 34n1, 35n6

Islamic Revolution 154, 162

Islamic State of Iraq and the Levant (ISIL) 2, 47, 49, 61, 129

Islamic Summit Conference, 1969 156

Islamic Unity of Afghanistan Mujahideen 44–45

Islamification 125–126

Islamism 5

Islamophobia 26

Israel 87, 136, 149n2, 162

al-Ja'afari, Ibrahim 104–105, 110, 111
Jabr, Bayan 105, 106
Jalal, Ayesha 26–27, 27
Jamaat-i-Islami 171
Jaysh al-Mahdi 110
Jerusalem 162
Jews 59
jihad 22, 24, 25, 33; Soviet-Afghan War 39, 45, 49
Jordan 87, 136, 139, 144, 162

Judgement Day 59
jurists and jurisprudence 9, 11

kalima, the 28–29
Kalyvas, Stathis N. 81
Karbala 13
Karmal, Babrak 41
Kashmir 16–17
Kaye, Dalia Dasse 140
Kepel, Gilles 44, 45, 46, 49
Khalilzad, Zalmay 108, 111
Khan, Adil Hussain 21, 34, 35n6
Khan, Mohammad Daud 40
Khan, Saiyid Ahmad 12
Khomeini, Ruhollah 2, 160–161, 163
al-Khuri, Bishara 70, 72, 73
Kukis, Mark 106
Kurds 91, 94, 94–95, 95, 96, 97, 98, 108–109, 119, 123; Iraq 131n13
Kuwait 138, 146
Kuwait Daily 158

Lebanese Armed Forces 77, 84–91; Chehabism 86; Christian dominance 85–86; civilian-military relations 87–88, 90–91; deployment 86–87, 90; integration 90; The National Pact 85; National Reconciliation Accord (Ta'if Accord) 1989 88, 98; organization 86, 90; post-Civil War 89–91; pre-Civil War 85–88; promotion 86, 89; recruitment 85–86, 89; sectarian politics 84–85; special units 90

Lebanese National Movement 85–86

Lebanon 64–76, 99, 136, 138; Census, 1932 70, 85; Chehabism 86; Christian population 65–66, 69, 70, 72, 84–85; Constitution, 1926 70, 70–72; Druze population 65–66, 84–85; European domination 68–70; Flag Service Law 89; imperial manipulation 66; independence 70–74; *Le Grand Liban* 69; Long Peace 67; mandate period 68–70; Merchant Republic 73–74; *mustafarriate* 67–68, 74; The National Pact 70–74, 85; National Reconciliation Accord (Ta'if Accord) 1989 88, 98; political mobilization 69; power-sharing structure 72; *Réglement Organique* 67, 69, 74; religious pluralism 72; roots of nationalism 67–68; sectarianization 72, 74–75; sectarian politics 84–85; sectarian solidification 69–70; territorial sectarianization 1843–1860 65–66

legislative prophets 30

Index 177

liberalization 138, 139, 148
Libya 145
Lijphart, Arendt 81–82, 97–98

Mada'in 104–105
Makdisi, Ussama Samir 65, 67, 74, 75
marriage 56–57, 58–59
materialization 122
methodologies 5
Miles-Joyce, Rennanah 148
military expenditures 140–141, 147
military institutions: civilian-military relations 84, 87–88, 90–91, 94, 97; command-and-control 83; deployment 83–84, 86–87, 90, 93, 97; dynamics 82; ethno-sectarian cleavages 91; and identity 77–99; identity formation 82–84; Iraqi case study 77, 91–97, 98; Lebanese case study 77, 84–91, 98; organization 83, 86, 90, 93, 96; promotion 83, 86, 89, 93, 96; recruitment 82–83, 85–86, 89, 92, 95–96; sectarianization 147–148; sectarian quotas 96
Mohammad, the Prophet 13, 25, 162; behavior toward women 59; claim of Prophethood 32; debate about 29–30; finality of 21, 28–29, 29–30, 35n7; Ghulam Ahmad as *buruz* 30–31; normative model 29–30; persecution 31–32, 33; prophecies 32; role of 22; sanctity of 26, 29, 31, 34; succession 153
Morgenstein Fuerst, Ilyse 26
Morocco 144
Mottaki, Manouchehr 163
Mubarak, Hosni 53, 60–61
Mughal period 10, 11
munazaras 13
Muqaddasi 8
Muslim Brotherhood 140
Muslim identity 22–23
Muslim World League 44
al-Muttawa, Abdul Wahab 53–54, 55–58, 59–60, 60–61

Naccache, Georges 73
Nakash, Yitzak 156
Nasr, Vali 5, 38, 130, 131n9, 171
Nasser, Gamal Abdel 52–53, 155
national identity formation 78–79
National Institute of Health 44
nationalism 2, 4; identity formation and 78–79; territorial roots 67–68
national security 80–81, 98
nation-building 77, 78

nation-states: legal idioms 9; role of 9; threat of 8
NATO 142–143, 143, 150n21
Negroponte, John 104
Netherlands, the 81–82
New York Times 48
Nixon Doctrine 47, 169
Nomani, Shibli 10
Noman, Raziullah 25
non-legislative prophets 30
non-state actors, threat of 8
norm conflict 148
Nunan, Timothy 43

Observer, The 160
Oman 154, 155, 157–159, 165
Operation Enduring Freedom 143
Operation Iraqi Freedom 118–119
othering 3, 5, 122
Other Muslims 25
Ottoman Empire 65, 67, 68, 84
out-group identity 80

Pahlavi, Mohammad Reza Shah 154–155, 156, 156–157, 158–159
Pakistan 2, 14–16, 17, 18, 42, 45, 120, 131n8, 169–170, 170–171; Ahmadiyya Muslim Community 21, 23–24, 29, 33, 34
Palestine, Islamic importance 161–162
Palestine Liberation Organization 87, 160, 161–162
Paul, Rand 153–154, 165
Peled, Alon 81
Persian Gulf, British withdrawal 156, 157
personality cults 11
political culture, fractured 81–82
political domination 75
political economy 5
political entrepreneurs 3, 39, 170, 171
Political Islam 1, 38–39, 120–121, 171
politicalization perceptive 65
Popular Front for the Liberation of Oman and the Arab Gulf 157
Popular Islamic Conference Organization 125
Popular Mobilization 2
positive sectarianization 138
Postel, Danny 2, 3, 4, 65, 74–75, 137
Poujade, Eugen 66
power 2, 23
power-holders 79
power-sharing 82
primordialism 3
privilege 2

profession of faith 28–29
prophecies 32–33
proxy conflicts 135
public disputations 13

Qatar 147
Quran, the 8, 25, 30, 31

RAND 140
Reagan, Ronald 45
Réglement Organique 67, 69, 74
religio-political landscape, shift in 120–121
religiosity 60
religious beliefs 8, 10
religious cleavages 80
religious freedom 11, 15
religious identity 2, 4, 5, 121, 122–127, 128, 131–132n14
religious pluralism 18, 72
Roy, Oliver 42, 49
Rumi, Jalaluddin 18

Saddam Hussein 2, 4, 92, 93, 94, 99, 101, 117, 145; Faith Campaign 125–126, 132n19; instrumentalization of sectarianism 118; and Iranian intervention in the Arabian Peninsula 158–159; legacy 121, 130; strategic utilization of identity 120, 122–127, 130, 131n6, 132n26
Saddam University for Islamic Studies 125
Salafi Islam 163
Salem, Tawfiq 85
Saud al-Faisal, Prince 139
Saudi Arabia 39, 42, 46, 47, 49, 50n9, 136, 137, 140, 144, 145, 149n2, 170, 171; anti-Shi'ism 156, 162–164, 165; Cold War background 154–157, 169; establishment of 155; pre-revolutionary relations with Iran 154–159, 165
sectarian competition 8
sectarian divisions 9
sectarianism 120; conceptual limitations of 10; focus 136–137; in India 10–14; lack of clarity 9; longitudinal histories 9; Muslim penchant for 10–14; negative connotations 9; in Post-Colonial South Asia 14–18; rise of 4; role of 1, 5; strategic utilization 1; temporality 137; understanding 1–5, 8–18, 64–65, 74–76, 136
sectarianization 72, 74–75, 149n2; armed forces 147–148; institutional 145–146; and securitization 136–137; silent space for 145
sectarian narratives 97–98

sect-based identity 2; strategic use 39
sect based violence 66
sect, definition 1
sects, parameters of 136
securitization 135, 136, 141; and sectarianization 136–137
security and stability paradigm 137–141
security elite 80–81
security maps 98, 99
security, sectarian lens 135
September 11, 2001 terrorist attack 20
seven deadly sins 58, 62n8
shahadah, the 28–29
al-Sharawy, Muhammad 54–55
Shariati, Ali 2
Shelef, Nadav 78
Shia Crescent, the 141
Shias . *also* Sunni-Shia conflict
Sistani, Ali 102, 103, 104
Smith, Anthony D. 3
socialization 89
social media 12
soft power 144–145
Soviet-Afghan Friendship Treaty 40
Soviet-Afghan War 38–50, 120, 131n7, 169–170; casualties 43; cost 43–44; foreign fighters 44; humanitarian crises 44; impact on the Soviet Union 43–44, 48; Iran's involvement 42–43, 46–48; jihad 39, 45, 49; legacy 49; mujahideen 40, 41–42, 43, 44–45; Operation Cyclone 45; Shia Mujahideen 39, 42, 44, 46–48, 49, 170; socio-political landscape 38–40; Soviet invasion 15, 16, 40–42; Soviet strength 40–41; Soviet withdrawal 40, 42–44; Sunni Mujahideen 39, 42, 44–45, 45–46, 48, 49; U.S. strategy 39, 42, 45–46, 48
Sri Lanka 17, 18
Stack, John F.Jr. 3
state formation 9, 77, 78
state security 98
Steele, James 111
strategic utilization 1
Suez Canal 53
al-Sulh, Riad 70–74, 72
Sunnis: sects 13. *see also* Sunni-Shia conflict
Sunni-Shia conflict 3, 4, 5, 6n1, 9, 47–48, 49, 75, 121; Cold War background 154–157; and the Iranian Revolution 160–161; Orientalist explanation 153–154; Pakistan 15; and Palestine 161–162; pre-revolutionary relations between Saudi Arabia and Iran 154–159, 164–165; religious basis 12–14;

Saudi-Iranian roots 153–165; Saudi roots 162–164
Supreme Council for the Islamic Revolution in Iraq 102, 108, 111
Syria 87, 136, 145, 147, 165n8

Tabatabai, Waleed 146
Tabet, Jacques 69–70
Ta'if Accord 88, 98
Taliban 49
Tantawy, Sheikh Muhammad Sayyid 54–55
Taraki, Nur Mohammad 40
Tareen, SherAli 29–30, 34n1, 35n6
tawhid 13
al-Tayeb, Ahmed 61
Tehran Eight 47
territorialization, of identity 65, 65–68
territorial sectarianization 65–66
terrorism, and sectarianism 141–142
theoretical framework 2–4
Time magazine 153
Traboulsi, Fawwaz 74
Troubilsi, Fawaz 66
True Islam 21, 22–23, 24–26, 28, 29, 31, 32, 33, 34
Trump, Donald 140
Tunisia 145

UAE 146, 147
UN Counterterrorism Committee 142–143, 144, 150n26
United Iraqi Alliance 103
United Kingdom 24, 156, 157
United Nations 43, 142–143, 150n19
United States of America 24; counterterrorism initiatives 139; democracy promotion 137–141; foreign policy 136, 169; imperialism 162; Iraqi Civil War role 101–114; Iraq strategy 103; lack of post-regime change in Iraq 101–102; Middle East policy 159; military and economic assistance 137, 138; military failure in Iraq 112–113; mobilization of Islam 131n7; National Strategy for Combatting Terrorist and Other Illicit Financing 140; provision of military training 148; Soviet-Afghan War strategy 39, 42, 45–46, 48; Twin Pillar policy 169
Universal Islamic Consensus 20
UN Office of Counterterrorism 143
UN Security Council Resolution 1546 112
USAID 137, 139
U.S. State Department 46
us versus them narratives 38, 49, 121

Valbjorn, Morten 3, 4
Vietnam War 155
visual imagery 71

Wahhabism 46
War on Terror 136, 139, 140, 144–145, 148–149
watershed moments 169
Wells, Madeleine 138
Whitaker, Beth Elise 144
World War I 68, 91

al-Yawar, Ghazi 100, 103
Yemen 144, 156, 157
Yom Kippur War 158–159
Yousef, Ahmed 160

Zarqawi, Abu Musab 105, 106–107, 128, 132n22
Zayd, Nasr Abu 62n13
Zia-ul-Haq 2, 15–16, 45, 120, 169, 171

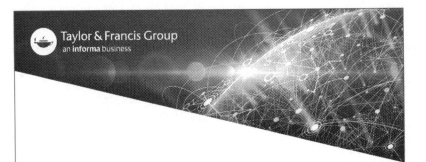

Printed in the United States
by Baker & Taylor Publisher Services